AFTER GENOCIDE

AFTER GENOCIDE
How Ordinary Jews Face the Holocaust

Sue Lieberman

KARNAC

First published in 2015 by
Karnac Books Ltd
118 Finchley Road
London NW3 5HT

British Library Cataloguing in Publication Data

A C.I.P. for this book is available from the British Library

ISBN-13: 978-1-78220-192-2

Typeset by V Publishing Solutions Pvt Ltd., Chennai, India

Printed in Great Britain

www.karnacbooks.com

CONTENTS

ACKNOWLEDGEMENTS

I am indebted to the many people who have helped me with this book.

First, to Liz Bondi, who took me under the wing of Edinburgh University and mentored me throughout. She believed in this idea from the start.

To all those who have, over the years, read part or all of the drafts and given me critical and valuable feedback: Sue Collin, Moris Farhi, Kate Lebow, Judy Sischy, Cathie Wright; and above all to Sue Macfadyen, for her insistence on meeting me regularly and her commitment to supporting me through the lengthy process of writing.

To Oron Joffe, for his invaluable technical help at the start, and to Karen Coleman for her efficient and enthusiastic transcribing of the interviews.

The epigraphs in Chapters Six and Seven are excerpted from *The Winter Vault* by Anne Michaels, copyright 2009 Anne Michaels. Excerpts reprinted by kind permission of McClelland & Stewart, a division of Random House of Canada Limited, a Penguin Random House Company; and by Bloomsbury Publishing PLC. Also by Alfred A Knopf, an imprint of the Knopf Doubleday Publishing Group, a division of Random House LLC. All rights reserved. Any third party use of this material, outside of this publication, is prohibited. Interested parties must apply directly to Random House LLC for permission.

Thanks to Roberto Cubelli and to Sergio Della Sala for permission to cite their research on memory; and to Dr. Alfred Garwood for his interest and support for me drawing on his invaluable paper on survivor guilt.

Thanks to Heather Valencia for providing the YIVO translation for Zeitlin's poem "*Kinder fun Maydanek*", and for sourcing the information about Zeitlin and the circumstances in which this poem was written.

I wished very much to contact Professor June Huntingdon, whose conference paper on "Migration as part of life experience" proved so helpful, but despite many efforts was unable to track her down.

Thanks are also due to:

Dudley and Rose Leigh, Sharon Miller, Roger and Caroline Moore, and Joe Raimondo, for providing hospitality at various stages in the researching and writing.

Oliver Leaman for his confidence that the book would be published, and for his many practical suggestions.

Roger Bacon for his love and thoughtful reflections.

Judith Fewell, for being such an invaluable resource of ideas for reading, and for her generosity in lending me many of her own books.

To the numerous others who loaned or gave me books and papers to inspire and help me: Jess Abrams, Roger Bacon, Lisa Barcan, Art Blokland, Steve Burkeman, Patrick Harkin, Hannah Holtschneider, Oron Joffe, Sheena McLachlan, Kay Menzies, and Heather Valencia. Particular thanks are due to Kirsteen Mackay for bringing June Huntingdon's paper to my attention, and for her tireless search for a copy amongst her own archives, especially as the UNSW can no longer trace it.

And above all, to my interviewees, who wanted to be part of this project and who offered themselves and their time to be interviewed. Without them, this book would not have been possible. For reasons of confidentiality their names have been changed.

ABOUT THE AUTHOR

Sue Lieberman grew up in London in an "ordinary Jewish" family and studied at Bristol, York and Bradford Universities.

After an initial career in community work she worked in local government, then for many years as an organisational consultant and team trainer.

Between 1988 and 2003 she trained in psychotherapy, first in a humanistic school and later in Group Analysis, and she works as an integrative psychotherapist. She lives in Edinburgh.

INTRODUCTION

"I don't know why it affects me this much"

What do these two speakers have in common?

> "About twenty years ago ... [...] ... it [the Holocaust] began to be much more important. And I got aware of it! ... It was through awareness of anti-Semitism that the Holocaust seemed to me to become more and more monstrous and more ... I started to watch every programme on television and read every book I could get hold of."

> "I can't think about it [the Holocaust]. I won't watch any programme that comes on [...]. I can't, I can't bear it. I know that's why you're here, for me to talk about the Holocaust, but .... All I can say is, I feel guilty for being alive. But I've felt that all my life."

These different expressions of feeling about the Holocaust come from two elderly Jewish women who have, on the surface, a great deal in common. Both were first or second generation British Jews, now in their eighties, who were born in London in the early 1920s. Both were teenagers at the outbreak of the Second World War; both were evacuated to other parts of Britain to escape air raids; and both learnt about the extent of the Holocaust in the aftermath of the war. Neither is orthodox, but both associate with Jewish activities and events. Yet despite the similarities between them, their internal relationships to the Holocaust differ; differences which derive not from the Holocaust itself or its many representations but more from the specific characteristics of their own lives. The first speaker, whom I shall call Doris, owes her sensitivity to anti-Semitism in large part to having grown up with an anti-Semitic housekeeper who came to look after Doris and her sister after the early death of their mother. The second, whom I call Pearl, was the sixth of nine children in an impoverished immigrant family. At an early age, Pearl learned from *her* mother that her mother had not wanted any more children after the first four and had "tried to get rid of" her. Guilt for being alive was for Pearl a sentiment established in her psyche well before the Holocaust.

Like Doris and Pearl, both British-born and with only distant family—if any—in Europe at the time of the Holocaust, the majority of Jews alive today do not have a direct connection to the Holocaust. We are neither survivors nor descendants of survivors; we are not descendants of Jewish refugees who fled Germany and Austria before the outbreak of war, nor do we have close family who were murdered. In all likelihood, we are descended either from the huge numbers of Jews who emigrated away from Eastern Europe during the last part of the nineteenth or the early twentieth centuries; or we belong to communities whose histories for many hundreds of years lie outside Europe altogether. In other words, our relationship to the actual events and horrors that took place in mainland Europe during the Second World War is distant. Naturally, we have a relationship to it: principally as Jews, but also through our various country nationalities and identities, and, of course, simply as human beings. But it is a relationship which largely seems assumed—taken-for-granted—rather than understood. In many people's eyes, it is a relationship that is even misused in order to justify continued support for certain policies by Israel towards Palestinians and Arabs. Therefore, both for the Holocaust's powerful position in Jewish life and for the impact of that in the wider political arena, it seems an overdue task to understand the intricate psychological and emotional relationship that the broad mass of Jews, who are only indirectly connected to the Holocaust, has with it. It is my central purpose in writing this book to explore this: to ask what it is that we feel, and to look more closely at why.

Not having a direct "lineage" from the Holocaust, so to speak, our relationship to it is complicated. If we cannot claim a direct family experience of the trauma of the Holocaust itself, how can we claim to be "traumatised" by it? What is it that "haunts" us? What is it that is difficult to "let go" about the Holocaust, and why is that? At one level, we *can* take for granted that we are affected by knowing about the Holocaust. At another level, the forms this takes are likely in many ways to be idiosyncratic, or else why would "Doris" and "Pearl" express such different reactions to the same information? Understanding the inner dynamics of our responses may, at the very least, be valuable personally. More critical in terms of its consequences is the question of the uses to which we put those reactions and responses: how we use them to construct meaning; to engage in—or disengage from—difficult debates; to shape cultural inheritance.

Of course, it is not only Jews who find themselves powerfully affected by the Holocaust. Many non-Jews also feel deep emotions. In public and private, non-Jewish people variously describe themselves as "haunted" by the Holocaust, or as having been "overwhelmed" in finding out about it; they, too, may feel angry, horrified, and nauseated. James Orbinski, for example, a past president of Médécins sans Frontières, who worked in Rwanda during the period of its genocide, recalls his earliest experience of coming across the Holocaust as a young boy in Montreal through seeing a programme on TV:

> What struck me then [...] and still stays with me was a realisation that we as human beings can do horrific things. [It was] a moment of complete dissonance

—a moment that for some time after left him disoriented, distressed, and incoherent (Orbinski, 2008).

Such feelings should not be underestimated. It is, surely, these which have driven not only individuals such as Orbinski to take heroic action in the field of humanitarian work but also an international agenda that now identifies war crimes *as* crimes to be prosecuted, and that has established the concept of genocide itself as a crime against humanity. The human capacity to identify with the suffering of others and to seek preventive or ameliorative action is a source of moral and social order, and non-Jews as well as Jews recognise the inherent violation of this by the Nazis. At the same time, other peoples can find in the Nazi Holocaust against the Jews a fit representation for their own suffering. Late in 2007, for example, the Young Vic put on a new version of Peter

Weiss's play, *The Investigation*, a German play about the 1964 Frankfurt war crimes trial. Not so unusual for the times to revive this play; only the Young Vic's version was performed by a Rwandan theatre company. In the publicity, Dorcy Rugamba, the play's director, asked, "Why do we, rather than tell the story of our own genocide, prefer to work on that of the Jews?" For this company, the meaning of the Jewish Holocaust was that it offers Rwandans a vehicle for approaching their own.

Jews, therefore, are not alone in feeling deeply disturbed when thinking about the Holocaust. Indeed, the very existence of Holocaust education and of Holocaust museums is predicated on the supposition that the events of the Nazi years are of importance to a much wider audience than a purely Jewish one. In many respects, therefore, what can be said about the reactions of "ordinary Jews" to the Holocaust could apply to anyone, and many non-Jews may see their own feelings reflected in some of the themes I explore. However, Jewish identification with the Holocaust and with the legacy of the Holocaust is extremely powerful. As J, a young colleague, put it,

> "my family may not have gone through the Holocaust, but I am *related* to it. We Jews are such a small minority worldwide. Losing so many, and all the subsequent generations, has a big effect."

Being able to turn away from the contemplation of horror is an important psychological defence, and non-Jews have the option to turn away from the Holocaust if they wish (as do Jews in relation to the genocides of other people). However, Jews can only exercise this option at the cost of something fundamental to their Jewish identity. We are, in effect, bound to feel particularly exposed to certain kinds of question associated with the Holocaust. For example, one anguished question which surfaced repeatedly in my interviews—"How could this have happened?"—has a subliminal counterpart of self-critique—"What is it about *us* that led to this?" (I explore this theme in Chapter Five). When Israeli film-makers such as Tamar Yarom (2008) and Ari Folman (2008) publicly comment about their own country's psyche that "the Holocaust has induced a state of paranoia in Israel" and "the Holocaust is in the DNA of Israel", it becomes clear that for many Jews there is no question but that the Holocaust has profoundly affected Jewish life in a way that is distinct from broader reactions. It is for this reason that, in this book, I focus only on Jewish responses to the Holocaust. While Jewish feelings are likely to speak to other experiences, perhaps particularly to other communities mourning equivalent catastrophes, this Jewish story has yet to be told in its own right, and it is, I hope, in the telling of this distinct story that we might realise more of the psychological complexity involved in our—or any other community's—ongoing relationship with historic disasters.

One of my central premises is that much of what passes for an apparently simple cause-and-effect ("Hitler would have killed us all, so we are all survivors" is a theme identified by one writer) is in practice something much more complex. The Holocaust is an historic event that, while it continues to resonate through the lives of the descendants of survivors, largely now lives in the realm of meaning and association; and to that realm we cannot fail to bring the material of our own lives, lives which are inherently full of personal hopes, longings, aspirations, and experiences. The Holocaust evokes reactions from us precisely because that material is already present and active, constantly forming questions to do with identity and images of self, safety and security, relationship, trust, meaning, and so on. It is indeed difficult to separate out the Holocaust itself as an historical event with profound moral, theological, political, and legal implications, from the intangible holocausts which we inevitably create in our own minds and through our own experience whenever we think about it.

> "Occasionally I have bad dreams … surrounding Holocaust imagery. … […] I'm not sure really what triggers that off … maybe watching something on TV or reading something … a book, something in the *Jewish Chronicle*." (Interview with "Ruth")

This psychological territory of "ordinary" Jews has been surprisingly ignored, even in the vast territories of Holocaust literature. While Holocaust survivors and their children write and are written about; while Holocaust scholars study the Holocaust from historical, theological, and political and even personal perspectives, often becoming embroiled in critiques of each other's positions; and while those engaged in Holocaust memorialisation (or what Norman Finkelstein (2000) has more caustically described as "The Holocaust Industry") assert, often aggressively, their own versions of "the truth" about the Holocaust and its ramifications, most Jews stay rather quiet, perhaps feeling guiltily that their feelings are of little importance in a field so overshadowed by those who suffered the actual horrors. Yet if we are to find out how to live in, and relate to, a world in which this Holocaust happened, without being driven by guilt, anger, blame, fear, internal conflict, or helplessness, I would suggest that our emotional reactions and responses to it, different *as they must be* from those who experienced it, need exploring in their own right.

Some recent writers are certainly aware that gaps in literature and studies exist. In his excellent study, *A Holocaust Controversy*, Samuel Moyn (2005) traces the evolution of a major controversy that, in his words, "rocked French and French-Jewish life in the mid-1960s" following the publication of Jean-François Steiner's (1966) semi-fictionalised account of an insurrection by Jewish inmates that took place in Treblinka extermination camp in August 1943. Moyn, an American historian, describes Steiner's book as a "fantastically successful text" which stimulated a debate in France that "tested popular understandings of World War Two, cast light on the state of the Jewish community, and involved many of the most significant, as well as numerous obscure, writers of the day" (Moyn, 2005, pp. xv–xvi). The controversy had a major impact on French interpretation of wartime events as well as catalysing a new focus for French-Jewish identity, and Moyn decided to study it not just because happening across it almost by accident it immediately drew his interest[1], but because he hoped that:

> the results might help illuminate a chronic, and enduring, phenomenon. Fierce arguments about the Holocaust are now practically a fixture of contemporary public and academic life, a fact that calls for recognition and analysis. (Ibid., p. xvii)

Through his own book, Moyn hoped to reveal how any study of the Holocaust takes place in its *own* cultural context and thus has to be a reflection of, and a response to, the cultural (an umbrella term which in this instance I mean to embrace the political and psychological) requirements of the particular era. A key chapter of Moyn's book is devoted to the biographical background: of Steiner himself and of his father, Kadmi Cohen, who was deported from Drancy in 1944 and died in one of Auschwitz's sub-camps soon after, when Steiner was eight years old. "Without reference to [the victimised father] it is impossible to understand the young son's conduct" (ibid., p. xvii): this refers to the way in which Steiner distorted significant parts of his own research in order to give his own meaning to the Treblinka insurrection, a meaning which the survivors whom he interviewed themselves disowned. "In many passages", one survivor wrote to Steiner, "you attribute sentences and words to me that I never said or wrote, and which contradict my sentiments and my actions as well as my past in the ghetto" (ibid., p. 125)

In wondering about the potential clashes which arise between an individual's (such as Steiner's) *subjective* need to give meaning to his personal experience, and the need for historians and political commentators to develop *dispassionate* theories as to the political and historical contexts in which events like the Holocaust arise, Moyn observes that:

> What the Treblinka controversy makes utterly clear is that there has been no single psychological course for the second generation to follow, and that different members of the second generation may develop antithetical identities based on their attempts to reinvigorate the same traumatic past at different historical moments. (Ibid., p. 153)

One could well add that this shifting relationship with the past also serves different purposes and needs at different moments in history.

Moyn continues: "neither the psychological nor the political interpretation of post-traumatic identity formation and cultural production is totally adequate, and no one has yet achieved a satisfactory account of their inter-relation" (ibid., p. 154). In other words, Moyn seems to be saying that no one—neither psychologists, political writers, nor historians—can fully explain how people come to think of themselves the way they do; or how the various parts played in this by someone's subjective inner life and the political and social contexts surrounding him or her from the day s/he is born, influence each other. By extrapolation, post-Holocaust Jewish identity is a fluid and changing entity that shifts in line with time, with cultural context, and with political imperatives. The historical events can and should be studied, but the meanings attributed to them are informed as much by an individual's personal experiences and social affiliations as they are by the cultural and political contexts of the day. Moyn does not attempt to bridge this gap; he observes that it is there and argues that both dimensions should be given equal weight in trying to grapple with the Holocaust as an historic event, and the impact of it through the lives of subsequent generations and cultures. "Though one could easily elaborate a typology of the psychic after-effects of parental or cultural trauma and loss [...], it is just as important to emphasize the political and historical contexts in which memory formation occurs" (ibid., p. 153).

Gary Weissman comes from a position similar to Moyn's. In *Fantasies of Witnessing*, Weissman deals with a phenomenon that he observes in the writings and productions of a small number of Holocaust "specialists", which he describes as "the non-witness's desire [...] to witness the Holocaust as if one were there."

> It is the unspoken desire of many people who have no direct experience of the Holocaust but are deeply interested in studying, remembering and memorialising it. It is a desire to know what it was like to be there in Nazi Europe; in hiding; at the sites of mass shootings; in the ghettos; in the cattle cars; in the concentration camps; in the death camps; in the gas chambers and crematoria. This desire can be satisfied only in fantasy, in fantasies of witnessing the Holocaust for oneself. (Weissman, 2004, p. 4)

Essentially, Weissman's book is a critique of a prevailing effort, evident in the proliferation of Holocaust museums and memorials, to persuade the present-day public that we can grasp the realities of "the Holocaust" through exposure to selective, "re-created" and often symbolic narratives. Weissman criticises this trend for a number of important reasons. One is that it blurs genuine distinctions between those who suffered directly and those (most of us) who have not, and replaces it with a different hierarchy, such as one based on one's courage and capacity to "feel the trauma". Further, the methods used actively encourage people to identify with Holocaust victims, and thus to believe that through identification they can "know" the Holocaust; as though being on the receiving end of the Holocaust is the only way to know what it was about[2]. Weissman finds himself deeply questioning of this now-widespread custom because in his view it delegitimises the crucial task of grasping the Holocaust *as* an historical phenomenon:

> Perhaps because [the Holocaust] is an historical concept comprising myriad events which no one person experienced directly, the Holocaust can *only* be understood historically. (Ibid., p. 94)

Unlike Moyn, however, Weissman is not an historian (in fact he is a professor of English). He is clearly concerned with the question of relationship between "non-witnesses" (primarily Jewish) and "the Holocaust"—that is to say, in what ways people experience and are able to express their relationship—and he tries to access this through speculating on what drives certain depictions of the Holocaust. As a result, he posits, in effect, a need to look psychologically below the surface of our own behaviours and assumptions. In *Fantasies of Witnessing* he argues that the way we think and feel about the Holocaust as an event that we, as "non-witnesses", did not experience is heavily influenced, if not driven, by our own psychological needs and characters:

> Something other than temporal distance and access to living witnesses determines how people relate to history. This other, more decisive factor is the tendency to privilege and identify with those histories that resonate with one's own sense of identity. (Ibid., p. 7)

And again:

> Holocaust educators frequently state that nothing connects us to the Holocaust more intimately and directly than the testimonies of survivors. Little attention has been paid, however, to how this connection is fraught with our own personal needs and fantasies, and further complicated by survivors' own difficult relationships to the Holocaust. (Ibid., p. 30)

In identifying a link between an individual's own life and what the Holocaust evokes for that individual, Weissman implicitly affirms a need to study more specifically not just the Holocaust per se but the dynamics of its impact within the wider Jewish community. However, Weissman does not undertake this as such. Instead, he limits his study to a select group of Holocaust scholars and film-makers: Alfred Kazin writing on Elie Wiesel; Lawrence L. Langer; and Steven Spielberg and Claude Lanzmann being his principal objects of focus.[3]

Having taken as his central theme the "unspoken desire" of "non-witnesses" to relate to the Holocaust by trying to experience it as though they had been *there*, Weissman is left to pose, but not actually address, a key question. His question takes different forms, but is essentially a puzzle for him as to *why* people seek to relate in this way:

> What obstacles do we face in our efforts to approach the Holocaust? Where do we look for the Holocaust? And, perhaps most important, what do we hope to find there? (Ibid., p. 27)

And

> Several decades later, we are still searching for ways to feel closer to that horror. The question we should be asking—though it may seem wrong, somehow improper or indelicate to ask—is why. (Ibid., p. 209)

It is the territory of that question—"why?"—that I seek to explore in this book. Weissman takes a particular phenomenon—people's apparent "desire to feel closer" to the Holocaust—and posits that this desire arises from a personal need, although he does not know what the need is. My starting point is different. I am interested in what people themselves say of their own thoughts, feelings, and reactions to the Holocaust; how they understand their own reactions; and how these reactions are positioned in their own lives. Like Weissman, I am interested in trying to name thematically some of those reactions. Throughout this book I explore what it is that fuels those reactions from the inside, both at the personal level of the individual and at the shared or meta-level of "Jewishness" and Jewish inheritance. I am not suggesting for one moment that the Holocaust was not the horror we know it to have been; but rather that we in the population of Jews disconnected from the Holocaust in space, time, and close family are the other party in a *relationship* with the "it" that the Holocaust was; and as such are active participants in its legacy.

Awareness of our relationship with the Holocaust *as* a relationship, and therefore as something we might be curious about, is a question generally conspicuous by its absence in the field of Holocaust studies. A feature of much Holocaust literature is what could be described as a battle between different protagonists as to "the truth" about the Holocaust; or, as Weissman puts it, who *owns* the Holocaust, and who, therefore, ideologically has "the right" to present specific views of the Holocaust and its meaning (if it can be said to have a single meaning) to Jews and the wider world. This is a central part of Weissman's own book. As he explores some of the conflicted territory of Holocaust interpretation, reflected in Kazin's changing, and fraught, relationship with Elie Wiesel, and Langer's apparent fixation on asserting the moral righteousness of his own views, essentially he argues that these individuals write seemingly without any awareness of what they themselves bring to the debate. Certainly, "truths" are often asserted—and received—within narrow interpretative frameworks, a habit which necessarily restricts a recognition of how someone's thoughts and feelings about the Holocaust are in practice actively co-created by them in relation to the historic events they grapple with.

An example of such a restricted viewpoint is to be found in Norman Finkelstein's book *The Holocaust Industry*. Finkelstein's book, which presents a radical critique of the ways in which American Jewish organisations and individuals have *used* the Holocaust for questionable purposes, and which caused a huge stir when first published, is by any definition a polemic. Finkelstein himself, in his foreword to the second paperback edition (2003) describes himself as having needed to get something "off [his] chest". In his introduction, he refers briefly to one of the prime motivators for his anger: an (one can assume) extremely painful childhood experience of having been abandoned by those around him to deal with the impact of his parents' Holocaust experiences alone:

> Apart from this phantom presence [this refers to his elusive sense of the disaster that had claimed the lives of both his parents' entire families], I do not remember the Nazi holocaust ever intruding on my childhood. The main reason was that no one outside my family seemed to care about what had happened. [...] I honestly do not recall a single friend (or parent of a friend) asking a single question about what my mother and father endured. This was not a respectful silence. It was simply indifference. (Finkelstein, 2003, p. 6)

What struck me about this statement was not the anger and distress that clearly must have lain behind Finkelstein's assertion "it was simply indifference," but its sweeping nature. It seems strange that Finkelstein's account does not offer the possibility of there being anything *other* than "indifference" behind his friends', and their parents', failure to enquire as to his parents' painful past. From his account, one is left to assume that for Finkelstein there is—and was—only one truth. Of course, I am British and did not know the particular cultural environment of 1950s and '60s Jewish America; but from my own experience I think it unlikely that indifference was the only possible interpretation. My parents had a number of friends who were refugees from Nazism, and my own best friend throughout adolescence was the daughter of Holocaust survivors. My friend and I talked often about what had happened to her parents; I wanted to ask and she, I know from much later conversations, found it important that I was there to tell. Judging, too, from the occasional comments I heard my parents make as to the people they themselves knew, they also were far from indifferent as to the experiences of survivors. However, coming from a generation in which—not uncommonly—they felt constrained from asking even their own parents and grandparents about their respective pasts, I think it more likely that they did not know *how* to ask; or what they would do with the answers if they received them. Self-protection, unease, perhaps guilt—all of these are indicated; but indifference?

That not all children of survivors (never mind the survivors themselves) deal with their cruel and devastating legacy in the same way can be seen by contrasting Finkelstein's book with Art Spiegelman's cartoon memoir, *Maus* (Spiegelman, 1996). *Maus* is a painfully honest effort to confront the sheer confusion that is left to subsequent generations living in the present world whilst dealing with a Holocaust past. In depicting his father's story, Spiegelman attempts both to honour his survivor-father's experiences and to illustrate his own confusion of grief, rage, and guilt at his parents' suffering then and their subsequent behaviours (not least of which was his survivor-mother's suicide when Spiegelman was twenty). Anger and rage are inevitably part of the Holocaust inheritance: while Finkelstein directs his at those who, in his eyes, "exploit Jewish suffering" (and by implication the suffering of his parents) for personal or political gain, Spiegelman wrestles with the contradictions of anger and guilt. Both are part of a bigger picture in which all of us who are interested in the Holocaust or concerned with its implications are simultaneously confronted with the historic facts and the desire or need on the part of our own confused[4] reactions to find outlet or meaning.

A similar strength of feeling to Finkelstein's can be found in Anne Karpf's memoir, *The War After*. Karpf, herself the daughter of Holocaust survivors who came to Britain in the aftermath of the war, like Finkelstein also rails against the "collective indifference" of indigenous British Jews to her parents' experiences. Unlike Finkelstein, however, she makes some effort to explain this, which she does through drawing on a socio-political critique of Anglo-Jewry and its reluctance to "rock the boat" of its perceived precarious acceptance in British society. Karpf gets closer than Finkelstein attempts to imagining what lay behind British Jews' failure to enquire:

> If British Jews had felt paralysed and shocked during the war, they must have felt even more so afterwards on seeing searing images of Jewish suffering and knowing how little pressure they'd attempted to exert from a position of relative safety. One can imagine their sense of guilt and discomfort in the presence of survivors, walking reminders of what they were doubtless trying to forget. (Karpf, 1996, p. 199)

Karpf is able to do this partly because the purpose of her book is different from that of Finkelstein's. He is arguing a thesis; she is writing a memoir. However, at the end of the day, neither writer can really write from an informed position as to what characterises or lies behind "ordinary" Jewish reactions to the Holocaust and its survivors because neither of them has actually asked.

It needs saying at the outset that whatever characterises our inner psychological relational dynamics with the Holocaust can never be purely personal in origin. There is a subtle interplay between personal and collective, or social, experience. We each construct our images of the Holocaust, I believe, partly in response to, and as a result of, the personal material of our own lives, material which develops through the interaction of our personalities with our experiences in and with our families. But family dynamics are themselves framed in the context of social experience. Since Jews as a group have been historically subjected to differential and often disadvantageous experiences, it is almost inevitable that those collective experiences would be re-enacted in and transmitted through individual families, and thus fed back into the formation of collective identity. So that references to the Holocaust as "a collective trauma" beg the question, when neither one's own family nor most of the families around were involved in the Holocaust, as to whether it is the Holocaust per se which is the source of this supposed trauma, or whether it *represents* other traumas which families, and therefore individuals in those families, did experience.

Linked to this question of collective identity is an observably unresolved question as to how we in the post-Holocaust generations identify ourselves in relating to the Holocaust: at the simplest level, how we refer to ourselves (or are referred to). Some scholars use the term "non-survivors", although this can confusingly imply those who did not survive the Holocaust itself. Weissman, having examined the various ways in which other scholars try to construct identities for the broad mass of post-Holocaust Jews, and, in particular, attempts to use an identity built around the idea of witnessing,[5] opts for the term "non-witnesses". This is key to his exploration of what he describes as the "fantasies" held by many that they can come close to the Holocaust by imagining their own presence in it. The problem, however, with "non-witnesses", as with "non-survivors" is that such terms define us by what we are *not*. It illustrates a perennial feature of what we might call our "post-Holocaust identity formation" as Jews: that is, that the Holocaust occupies such a central position in our recent collective past that it is deeply challenging to think of who or what we are without reference to it. Yet negative self-identity does not in itself clearly lead anywhere. If I am *not* a survivor, *not* the child of a survivor, *not* a witness, *not* a refugee, then as a Jew what am I? It is in effect a major challenge to us to know "who we are" post-Holocaust. For me, this is reflected in the task of coming up with a way of referring to the people whose feelings and thoughts about the Holocaust I have explored without defining them as "not" something. For the time being, I use the simple shorthand of "'ordinary' Jews"; though of course this in itself implies that those who fall (or fell) into the categories of victim, survivor, refugee, and so on are (or were) "extraordinary" Jews, rather than Jews who were unenviably caught up in extraordinary circumstances.

Underlying the struggle even for terminology is the difficult fact that the Holocaust eradicated numerous reference points for Jewish identity. It is important to remember that significant numbers of Jews are *not* descended from European Jewish communities, and that the relationship of, say, a Jew of Iraqi or Yemeni origin to the Holocaust is bound to be different in some measure from that of someone descended from the *shtetls* of Eastern Europe. However, most Jews *are* descended from European communities; the Holocaust thus poses tremendously difficult questions as to our relationship with our own history: a 1,900-year history which ended catastrophically in barely a single decade. Being Jews of European descent means in a real way that when we think of our history and the lands our forebears came from, what we now relate to is an *absence*. This may explain the "haunting" quality referred to by many writers in relation to the Holocaust. "Haunting" refers to something lost, to a ghostly vestige of itself which cannot be grasped. In this sense, we are left with phantoms. Loss and our relationship with history are two of the themes I explore in this book.

When Weissman poses the question of why it is that people—Jews in particular—now seek "to feel closer" to the horror of the Holocaust, there are a number of possible answers. Some writers approach it in politico-cultural terms. For Finkelstein, the embracing of Holocaust memory is political exploitation, the deliberate use of the Holocaust for the material advancement of individuals running significant American Jewish organisations, and for the political benefit of the Zionist cause. Peter Novick (1999), another historian, sees it more as a cultural tool around which, with the changing Jewish demographics and cultural climate in America during the 1970s and '80s, a needed new form of American Jewish identity could coalesce. Novick is surely right to point out the enormous importance of cultural contextualisation in how any historic event is perceived and used (or forgotten) by later generations[6]. At the same time, his oblique suggestion that "the centering of the Holocaust in the minds of American Jews" constitutes "excessive or overly prolonged mourning" (which in itself runs counter to Jewish teaching) appears to marginalise the need to reflect on the Holocaust *as* a genuine object of mourning (Novick, 1999, pp. 10–11). Literature on mourning and bereavement indicates that grieving is a process highly subject to complications arising from the relationship with the bereaved and the circumstances of the bereavement. So even if the Holocaust *is* used to serve needs which Jews feel today, this does not obviate the possibility of there existing a legitimate psychological pressure behind this phenomenon.

Weissman himself suggests that one drive for what he sees as "the need to feel closer" is simply the passage of time. The further away in time we get from the Holocaust, the more energy seems to accrue around the need to remember it: the more important it seems to become to *hold on to* it. Yet a need to hold onto the past presupposes fears about loss and betrayal. To let go of the past involves shifting the focus of one's search for identity and meaning into the present: a challenging process which can leave people disoriented, fearful of losing reliable points of reference as to who they are. The significance of the Holocaust for Jewish identity—what "it means to be Jewish" in the wake of the Holocaust—cannot be underestimated. The reverberations of this continue in, for example, clashes over whether we should see ourselves nowadays as victims or, in the conflict between Israel and the Palestinians, as victimisers; and the quite different outcomes that flow from those two positions. The fact of the Holocaust creates a pressure for new forms of Jewish identity to emerge; "who we are" now has to take account of this event—and this is not necessarily a bad thing. Jews no longer live in a world in which we have to accept appalling forms of racial stereotyping. True, they exist; but so do legitimate and well-founded arguments for countering them. The pressure around identity may be partly to do with the challenge of emerging from a persecutory world in which we would seem to have *no choice* but to defend ourselves from the constant threat of persecutory attack, into one where we can in our minds, as well as in daily living, see ourselves as equal. The sentiment of this challenge, although of course in very different circumstances, is captured in an article by Ben Okri, who interviewed numerous ordinary black people in the aftermath of the election of Barack Obama to the US presidency in 2008. Daryl Johnson, a pastor in Mound Bayou, Mississippi, told Okri that "the presence of Obama revolutionises the black man's mind, the old plantation mind from the south. *We don't have to be what we used to be*"[7] (Okri, 2008; my emphasis).

Most of the literature I have referred to so far has been by American Jewish writers (although Moyn, of course, is writing about a French episode), and it is impossible to get away from the fact that so much Holocaust literature is produced by American Jews writing in an American environment. This poses a significant question as to how the culture of American Jewry unconsciously slants perspectives, fostering an implicit idea that the American Jewish experience *is* the Jewish experience. As Novick points out, how American Jews see the world is in part how Americans see the world. The cultural domination of world Jewry by American Jews (much as Israel might like to claim that it speaks for all Jews, it is far too concerned with its own survival to be interested in diaspora affairs) is one tragically tangible outcome of the Holocaust, with its eradication of vastly diverse, intellectually and culturally alive centres of Jewish population in Europe. So while practical considerations dictated that it was much easier for me to interview Jews living in Britain, there was a good principle behind this choice. British Jews have a similar, but by no means identical, history and social experience to American Jews. The Second World War itself was a totally different experience for British Jews, as it was for Britons, than it was for American Jews. The only two members of my family who died in the war both died in air raids (my father's sister and my mother's uncle), events to which Jews and non-Jews were exposed without discrimination. For British Jews, Hitler was not some remote threat across the other side of the Atlantic but frighteningly close, a closeness which quite probably escalated post-war anxiety as to "how near we had come" to sharing the fate of Jews in mainland Europe and which may even now play some part in the nervousness in some British Jewish quarters as to the prevalence or otherwise of anti-Semitism. While the Holocaust is a shared fact of Jewish history to which all Jews have to relate in one way or another, the contextual differences in which Jews live play a role in forming differences in post-Holocaust Jewish responses.

All my interviewees live in Britain, although not all were born here. I have tried to interview people across the range of age, gender, religious affiliation, and origin[8] so as to explore how these differences might influence people's sense of relationship to the Holocaust. Without people's willingness to give up time to be interviewed, and to go through what were often deeply felt explorations, it would have been impossible to write this book, and I am immensely grateful to them all. Some people wrote to me independently of being interviewed; and I have had innumerable conversations over the years of researching this book with people who were absorbed by the subject and "had things to say". To a greater or lesser extent, all of these have been influences on my own thinking.

From the interview material and other personal contributions, and from widespread reading (one quickly learns the sheer impossibility of reading more than a fraction of the literature around concerning the Holocaust), I identified certain themes which emerged in some way as particularly significant. Key as a unifying theme is the concept of trauma. Many people—non-Jews as well as Jews—spontaneously refer to the psychological impact of the Holocaust on the Jewish population at large as "a collective trauma". What this means in their minds, however, is never really clear: "trauma" has become a useful, catch-all phrase. Nevertheless, it does mean something. Trauma is a multi-faceted and complex experience which has been, and continues to be, studied in enormous depth in the clinical setting of psychoanalysis and psychotherapy. In terms of individual suffering, much described as "trauma" has been thought about and elucidated, and it therefore seems probable that, by extrapolation, there may be similarities with what one might call a *collective* experience, even though played out quite differently. Since, too, during the course of interviews, many feelings were referred to which have clinical relevance to the theme of trauma, it became fairly obvious in my mind that "trauma" could offer a valid framework for exploring the post-Holocaust Jewish collective experience. For these reasons, the chapter headings and subjects for much of the book follow what are agreed clinically to be key constituents of trauma.

"Trauma" is a word applied to a complex emotional experience which, clinically, can take years for an individual to work through sufficiently to be able to get on with life in all the fullness of its present possibilities, as opposed to being hounded by the past. Whatever the source of trauma, it seems to be intimately linked with an experience of searing loss, commonly associated with other intense emotions: shock, pain, anger, fear, guilt, shame. Traumatic loss fundamentally challenges human beings in the territory of their identity: "Who am I?" and "Am I of value as who I am?" being questions intricately tied up with the quest for self in the face of an experience of *loss* of self. Most of the chapters therefore follow these themes. Chapter One focuses on trauma per se. In that chapter, I begin to unravel what it is that "ordinary Jews" mean when they describe themselves, or Jews collectively, as "traumatised by the Holocaust." Chapter Two focuses on loss, one of the most deeply felt associations with the Holocaust. In exploring loss, I suggest that there are two particularly powerful dynamics at work. One is that, because the losses involved in the Holocaust were so multi-layered, it has enormous *symbolic* power to reach into and connect with the changing realities of our own lives. The second is that the Holocaust not only evokes but compounds the emotional consequences and unspoken-about losses derived from one history which *is* shared by most Jews today: that of the mass migration of Jews from Eastern Europe which took place just over a hundred years ago.

Chapter Three focuses on anger. While Jews are bound in a simple sense to "feel angry about the Holocaust", something more is involved in these reactions. This "something more", I think, speaks partly of an angry frustration at the sheer struggle to articulate and comprehend so much that is evoked by this massive betrayal we feel to have been, and call, the Holocaust. Anger is not easily separated from fear; therefore Chapter Four considers fear and its too-easy association with anti-Semitism. Our fear is more complex, I suggest: it emerges in some ways from a deeply layered doubt as to our own acceptability in the world, and in that sense leads both back to anger and forward (in my sequencing of chapters) to our feelings of guilt and shame. In Chapter

Five, I explore guilt—a perturbing feeling for Jews in relation to the Holocaust, but one still present; and I wonder how much unconscious charge is given by guilt and the hidden, barely mentioned associated trauma of shame to the pain and anger which Jews feel more explicitly. Chapter Six explores how all these feelings and questions have become bound up in our complex relationship with, and need for, Israel, both as an actual state and as a symbolic repository of our hopes, fears, and longings.

Finally, in Chapter Seven I return to the elusive question of collective trauma and its impact on the ways in which history and identity are perceived. I suggest that for ordinary Jews, being on the periphery of this communal catastrophe has its own impact, not least in generating underlying anxieties as to their own legitimacy in speaking of the Holocaust when it is not a directly shared experience. I argue that while the Holocaust is constantly talked *about*, in practice most Jews are uneasy speaking about the way it impacts on them, and this reticence fosters a communal silence which in turn perpetuates its own version of trauma. As with the working through of personal trauma, developing ways to speak authentically about the traumatising impact of this history is critical to our capacity to free ourselves from its terrible legacy of victimhood and otherness.

For Auntie Rita

CHAPTER ONE

"A traumatised people"?

To speak of the Holocaust in one breath almost implicitly seems to involve the word "trauma" in the next. "Jews are", said Caroline, "a traumatised people." Sonia thinks that "we all suffer a collective trauma", and for Louis it is also a matter of "a collective trauma". Avigail Abarbanel, an Israeli-born psychotherapist, believes that it is "Jewish trauma [which] is behind the aggression of Zionist ideology, the colonisation of Palestine, the ethnic cleansing of 1948 and the way Israel has been treating the Palestinian people in the last 56 years" (Abarbanel, 2006). Abarbanel continues her line of thinking (although she does not specify what the "foundational myths" she refers to are), asserting that "Jewish foundational myths show very clearly that we, the Jews, have always been thinking and acting out of trauma." Richard sees an historic and continuous Jewish trauma derived from the practice of circumcising tiny babies: an experience which, in his view, sensitises Jews to later traumas such as the Holocaust: "it's utterly traumatic, the child does not understand this." Another interviewee completely refuted this idea. My interviews contained many references to trauma and, often, to a kind of trauma that was thought of as generic and shared. Post-Holocaust, a concept of common trauma seems to have become part of a Jewish vocabulary of self. But it is apparent from the brief quotations above that whilst Jews are interested in the idea of trauma as a Jewish experience, especially when related to the Holocaust, there isn't necessarily agreement on what it means or how it arises. Can we accurately speak of Jews who did not suffer the Holocaust as collectively traumatised by it? And if we are traumatised "by" it without having gone through it, how has this happened?

In recent years "trauma" seems almost to have become *the* defining characteristic of the Holocaust; consequently, this makes it unavoidable as a starting point for my explorations. But discussing trauma, much less "collective" trauma, is no simple task. Trauma is a complex and variable phenomenon, theories and practice around which have been evolving for more than a century, mainly for the purposes of clinical treatment. Some degree of consensus has formed as to the nature of trauma in its clinical manifestations, although it has to be said that the field of trauma studies is still characterised by considerable diversity and, as often, disagreement. What, then, are we to make of "collective" trauma? Not only is the concept itself on the whole new, but the expression is made additionally problematic by its very composition, for it is formed by linking two terms ("collective" and "trauma"), each of which suffers from its own definitional challenges.[1]

There are, of course, links between personal and "collective" experience, between personal and "collective" trauma. No collective (however defined) exists independently of individuals. But what these links are; how they work; the relationship between external traumatic events and internal traumatic responses; the issue of memory—what gets remembered and what gets forgotten in the formulation of cultural "memory": all these and more are questions central to developing our understanding of what constitutes "collective" trauma. Without addressing them, all we have are half-formed assumptions attached to an idea whose meaning is shadowy and vague. Yet if we are to take seriously an instinct which dictates that events as catastrophic as the Holocaust have serious and lasting consequences for individuals, communities, countries, and our very notion of civilisation, such questions must be addressed, however difficult they may be.

Theories and practice from the clinical field of personal trauma offer useful guidance to this exploration, and in subsequent chapters I explore in some detail how different dimensions of trauma manifest in "ordinary" Jews' narratives at both individual and shared levels. In this chapter, though, my focus is on the generic theme of "trauma".

It is a complex phenomenon with many layers and associations. As I present the thoughts and experiences in relation to the Holocaust of the "ordinary Jews" whom I interviewed, I observe that there are numerous influences at work; for no two people have exactly the same relationship to trauma but must first approach it through the individual experience of their own lives. I suggest that in many respects the Holocaust acts as a magnet to which traumatised reactions attach; and that it is not necessarily the Holocaust as such which is the trauma for "ordinary" Jews so much as its evocative power to disturb and provide a focus for other experiences, inherited and actual, in people's own lives. At the same time, there are distinct features associated with the Holocaust which are relayed through the cultural and communal connections Jews live with and which have their own impact. Individual and shared domains overlap; there is nothing about this subject which is easy.

Trauma and the Holocaust

In introducing a collection of theoretical readings on the Holocaust, Neil Levi and Michael Rothberg refer to the rise of trauma as a specific category of study in relation to the Holocaust. "The recent fascination with traumatic memory [...] comes to mind as one example of a phenomenon that links collective, historical experiences—such as war and genocide—with the psychic suffering of individuals." "The concept of trauma" has become, they say, "a key to understanding a range of individual and collective histories (including slavery, war, and sexual assault)" (Levi & Rothberg, 2003, p. 15).

To Levi and Rothberg, it is traumatic *memory* that links the individual with the collective. This begs its own question, and I return to this later, in Chapter Seven. For now, I focus on the idea of trauma as a theoretical "key" to certain histories. It is undoubtedly true that trauma has become of great interest in academic circles, particularly in the humanities, with whole departments now dedicated to trauma studies. However, extensive study has not in itself led to whole-hearted agreement as to what constitutes trauma. Furthermore, the idea of traumatic memory as the means through which indirect experience of a large-scale trauma such as the Holocaust percolates into a wider community contains its own difficulties, not least because "memory" itself is notoriously malleable. Cathy Caruth, who according to Weissman has become "the leading 'trauma theorist' in the humanities" (Weissman, 2004, p. 133), says of trauma's clinical uses that "this powerful new tool has provided anything but a solid explanation [...]." (Caruth, 1995, cited in Levi & Rothberg, op. cit., p. 192). To an extent, Caruth is right. Even in the clinical field, there are considerable variations in how different disciplines describe and approach trauma in order to treat it. Clinicians also work largely with individuals. By contrast, in the humanities academics consider trauma largely from a theoretical and speculative position, reflecting an effort to apply the concept of trauma speculatively to social patterning and cultural expression. Neither of these fields reach the more indefinable levels of collective experience. So whilst the idea of collective or shared trauma may be the best that Jews themselves can come up with in this post-Holocaust era, it still exists in something of a conceptual vacuum.

At one level, it is not difficult to see how, in thinking about the Holocaust, Jews might describe themselves as traumatised. A horror is deeply felt. Since the Holocaust presents to our gaze repeated depictions of events, images, descriptions, artefacts, and pieces of information which are highly disturbing and, not least, extremely frightening, "trauma" offers a kind of shorthand explanation for those disturbed personal feelings. At the same time it may not on its own be a sufficient explanation. Why, for example, should the Holocaust disturb me more than, say, watching a brutal murder in a film such as *The Talented Mr. Ripley*? (Minghella, 1999).[2] The fact that the one really happened, and the other is a fictional representation, is in a certain way immaterial, since I—like most Jews—know both largely through representation and narration, not through direct experience. Both speak to my personal capacity to be appalled and frightened at human propensity to inflict horrifying death and injury on others, but neither has factually happened to me. There is, of course, a difference. I can put down a disturbing novel or leave the cinema secure in some measure that what I have read or seen was only fiction. This is not possible with the Holocaust. Part of this trauma is that the Holocaust cannot easily be "put down"—relegated to a back shelf or donated to Oxfam. For better or worse, it is ours.

In *Kalooki Nights*, Howard Jacobson constructs a whole novel around one post-war-born Mancunian's inheritance of the Holocaust. Referring sardonically to "two sorts of Jews [...] those who went through the Holocaust and those who only thought they did", Jacobson satirises what he sees as a tendency amongst Jews who have not themselves suffered greatly in their own lives to identify with a common lot of woe, rather than as the fictional father does, "to seek deliverance … to ditch the J-word as a denomination of suffering altogether" (Jacobson, 2006, p. 18). Yet Jacobson is as aware of a central anomaly in the experience of second- or third-generation British-born Jews as he is also aware that the Holocaust casts a heavy shadow, calling this "the death-in-life grip those slaughtered five or more million had on our imaginations" (ibid., p. 8). Through the mouth of Max, his central character, Jacobson poses this anomaly:

> By any of the usual definitions of the word victim, of course, I wasn't one. I had been born safely, at a lucky time and in an unthreatening part of the world, to parents who loved and protected me. I was a child of peace and refuge. […] But there was no refuge from the dead. (Ibid., p. 5)

Jacobson's novel is almost unique in the English language. It takes an "ordinary" Jew, born after the war to English-born parents, and looks at the Holocaust, and more particularly at *the meaning* of the Holocaust, to this central character. It cleverly weaves a narrative in which arise many of the questions which someone born in these circumstances might ask: Where did we come from? Who are my parents? What does it mean to be Jewish? Why don't we talk about what happened? Fictional as it is, it nevertheless presents something recognisably from that time, and a curious question arises: where is the trauma of the Holocaust to be found? In the fictional character Max's experience, was it in his shock of learning about it through a book,[3] and realising that his parents had avoided talking about it? Was it already in the family experience, having lived in and then left the village Jacobson caustically dubs "Novoropissik"? Or was it conveyed through the disquieting attitudes of his friend's deeply orthodox parents, which made his own friend somehow worryingly "other"?

What is "trauma"?

There are central problems associated with any discussion of trauma, and even more so with a presumption that the Holocaust as an historic event is, especially in this by now much later period, not only *still* but *particularly* traumatising for Jews. One obvious problem is that the word has so invaded normal daily language that its value as a term which might meaningfully describe experience has become quite eroded. People regularly can be heard describing themselves as having had "a traumatic day" or "a traumatic journey"; by which, usually, they simply mean that they have had a difficult day (or journey) within the normal parameters of daily life. But if "trauma" is to be taken seriously as a concept—and particularly as a clinically useful tool—it has to mean something more than the normal difficulties which arise in the course of daily living. Ruth Leys begins her book, *Trauma—A Genealogy*, by citing two public instances to illustrate the wide discrepancies in situations to which "trauma" finds itself applied. Her first example focuses on the abduction and enforced involvement in violence of about twelve thousand Ugandan children by a Ugandan guerilla group in the ten or so years after 1988. The second example takes the case of Paula Jones, who famously brought a case for sexual harassment against the-then President Clinton, citing post-traumatic stress as evidence of the harm she had suffered. Leys observes that "it is hard not to feel that the concept of trauma has become debased currency when it is applied both to truly horrible events [such as the Holocaust, and the appalling outrages inflicted on the kidnapped children of Uganda] *and* to something as dubious as the long-term harm to Paula Jones" (Leys, 2000, pp. 1–2).

Widespread popularisation of the term "trauma" is one issue, although of course it has to be said that this is not the way in which Jews who think of the Holocaust as "a collective trauma" usually use it. More to the point is the fact that even in clinical[4] settings, where the very concept of trauma arose and where people are centrally engaged with trying to understand traumatic experience for the purpose of therapeutic healing, there are different perspectives on what trauma actually *is*, and therefore the extent to which, and how, it can be healed. In her densely written book, Leys traces the evolution of thinking about trauma over the course of a century, beginning with Freud and working through a succession of chapters focusing on particular psychoanalysts, psychotherapists, psychiatrists, and psychologists, before ending with the Holocaust-focused, post-modern work of professor of English and comparative literature, Cathy Caruth. Leys concludes that "from the moment of its invention in the late nineteenth century the concept of trauma has been fundamentally unstable, balancing uneasily—indeed veering uncontrollably—between two ideas, theories, or paradigms" (ibid., p. 298).

From an overview of the historical development of clinical thinking around trauma, one thing is particularly obvious: there are different dimensions to trauma, and often, therefore, different formulations at work. Broadly speaking, these are reactions to defined and material *events* which result in symptoms usually grouped together under the heading of post-traumatic stress disorder (PTSD); and what can be thought of as more *systemic* forms of trauma: that is, traumas which have become built into an individual's (or possibly a group's) system of psychological organisation in the world. The PTSD traumas are traumas of conscious life, even if the memory of those traumas has been pushed away. Experiences in the concentration camps, or the experiences of the Ugandan children Leys refers to, fall into this category. "Systemic" traumas are less specific *events* than they are certain kinds of *experience* which have occurred in early life, usually before the development of language, thought, and therefore of conscious memory. By definition, they are more elusive to grasp and can often only be inferred from later behaviour, attitudes, and orientation in and to the world. However, within any individual, these two dimensions are bound to overlap, thereby fostering considerable variation in how different individuals respond to the same external event(s). Thus Ruth Kluger, a Holocaust survivor, insists that while the camps were unremittingly grim places where one's chance of survival depended as much on whim and luck as on personal character, no two survivors experienced the Holocaust in the same way: "Though the Shoah involved millions of people, it was a unique experience for each of them" (Kluger, 2001, p. 66).

From a clinical point of view, trauma is essentially a deep wound of complex character. Doctors use the word in specific physical terms to refer to a blow or injury to the body that will take weeks or months to heal. The complexity of character refers to the way the injury impacts on different parts of the body's system: while a simple fracture is "simply" a localised break in a bone, a complex fracture will also involve damage to surrounding tissues or structures. A particular experience of my own, however, illustrates how even a physical trauma may be *more than* an event: how it can impact on the whole self in complex ways, and how it sits within a context. In the early stages of researching this book, I suffered a serious trauma when, for unknown reasons, I catapulted over the handlebars of my bicycle and landed on my (unhelmeted) head. I sustained a head injury; because this came from a blow to the head, it impacted on my nervous system. My most vivid memories of the days following the accident are of the utter terror that overwhelmed me as my brain and body no longer seemed connected, and I could not physically move without intense fear of falling. Yet, overwhelming as these experiences were at the time, I was almost completely recovered within weeks and never suffered afterwards from nightmares, flashbacks, or any of the other symptoms associated with some traumas. It was, after all, an isolated, contained, and unprecedented event with no other human agency involved and with comparatively little reason to fear that it would happen again. However, if my childhood history had been different—if it had included, for example, experience of a terrifying accident in which someone had died, or of physical violence, my long-term reactions might have been very different. In other words, many traumas are isolated events: they may be overwhelming and disturbing at the time, but they can be recovered from. Other traumas are different: they sit within a history and, consciously or unconsciously, demand meaning. The Holocaust is one of these.

Sometimes it seems as though the very word "trauma" evades definition: that it is, in consequence, itself a shorthand word for many overlaid experiences. Colleague psychotherapists have spoken to me of trauma's "vortex-like character", referring to the way in which trauma seems to suck all experience into itself; and to "the frozen quality that develops when people 'play dead' in the face of overwhelming threat." Psychoanalyst Christopher Bollas sees deadness—that is, the killing off of feelings—as a central quality of trauma (Bollas, 1995).[5] Recovery can only happen (if it can happen at all) when the living feelings, with all their potential for the creative force of life, have themselves been recovered from an internally deadened landscape. In similar vein, theologian Zachary Braiterman sees the most profound "depiction" of the psychological landscape post-Holocaust in the deadening and eerie quality of one of German painter Anselm Kiefer's post-Holocaust paintings. *Shulamite*, Braiterman tells us, presents an ashen, burnt-out, claustrophobic interior without illumination or way out: in Braiterman's own words, a "crematoria image" presenting the "grim certainty" of death (Braiterman, 1998, pp. 171–174). One outcome of such deadness is that it kills (either psychologically or actually) meaningful action, thus adding further layers to a felt experience of trauma by reducing the traumatised individual to an object without power or agency. In this respect, it seems clear from the writings of many Holocaust survivors that one of the ways in which they managed *psychologically* and ultimately *physically* to survive was by holding on to an experience of themselves as someone able to act; whether, like Viktor Frankl, through realising in the camps that his last human freedom was to *choose his attitude* in the circumstances surrounding him; or, like Kluger's mother, being determined to manipulate the system in whatever way she could so that her daughter could survive (Frankl, 1946, p. 86; Kluger, 2001, pp. 104–106).

Other writers associate trauma with loss, and others again with shame. For example, psychoanalysts Susan Levy and Alessandra Lemma call their book on trauma *The Perversion of Loss*, signifying that in their eyes trauma has to do with a failure to grieve (Levy & Lemma, 2004). I write about loss as a particular dimension of Jewish feelings about the Holocaust in Chapter Two. For now, I will simply observe that there seems to be a quality about traumatic loss that entails an attack on, or violation of, the unconscious "givens" of human existence. Thus in John Bowlby's seminal works on adult depression and loss, he observed that people who, as adults, became overwhelmed by complicated—typically endless—grieving for a current bereavement had usually experienced a particularly painful loss of a parent at a very young age—in a child's life a time when parents are "supposed" to be present and loving, not absent or dead (Bowlby, 1973).

All this makes any construct of the Holocaust as a trauma *collectively experienced* by Jews who were not there exceedingly difficult to pin down. Traumatising elements clearly exist: Jacobson's description of "the death-in-life grip [...] on our imaginations", for example, bears out Cathy Caruth's observation of the *possessive* quality of trauma and Bollas's reflections on the way the deadening impact of trauma absorbs life (Caruth, cited in Levi & Rothberg, op. cit., p. 193). To think of all Jews as equally traumatised, however, muddles important distinctions. Obviously, someone who was not caught up in the Holocaust itself cannot possibly be traumatised in the way its actual victims were. Nor is it possible for the descendants of people safely living in Britain or America during the war to suffer the same kind of emotional after-effects as the children of Holocaust survivors. Here again there are distinctions to be drawn: Ruth Kluger, a Holocaust survivor living in the USA, finds that "Europeans who have sat in air-raid shelters have something in common with me that Americans don't" (Kluger, op. cit., p. 12). In other words, whilst we may relate traumatically to the Holocaust in our minds, our levels of exposure have been very different. Moreover, Kluger refuses to be defined merely by her Holocaust experience, but asserts her right to have a personal life unique in its own terms. At a Limmud[6] seminar in 2008, a lecturer on Holocaust literature expressed puzzlement that Kluger should have spent part of her book "complaining about her parents", as though such "petty" feelings should have disappeared in the shared solidarity of victimhood. Yet why not? Remembering her living self as a protesting self is Kluger's way of still being alive in every sense, and in that way represents her personal triumph over the Nazis. Even direct "victims", therefore, find creative ways to confront their trauma, rather than sinking into the simple identity of "Holocaust survivor."

For those of us who are "ordinary Jews", too, how we each relate to the Holocaust, to something we know *about* but did not actually *know*, is a deeply personal experience. Importantly, it should be noted that none of the people I interviewed for this book described *themselves* as "traumatised" by the Holocaust. Whenever the term arose, it tended to do so in reference to *other* Jews: Israeli Jews, Jews-as-a-whole, the Jews of history. Yet for most Jews, there is still a sense that this is something shared; something that "belongs" to us, even if we don't really understand how. Many "ordinary Jews" still experience a struggle to get past the shock and the disturbance: to surface and to communicate the depth of reaction that our (relatively limited) knowledge touches. As Sonia puts it,

> "it's so ugly […], these things that were done […] were so ugly, you have to sit and think about it and give it space and you realise, it's terrible. […] … It can't even be put into words, the magnitude of 'terribleness', but you've got to get on with life … ."

In the rest of this chapter, I explore certain experiences that help explain how individual Jews make personal associations of trauma with the Holocaust. These lines of thinking have emerged from personal narratives which I present at some length, and they act as a preamble to a more detailed examination in the following chapters of specific themes associated with trauma, such as loss and shame. I conclude this chapter by considering historian Orlando Figes' (2007) study of transgenerational "collective trauma" in Russia and its potential relevance to the post-Holocaust Jewish legacy.

Meeting the Holocaust

Knowing survivors

It is, of course, a dying generation, but one of the most direct ways in which non-survivors have "met" the traumatic effect of the Holocaust is through knowing survivors. Survivors' stories, even their simple presence, evoke complicated feelings and unanswerable questions as to what it is like to meet face on the horrors of mass murder and industrialised genocide, and to have to deal with the way it changes an individual life forever.

The chances are that most Jews who grew to adulthood during the half century following the war will have met at least one Holocaust survivor. As a child I knew a number, who were either friends of my parents, or parents of my friends. It is impossible to say now whether my memory of those encounters is of my actual experiences then, or have acquired a certain kind of *post hoc* rationality, influenced by later reading and more explicit exposure. Looking back, it seems to me that the people I knew shared certain characteristics. Certainly, accent and way of speaking alone would have been enough to set them apart; but over and above that, nearly all seemed to convey a sadness of face, a plangency of voice, and a retreated energy suggesting that it would be better to fade into the background; an aura which Anne Karpf pointedly describes as a "subcutaneous sadness". Their homes were imbued with a mutedness that contrasted strikingly with the loud, histrionic atmospheres of the made-good, former East End Jewish social world to which my family belonged. My parents seemed to speak of survivor friends and acquaintances almost reverentially, alluding to narrow escapes and lost relatives in tones that implied one had to be very careful in what one said. Or perhaps I looked at the gaunt face and haunted eyes of one of my father's dearest friends, and drew that assumption myself. If so, I was not alone. Gideon, who grew up in Israel in the 1960s, spoke of the children he knew and of their impact on him:

> "There was a kind of darkness about Ashkenazi children—German Jews, people whose parents were Holocaust survivors. You always felt that you weren't supposed to be too happy."

Not all childhood encounters with survivors, however, were conscious ones, and, indeed, appearances could vary. Bernice describes meeting again someone whom she had first known when a child. Less specific than was Gideon's experience to a consciousness of the Holocaust, she nevertheless describes an experience of "otherness" within her community of familiarity:

> "I now know one particular person who I met [again] only a couple of years ago. [...] I was ten years old [when I first knew him]; he was the

> first real, dapper, continental man I'd ever seen and we used to come home from *shul*[7] together. Now, he was a '*kind*'… […], he came out of Austria when he was seventeen.[8] As a young person […] it never crossed my mind […]…. the Holocaust never came…. he was just a nice man and used to talk to me on the way home from *shul*."

Nearly everyone I interviewed over the age of forty knew survivors. Often struggling to describe the varying impacts this had on them, what interviewees found themselves saying testifies to a deep dilemma facing all of us in this enterprise: both to know, and not to know, may in their own ways be traumatic. Allowing ourselves to know and to feel something of a survivor's experience exposes us to things we would rather not know about; yet if we do not actually *know*, we are forced to *imagine*, and one of the constant difficulties we face in relation to the Holocaust is, in "normal" terms, its unimaginability. David Grossman's (1989) novel, *See Under: Love*, is, in Hartman's words, "a touching account of what it feels like to grow up with adults who try to protect youngsters from a disastrous knowledge, but leak it anyway and compel them to imagine their own Holocaust scenarios" (Hartman, 1996, p. 8). "Knowing" also invites the possibility on both sides—the survivor and the seeker of knowledge—of breaching a boundary. Does the survivor wish to be known? Do I wish to know?

Yet some kind of knowledge of the survivors we know must and does take place. We may not, as James Young did, spend "long days and nights in the company of survivors, listening to their harrowing tales", but something of "their lives, loves and losses" does get absorbed, and all leave an impact (Young, cited in Hartman, p. 9). The impact, however, may not always be the same. As Ruth Kluger reminds us, survivors are all individuals, as are we; their experiences of the Holocaust were all unique, and our experiences of life, too, differ. All encounters with Holocaust survivors must inevitably interweave with already existing experiences and orientations; and in this sense any trauma "received" from knowing survivors is likely to be neither equal nor uniform.

In his twenties, Edward knew a boy whose father and uncle had both been in Auschwitz. He was greatly disturbed by the unpredictability and contradictions revealed by these brothers:

> "his father had lost fingers of one hand, and his [*the father's*] brother had lost fingers on the other hand and I think that's because they

> shared gloves at Auschwitz. One used the right hand, one had the left hand and they had lost fingers in the frostbite. Now [...] these men had become very rich [...] and then the two brothers had fallen out over money. That made a profound impact on me. I remember thinking ... How can you ... they're so rich, ... they had more money than they could spend and they'd fallen out over money when [...] twenty or twenty-five years earlier in Auschwitz, they had shared gloves [...] I remember thinking the irony of ... the psyche of that [...]. I found (it) deeply worrying."

Bernice spent fourteen years as secretary to a synagogue whose members were largely German refugees and survivors. It opened a world to her very different from the protected one she had grown up in. The effect was to evoke in her a reverence that masked an underlying unease at what the different members of this community had had to endure in order to live the values they now expressed:

> "I was interested and I wanted to know more and the people were so lovely. [...] I mean, when you hear their stories, you ... . just think how lucky I was and our family and how just lucky we were. You know, terrible things that happened, and how lucky they were to be alive and their attitude to life as well, a slightly different attitude to life. A little bit of living for today [...]. It did go in deeply because I was in awe of the people, how they'd gone through so much and how they'd come out of it such wonderful people at the other end. Not all of them were wonderful but the majority, and I loved their values."

Diana also worked with Holocaust survivors over a period of five years in order to produce Holocaust educational materials. She could hardly restrain her tears as she talked about the intense impact this work had had on her:

> "I'm seeing someone today [...] a ... woman who survived Auschwitz, her mother didn't, she thought nobody had survived the war, her father and brother were murdered in Russia by the Nazis and [...] one brother did survive. We stayed friends [...], she's a wonderful woman, a difficult woman, she's been in psychiatric care for four months, I'm going to see her tonight [...]. She had [...] a life after the Holocaust,

> but of course her whole life was affected and informed by what had happened. Periodically she has these terrible depressions. She used to come and do things with kids I taught, and her husband blames this project partly—she's such an effective communicator, and that's part of her dealing with what happened to her, [...] I remember thinking when she stayed, 'How can she sleep? Would you ever go to sleep after? How can your mind not think about what has happened to you?', but of course that's how people survive."

Leah's experience had a more direct and horrifying impact on her own family. Leah is a member of an ultra-orthodox community whose members include(d) a high proportion of Holocaust survivors. One such worked in the community as a childcarer. When her own children were small, Leah entrusted them to this carer, only to discover that the carer was abusing the children she looked after. Years later, Leah is still deeply affected by this experience:

> "When I encounter examples of child abuse, it's often said [Leah's voice became very quiet at this point] that this can be related to ... Holocaust-related experiences in the parents or grandparents. [My] first exposure to this was a woman ... a very tragic figure, who was a camp survivor. She'd been in concentration camps as a child and she was a childminder, and I used to leave my children with her. She suddenly had some kind of breakdown and began damaging all the children that she had ... she had two or three children in her care, including mine. [...] The kinds of things she was doing were ... basically very crude violence—you know, smashing the children around—and very likely to have been the kind of things she would have experienced as a young child. The mothers got together and went to the Rabonim[9] [...]. My husband said, 'We just have to put this all on Hitler's *cheshbon*'."[10]

Meeting the Holocaust through encounters with survivors is therefore not an easily categorisable experience. In part, it is an experience mediated through the human capacity for empathy. Through observing very young children, Robert Winston suggested that most human beings seem to be born with an innate potential for empathy (Winston, 2004). This concept, central to the practice of psychotherapy, is founded in an understanding of human beings as essentially *relational*; by which is meant that human beings acquire a sense of life's meaning primarily through the experience of self in relation to others—a concept also central in Talmudic writings (Cooper, 1988, pp. xxi–xxii). The neurological development of the potential for empathy probably has an evolutionary function: empathy binds us in interpersonal connections and therefore sustains community bonds, a factor vital in the evolution of human society.[11] Therefore meeting Holocaust survivors is an empathic challenge: their anguish—hidden or otherwise—almost literally gets "under the skin" of those exposed to it, to the subcutaneous level that Anne Karpf describes. But the encounter between a survivor and an ordinary Jew is also an intersubjective one: there are two separate subjects (individuals) who meet, and each brings his or her own individuality to the encounter. Survivors may have suffered similar horrors, but they cannot conveniently be parcelled up into a box labelled "survivors", as though that defined the totality of their lives, any more than ordinary Jews can be categorised by the conditions of their lives. As Bernice observed, while some survivors evoke feelings of respect and affection, others can be very challenging to be near:

> "some people are depressed people … […]. A lady died recently, who … used to be the bane of my life. She was the most depressed person I'd ever come across. Every year her *shul* bill would go out, … everybody would wait for this phone call and […] she'd just cry for half an hour. She did have a terrible life but […] it became her life to be a miserable person. I think that was her only pleasure, to be miserable. And it was sad because you wanted to … point out good things to her and she couldn't …"

I have only gradually realised, myself, how such a "normative" experience of background encounters with Holocaust survivors has its own impact. Until I began discussing what I was writing with friends and colleagues, many of whom are not Jewish, it had not dawned on me quite how much these experiences were embedded in me and in my growing up, and in the similar growing up of most Jews of my generation. In unconsciously taking this for granted, "we", that is, ordinary Jews, may forget to give the space needed to absorb its psychological impact on us. Only when I see the reactions of friends, meeting this accumulation of experience in a community for the first time, does it occur to me that it was never entirely normal.

Through the lens of personal trauma

"Ordinary Jews" also meet the Holocaust through the powerful experiences afforded them by their own personal trauma and private sorrows. It is difficult to see how this could be otherwise. Personal experience, especially in early years, provides the basis for our way of relating to and interpreting the world, including precisely the potential for that empathy and "empathic unsettlement" that historian Dominick LaCapra espouses (LaCapra, 2001, p. 78).[12] My personal trauma colours how I see the world and influences the quality of my emotional availability. Those whose job it is to study childhood development have long observed that childhood, partly through events but more significantly through relational dynamics between children and their parents, contains traumatising experiences which can become embedded in later personality development.[13] As Jews who lack the direct experience of the actual historic events, what we do have is access to our own trauma, and the possibilities—both creative and destructive—this affords us to connect with those events.

In his early thirties, Edward came across the work of Primo Levi, and in a certain kind of way, "fell in love" with him. He immediately read all Levi's books and became in his own right an authority on someone whose body of work on the Holocaust has now given the writer an almost iconic status amongst Holocaust witnesses.

Edward is someone for whom questions of social justice and caring for those less well-off are of paramount importance. He was deeply affected by Levi's writing:

> "I found … *If This is a Man* and *Moments of Reprieve* […] profoundly uplifting […]. In *Moments of Reprieve* I was attracted to this idea [that] even in the depth of the despair, there were these moments … . […] In particular the story of Lorenzo … Lorenzo was an Italian forced labourer near Auschwitz, non-Jewish of course. … Because Levi was Italian, [Lorenzo] brought [him …] food almost every day. […] One day [… he came] during the middle of an air raid to bring Levi his soup. […] I was profoundly uplifted by that concept of humanity."

Levi's later works, darker and more pessimistic, confronted Edward with the ambiguities of human behaviour and feeling, and the complex figure of Levi himself became someone through whom Edward could wrestle with his own political, philosophical, and moral sensibilities.

> "When I talk about guilt, I'm talking about … 'survivor guilt', which must be healed … I don't think Levi led a particularly … he was an individual in the camps … he talks about … who survived Auschwitz. To survive Auschwitz, you had to be willing to steal, you had to be willing to collaborate … of course he didn't … […] I think he made compromises to survive, but …that's different from collaborators and the awful collaborators of the … even then, you've got to understand why the Jewish ghetto leaders would collaborate with the Nazis and run the ghetto. So these are deep, difficult questions but nonetheless, for some people it engenders a guilt, doesn't it? … He argues, the best all die … in Auschwitz the best died trying to help people. Trying to look after other people means that you would die. Who survives? The brutal, the selfish, the collaborators, those who've got a skill that the German needs … ."

When Levi died in 1987, apparently through suicide, Edward was profoundly affected. Levi's death intensified for Edward deep and significant losses in his own life.

> "It came at a bad time in my life. … We had … twins … born prematurely … who lived for only a few months. So it was a difficult time in my life […]. … Levi died in the April, this happened to me later in the year, roundabout August/September … but it [Levi's death] had a profound effect on me in the February. It was … a severe … sense of loss … a sense of loss which … […] it's a terrible thing to say, but it was … up till that point, I think, the greatest sense of loss that I'd felt, even a greater sense of loss I think than when my father died. It's a terrible thing to say and I can't explain it. But then probably, twenty years earlier, I was twelve or thirteen years of age and my father's death … it affected me, I think, quite profoundly but I didn't … I had a sense of loss but I've got a greater sense of loss for my father now …"

Alex is now in his fifties. When I first mentioned my research to him, his immediate reaction was to tell me that, as a young man, "I didn't think I qualified as a proper Jew, because I hadn't suffered enough." Deeply struck by this remark, I invited Alex to meet me for a more in-depth discussion.

Alex's conscious relationship to the Holocaust was one of distance: "I can't go near it … It's too horrifying." When, some years before, he had seen the film *Schindler's List* (1993), he had felt ashamed that he knew so little about the Holocaust, but still had not wanted to delve more into it; to that date he had read remarkably little for one of his generation and background. He explained his original comment to me in the terms that "you can't really be a Jew until you've looked the suffering in the face." He reserved his feelings of anger and outrage for the current situation in the Middle East: Israel, he thought, was failing to match up to the ethical standards required of "any human being, but Jews especially" in the aftermath of the Holocaust. Being angry towards Israel was useful, he thought, as it offered him the possibility of doing something constructive. "I can do nothing about what happened sixty years ago."

Behind these feelings of anger and helplessness on the one hand, and avoidance of horror and suffering on the other, lay two catastrophic experiences in his own family. Some decades before the Holocaust, Alex's paternal grandmother had committed suicide when Alex's father was only seven years old. As our conversation was winding to a close, Alex suddenly revealed that his own father had also committed suicide, when Alex himself was thirteen. More intensely and directly traumatised than most non-survivors by this family history, Alex's decision to "keep away" from the Holocaust and what knowledge of its horrors might evoke could be understood as an unconscious way of keeping his own psyche intact.

Richard is a British Jew of Middle Eastern descent. Consciously, he grew up without much feeling around the Holocaust; when I first met him, he described the Holocaust as belonging to "other" Jews, and expressed some perplexity at that separation. In our interview some years later, he described the moment when that changed. It happened as a result of reading Anne Michaels' (1996) *Fugitive Pieces*, a sensitive and haunting novel about the rescue and protection of a young Jewish boy by a Greek man during the war years. Richard's father was British-born and living with his family in North Africa at the outbreak of war. Thus he fought with the British Army in Greece, where he was captured and served as a prisoner of war.

> "[When I read the book] I went ballistic. Then I realised that though Auschwitz never affected me personally, the Germans in Greece had. I didn't even know I was anti-German till I read that piece. The

> Holocaust didn't affect me, but it did, because when I see what they did in Greece, it evoked …
>
> You see, my father had a breakdown after being a prisoner of war in Greece. He went back to where the family was, and they thought he should get married as a way of helping him settle down. It was a semi-arranged marriage with my mother, and it was a catastrophe from day one. So in my unconscious there's, 'If the Germans hadn't invaded Greece, my father wouldn't have had a breakdown, he wouldn't have married my mother, and … I wouldn't have had to contend with this catastrophic marriage'. It did impact on me, not in a way to do with the Holocaust, but to do with the war. …
>
> It was so strange, because I had thought, 'Well, I haven't got a big deal about the Holocaust', then for two days I could barely contain my rage towards the Germans. I couldn't work out […] why reading *Fugitive Pieces* set me off in a kind of psychotic rage. Then I thought, 'It's because of my father'. I didn't immediately make the connection, it took me about two days."

As time went by, he realised that images to do with the Holocaust were embedded in his unconscious:

> "I was doodling, and I saw afterwards […] that I'd drawn the entrance to Birkenau—you know, the railway lines going in and the whole thing. And I went, 'Shit, it's hidden in my unconscious'. Then I noticed that whenever I saw a barn with an entrance, I immediately went 'Auschwitz', or if I saw poplar trees … […] there are poplar trees [at Auschwitz]. So it's living in me."

The unexpected arising of these pictures and thoughts again had associations to Richard's relationship with his father. Combat experiences in the war had traumatised Richard's father and this in turn had affected the relationship between them; the Holocaust thus offered archetypal imagery to describe Richard's inner devastation at the loss of the relationship he would have wanted with his father:

> "We weren't on good terms and a lot had happened … I went to visit his grave. I was looking for it—I hadn't been back since he died. I heard a dog bark and […] I thought, 'That's an Alsatian, the

> Germans are going to come and get me, I must get to the grave before the Germans find me'. I was Richard aged forty, knowing full well that I was in [England], and another part of me was psychotic. I was running around looking for the grave as if I only had twenty seconds to find it in. It was triggered by a dog barking. I was really perplexed by that, because it was psychotic.
>
> On an archetypal level, you could say I was obsessed with the Holocaust ... I'm not suffering at all directly from it, but I was quite astonished ... It's living in me."

These are three men of similar age but different backgrounds. For each of them, a major effect of *thinking about* the Holocaust has been to evoke a deep personal experience of loss; but each of these losses is particular and cannot be ascribed to the Holocaust. Perhaps rather than traumatise us directly, what the Holocaust does is allow us to feel, and give us images for, those particular traumas already residing inside, as Simon's story, below, graphically illustrates.

In 1990, as part of a "very difficult and painful process" of "coming out" as a gay man, Simon took up an invitation to attend group therapy during a visit home:

> "This was the height of the AIDS crisis and most of [the group] were men with AIDS, dealing with their mortality. [...] This was when people were really dying in great numbers and [...] I was aware that most of the other guys in the room ... [...] had AIDS, so were in a very different situation from me ... My issue was [...] about coming out, and specifically at that point, it was about coming out to my parents [...].
>
> [As] part of the session, he [the therapist] played some music and invited us to meditate on [... it]. It was a piece of music I knew very well, the first movement of Mahler's Resurrection Symphony [...] ... that first movement [...] has great climaxes in it that the orchestra works up to very slowly [...]: I always loved that [...] and [...] I'd always related to that piece of music [...] very joyously.
>
> That day, we all sat there with our eyes closed while he played this ... [...]. When we were asked to share what we'd been thinking or visualising while the music played, most of the guys ... [...] spoke [...] about healing and hope and that kind of stuff. My experience [...] was totally different and really shocked and took me by surprise. [It]

> definitely was tapping into something unconscious at that moment because … [while] working up to […] this great massive climax, the image that completely possessed my mind […] was of pyramids of corpses in a gas chamber. I don't know where I'd seen pictures of that, I obviously had at some point, but maybe it was from verbal reports of it that I'd visualised it myself … [T]he way in which … when the gas started coming into the gas chambers, everybody tried to get out through the only opening, which was a vent in the ceiling which is where the gas was coming from and so people … would literally climb on top of one another and die and end up in a […] pyramid pile of corpses. And this … I still cry when I think about it … this was what filled my mind. I didn't quite know why, and […] I suppose the obvious thing is that those other people in the room with me were seriously ill … but I don't remember it being about […] those other people. I remember it being about me and about my fear and anxiety. […] I was in a mess at the time and that was the kind of imagery that was able to emerge."

"Vicarious traumatisation"

If personal trauma enables ordinary Jews to make an emotional connection to the Holocaust, how could this translate into Jewish "collective" trauma?

Ruth, a clinical psychologist, believes that "vicarious traumatisation" offers the best way of understanding the impact of second-hand horror:

> "It's vicarious trauma, isn't it? I think that's the best word isn't it? I think if you have a modicum of imagination and empathy, it's all too easy unfortunately to imagine some of these extreme horrors, sadness that other people endured."

"Vicarious traumatisation" is a concept that has developed in the fields of psychology and psychotherapy although the phenomenon is also applied to people working in any field where they are routinely likely to come into contact with individuals on the receiving end of trauma—such as paramedics and doctors, police, social workers. It extends to people who do not directly *see* or *hear* a traumatic event, but have to become familiar with often gruesome details; this is commonly the case for those who work in the criminal justice system, but as Holocaust historian Saul Friedlander points out, the historiographical work involved in studying documentary and eyewitness evidence has its own cumulative effect on the historian (Friedlander, 1993, extracted in Levi & Rothberg, 2003, pp. 206–213).

Trauma therapists Pearlman and Saakvitne describe vicarious traumatisation as "the cumulative transformative effect upon the trauma therapist of working with survivors of traumatic life events" (Pearlman & Saakvitne, 1995, p. 61). They discuss how particularly traumatised individuals—in the case of their clinical work, people who have been sexually abused in childhood—communicate their intense feelings (disgust, terror, impotence, guilt, betrayal, devastation) in ways which therapists pick up non-verbally and have to find ways of exploring. At the same time, this work also exposes trauma therapists to detailed material of a very disturbing nature: "this material includes graphic descriptions of violent events, exposure to the realities of people's cruelty to one another, and involvement in trauma related re-enactments, either as a participant or a bystander. It includes being a helpless witness to past events [...]" (ibid., p. 31). Pearlman and Saakvitne describe the cumulative impact on therapists themselves of repeated exposure to such experiences; and argue for therapists to establish supportive frameworks around themselves so that they can also process material and recover.

Like "trauma" itself, the concept of vicarious traumatisation has its own difficulties of definition. A colleague who herself works with adult survivors of child sexual abuse prefers to use the word "impact" to describe the challenge for her in meeting and responding to material of an often horrifying nature. Either way, what is central is some idea of a dynamic exchange of emotional experience and disturbing imagery, whether through personal encounter with survivors or through exposure to Holocaust material—literature, film, historical account, archival material, witness testimony. However, perhaps the key link between the impact on a given individual and any concept of *collective* trauma lies in that part of Pearlman and Saakvitne's work which emphasises therapists' need *themselves* to process the material they receive. Holocaust experiences are "around" within Jewish communities and in wider society in ways which are unlikely to be fully digested. While ordinary Jews are unlikely to be as exposed to the material in the way that psychotherapists are unless they choose to be, there is no equivalent way in which it is talked *through*, as distinct from being talked *about*, and thus it may remain unintegrated: a constantly disquieting experience "on the side".[14] Hence Bernice and Diana, who voluntarily exposed themselves to the experiences of Holocaust survivors over a number of years, eventually experienced burn-out. In Bernice's words, she became "Holocausted out"; while for Diana, "The idea of working on the Holocaust again, I couldn't bear it. I could do it for five years".

Being traumatised vicariously is a consequence both of the content of the material/experiences that are conveyed, and the extent to which the recipient subject is able to receive and process this "stuff". Cathy Caruth, amongst others, focuses (understandably) on the importance of offering empathic support to the victims of the Holocaust; but even the comparatively low level of exposure ordinary Jews have to disturbing material may, if unaddressed, accumulate over time into a confused state of unease that is never quite disentangled from the personal traumas of people's own lives.

Collective trauma?

In speaking of his book *The Whisperers* on BBC Radio Four, historian Orlando Figes discussed how the impact of collective trauma can be recognised in the adaptive behavioural patterns developed by a given population (Figes, 2007). Figes' book concerns the cumulative effect on the mass of Russian people of living under decades of totalitarian control. Under Stalin, ordinary individuals had to repress any views which could be picked up as potentially dissident, out of fear of denunciation, imprisonment, internal exile, or worse. Probably not altogether different in *kind* from the repressions of Nazism, the key difference is the length of time Stalin's system continued for: upwards of twenty-five years; in effect, one complete generational birth-cycle. Figes followed the impact of this through hundreds of interviews, including with the children and grandchildren of those who lived under Stalin. He concluded that the traumatising effect on *individual* families not only results in measurable changes of behaviour within those families but, over enough people, eventually translates into an accumulation of changes that could be called "collective trauma". "The repression of one person doesn't just affect that person," he says, "it affects everyone around and affects several generations." Inbuilt loyalties and conditionings develop, which continue even after the original cause has passed. "The Soviet experiment shows that even by default, [...], simply by the traumas brought to families and the way that families react in order to survive, it does change human nature. Russians have been fundamentally altered by their history. They're still traumatised."

Figes' study relates to the growing body of psychological work concerned with "transgenerational trauma", a process through which unresolved and painful experiences in one generation get "passed on" to subsequent generations through the behaviours and attitudes of parents. For example, *rationally* derived fears for personal safety in one generation (as in Figes' study) can, even though decontextualised, profoundly influence orientations and behaviours in the next generation, the vehicle for this being the way in which parents unconsciously react to, and shape, their infant children's needs and expressions of self.

While Figes' study does not directly relate to ordinary Jews and the legacy of the Holocaust, one area of the Jewish world in which it fruitfully comes together with the concept of vicarious traumatisation is that of Israel. Between 1946 and 1948, the population of the territory which became Israel in May 1948 was heavily swollen by refugees from the devastated Jewish communities of Europe. In Simon's view, the trauma brought into the very foundation of Israel by the mass influx of what were, by any definition, deeply traumatised individuals has never been addressed:

> "A lot of what has gone on in Israel [...] has been the result of the Holocaust. [...] it's not that the experience justifies whatever Jews in Israel do to, as they see it, guarantee their survival or their safety; but Israel as a country, as a population, is still traumatised sixty years on ... Sixty years is little enough for an individual who's gone through that kind of experience, but for a whole community or nation which has collectively experienced ... sixty years is no time at all [...]. I think Israel is still living through that trauma and acting out that trauma and a lot of it's because ... [...] it was suppressed in the early years. Until the seventies, people didn't delve into it and talk about it that much, and in Israel particularly the whole focus was on being strong, being heroic, being manly and militaristic [...]; but at the same time an overwhelming conviction of the complete innocence and rightness of everything they did ... a sort of purity. Nothing was analysed, nothing

> was worked through of that terrible trauma. It was denied [...] as though Israel makes all of that okay [...]. I think that's why Israel has so often either overreacted [...] or behaved unnecessarily brutally or denied the possibility that it could be wrong and other people might be the real victims here. It's something that is still not fully acknowledged a lot of the time by Israel. Yes, that's one of the things that made that whole conflict so intractable."

Although the Holocaust lasted for much less time than did Stalin's repressions, Holocaust experiences were marked by an unprecedented depth and complexity of trauma. Figes' view of collective trauma would suggest that such trauma becomes collective when it operates at a level at which significant behaviour change across a population sets in. In that sense, the Jewish—and perhaps non-Jewish—population of Israel could, as Simon suggests, well be described as collectively traumatised by the Holocaust because from its inception Israel absorbed a "critical mass" of individuals deeply traumatised by Holocaust experiences that were for a considerable period neglected and even disparaged, as Gideon describes:

> "In Israel [...] there was this conscious effort to portray Holocaust survivors as, well, Ben Gurion called them 'human dust'. To think of them as *'miskanim'—'miskan'* means poor old so-and-so. Wretches. [...] As a young child, the disparaging part was really quite remarkable."

Such early belittling of Holocaust survivor experience in the Israeli state would not only have consequences for the survivors themselves. It would also mean that ordinary Jews settling in the new state were exposed to the indirect expressions of disturbance without a way of processing it. Following Pearlman and Saakvitne's line of thinking, this in itself could have been enough to "transform" (not necessarily for the better) Israeli behaviour at a meta-level.

But what of the diaspora? Although many survivors settled in the UK, the USA, and elsewhere, as a proportion of the total population—even the total Jewish population in those countries—they would have been relatively small. How, in these circumstances, can "collective" trauma be said to operate? The answer, I suspect, lies partly in the experiences to which those Jewish populations *were* historically subject.

In the next chapter I focus on loss. In trying to disentangle what often gets woven together under this one grievous heading, my central proposition is that the pre-Holocaust inheritance that lies behind present-day patterns of Jewish settlement in the diaspora, itself forms a crucial background to the experience of loss embedded in this sense of a "collective Jewish trauma".

CHAPTER TWO

"A profound sense of loss"

From a Jewish perspective, loss is inseparable from any discussion of the Holocaust. Invited, as we so often are these days through memorials, museums, and archive film, to contemplate the faces of those packed into ghettoes, deported, or simply shot; the carefully-displayed remnants of artefacts once produced by living communities; or the laboriously inscribed names of thousands of murdered Jews, as on the walls of the Pinkasova Synagogue in Prague; there is simply no escaping an equation of Nazi rule with loss—the loss of individuals, of whole families, communities, institutions, of virtually everything that formed the substance of Jewish life in much of Europe prior to 1939. From her particular experience of working intensively with Holocaust survivors, Diana observed that "it would be really weird if we didn't start crying"; and hers is simply one of many voices in which "ordinary" Jews speak of the oblique feelings of loss which thoughts of the Holocaust summon up:

BERNICE: "Loss … . I do grieve … I do grieve about the loss of … when you think of how many … how many people there would be now."

EDWARD: "I do feel loss, […] a sense of loss. […] I've a sadness. […] I do feel sadness about the whole thing."

RUTH: "It's difficult for me to know how to answer this, but I suppose if I'm thinking about the Holocaust, [...] yes, I think grief and sadness."

GIDEON: "The first thing that happens, which didn't used to happen, is that I get very upset. When I read [...'s] account of his experience, it brings tears to my eyes."

In many respects, loss is not only an unavoidable material *fact* of the Holocaust, but a central component of our psychological relationship to it. Almost for this very reason, it is enormously complicated to explore, not least because the sense of loss and the losses themselves go in so many different directions. People become "lost for words" in trying to grapple with their confusion and sheer incomprehension as to *"how it happened"*. Those who know or have known survivors to any degree pick up on the almost inexpressible grief at lost families, lost friends, lost homes, lost pasts innocent of Holocaust experience, which those individuals carry throughout their lives. A Jewish colleague whose mother successfully escaped to Britain from Germany in the 1930s refers to her mother's unspoken anguish at the loss of her "German-ness". Yiddish writer Kadya Molodowsky, whose 1946 book of poetry *Der meylekh Dovid aleyn is geblibn* was produced in the immediate knowledge of what had happened in Europe, thought of her book as "a tombstone for a life [...] vanished", a theme of painful finality echoed by many subsequent writers close in family connection or personal history to the geographies of the Holocaust (quoted in Valencia, 2006, p. 13).

Coming from a more removed position to a question of what to think or what to feel about the Holocaust, many ordinary Jews simply feel confused: recognising feelings of loss but unclear as to what exactly to attribute their own feelings to. While Bernice mourns the numbers of people lost and the impact of such losses on the size of the whole worldwide Jewish community, Gideon weeps for an individual survivor's experiences in the death camps, touched by that survivor's capacity *not* to lose his ability to "look outside at the stars, and [... see the] incredible [...] beauty in life". Diana relates painfully to the loss of people's belonging to the societies of which they had thought they were part, and Ruth and Edward each feel a pervasive sadness linked to their own personal experiences of loss. For ordinary Jews the losses function on so many different levels: tangible yet simultaneously elusive; both specific and general; felt at a personal level whilst not personal as such.

With all this confusion present, it can appear almost impossible to know how to begin coherently discussing a theme which at one level seems so obvious and at another is so difficult to grasp.

The difficulty of coherently discussing loss in relation to the Holocaust has something to do with its sheer enormity. The Nazis and their collaborators did not simply murder very large numbers of Jews. They did so within a programme and an ideology that sought to—and very nearly succeeded in this—eradicate Jewish lives and Jewish life from Europe. The enormity of this is difficult to comprehend. It is not just a question of the bodies. It concerns what those bodies when alive, and still in imagination, *represented* of Jewish presence in history, in cities and villages, in European life; and of what that presence reflects back to Jews of their participation in European history. Synagogues can be rebuilt and new communities established, but the continuity of Jewish life in Europe has been dealt a shattering blow. For many Jews, travelling around Europe can become an endless litany of loss as they rehearse in their minds all the countries and all the conditions in which Jewish life there was removed. In 1987 critic Bernard Levin, an "ordinary Jew" travelling down the Rhine, captured this feeling in relation to German Jewry when he wrote,

> Germany has not been able to repair the loss to German life which resulted from the destruction of German Jewry; and it shows. Perhaps it shows most clearly in Cologne, and perhaps that is what I had sensed when I felt that there was something missing in the greatest, richest and most powerful of all the cities of the Rhine. (Levin, 1987, p. 216)

The numbers of Jews killed, of course, is an inescapable fact of the Holocaust, and demographically this certainly has had a great impact. Even today, the Jewish population worldwide numbers only around fourteen million; it can be reasonably assumed that the Nazis successfully wiped out something between one-third and one half of the then-European Jewish population, representing about a quarter of what might have been today's global Jewish population. For Jews who, in their own minds, have been tenaciously fighting a rearguard action against disappearance since the time of the Romans, the loss of six million actual people can be deeply worrying. Dan wrote to me that "none of my direct family were killed, though I must say I feel that six million of my family were murdered". Huge as the numbers were, however, if the Holocaust was simply a story about numbers it may well by now have faded in significance. When Howard Jacobson's fictitious hero, Maxie Glick, talks with an almost salacious horror about "five million Jews",[1] it is a form of shorthand. Something associated with numbers but much more than numbers has been lost. For Jews, the Holocaust seems to *symbolise* loss in a way that no other historic event truly can. This is how Sephardi-born Esther tried to explain the complexity and bewilderment that it involves for her:

> "I do feel it's my loss … it was a loss to humankind, it was a loss to humanity let alone my people, and I do think it was a loss to my people … through the suffering. The incomprehension is, yes, how did that machinery get going? How did it all happen in what we thought was a civilised developed world? […] [It's] a loss of security, a loss of … a loss of people. A loss of the ideas in the civilisation that went with it. […] It's a concrete loss of who was lost, but it's also loss of hope."

One of the complications in understanding the dynamics of this is that each individual's psychological relationship to the Holocaust in itself is deeply affected by the personal fabric of his or her own life, and what that individual is already "attuned" to. Loss, anger, bewilderment, guilt, fear, shame—all these feeling states are normal parts of most people's emotional repertoire, derived simply from the experience of having grown up in human society and being exposed to events and experiences in which those feelings are likely to arise. A massive and multi-layered loss like the Holocaust cannot fail to tap into personal sadness and losses, evoking either more, or less, powerful responses or certain kinds of responses according to how personal losses already "sit" in our own lives and awareness. Ruth, for example, who, like Edward and Alex lost her father at a painfully vulnerable age, recognises that losing such an important figure early in her life has had an important impact on her emotional responsiveness and on her choice of profession:

> "Grief has affected me from the time I was fairly young. I was fifteen [when my father died] but he'd been ill for a year before that as well, so […] illness … both my parents were quite frequently unwell and I think it must have sensitised me to themes of loss and grief. Maybe it

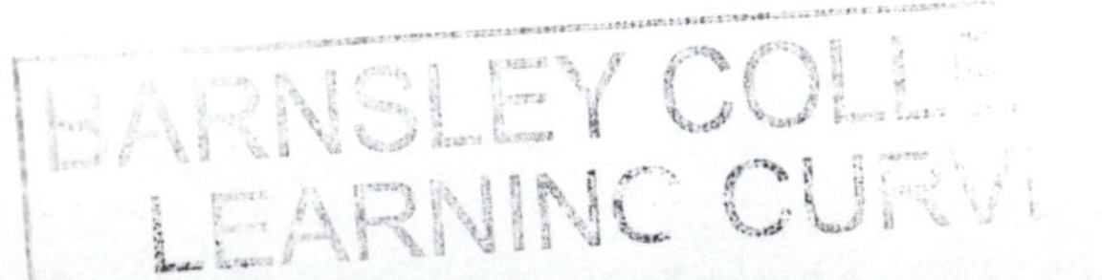

> was part of the background to wanting to be a psychologist, to help others."

For Edward, again, the death of Primo Levi evoked not only that much earlier loss of his own father but the painful loss of a role model:

> "I've got a greater sense of loss for my father now ... [... o]r as I was ... when I got into my twenties and thirties when he wasn't there, than I felt when I was twelve or thirteen. [... Levi's death] was profound, it was a sense of loss, [...] ... it was [...] like losing a member of your family... [...] I'd become very entwined in the writing which I'd only then discovered, two or three years before he died. I don't know how else to describe it other than [...] a profound sense of loss. [...] I felt [...] closer to him as a writer than I've felt to any writer before or since. Never read anybody whose works have moved me in quite the same way. And I think what moved me most about his works [...] was ... the constant attempt by individuals to hold on to their humanity in the depth of the most difficult circumstances. [Levi] represents for me how you would like to act if you were ... if you were in that situation, but you're not sure you ever would. I still feel a sense of loss about it."

In reality, lacking any direct connection with the Holocaust's actual events and all its myriad losses, the only way ordinary Jews *can* connect with it emotionally is through the prism of their own personal lives and experiences, for it is only in one's own life that emotional experience is born. My emotional experience may be personal to me, but it potentially gives me access to grasping the impact of certain of the Holocaust's realities. Given the impossibility of ever fully grasping the enormity of the whole event this, surely, is as valid and important in its own terms as the experiences of any individual survivor. The risk in this process, it would seem, is the potential to be "taken over" by the Holocaust and to attribute to *it* the cause of the sadnesses in one's own, non-Holocausted, life. Many years ago, towards the end of a week-long training event near Munich during which those of us who were Jewish had taken time to visit Dachau, I was reflecting on my own feelings of loss. "Of course you feel loss", suggested one well-meaning Dutchman, "You've lost six million of your people". It was not the reason for my feelings; but I was struck by the fact that he thought it should be.

In *The Lost: In Search of Six of the Six Million*, Daniel Mendelsohn describes in great detail his own long journey to uncover some of the Holocaust histories in his extended family. Despite its length (over 500 pages) the book is a cameo; in effect, Mendelsohn shows how the details of what happened to actual people who are significant to us encapsulate the larger picture, and that through revealing them something of the whole terrible history of the Holocaust can be communicated. Mendelsohn constantly asserts the importance of detail. On his visit to Auschwitz, en route to Bolechow, the small town in the Polish-Ukrainian territories where his mother's family came from, he reflects:

> Auschwitz, by now, has become the gigantic, one-word symbol, the gross generalisation, the shorthand, for what happened to Europe's Jews—although what happened at Auschwitz did not, in fact, happen to millions of Jews from places like Bolechow, Jews who were lined up and shot at the edges of open pits, or, failing that, were shipped to camps that, unlike Auschwitz, had one purpose only, camps that are less well known to the public mind precisely because they offered no alternative to death and hence produced no survivors, no memoirs, no stories. But even if we accept Auschwitz as the symbol [...], there are problems. It had been to rescue my relatives from generalities, symbols, abbreviations, to restore to them their particularity and distinctiveness, that I had come on this strange and arduous trip. *Killed by the Nazis*—yes, but by whom, exactly? The dreadful irony of Auschwitz [...] is that the extent of what it shows you is so gigantic that the corporate and anonymous, the sheer scope of the crime, are constantly, paradoxically asserted at the expense of any sense of individual life. [...] [F]or me, who had come to learn about only six of the six million, [...] the vastness, the scope, the size [of Auschwitz] was an impediment to, rather than vehicle for, illumination of the very narrow scrap of the story in which I was interested. (Mendelsohn, 2007, p. 112)

Mendelsohn does complete his mission, through a journey lasting several years and involving travel across three continents. Ultimately he gets what he wants and is able to rescue from being "lost" the names and something of the personalities of the six members of his family who died, along with the details as to how, when and where they had died. In so doing, he is able to restore the dead family to a living place in the memory of the family whose immediate forebears, unlike murdered Great Uncle Shmiel, had fortuitously chosen to seek their fortunes in the USA some twenty years before the start of the Holocaust.

Many ordinary Jews might think that Mendelsohn is fortunate. Enough of his family had moved to America, and relatively close in time to the Holocaust, for significant memories and family information to have been retained, information which Mendelsohn eagerly exploited from childhood. Besides this, Mendelsohn had a very close relationship with his grandfather, Great Uncle Shmiel's younger brother Abraham, who committed suicide in 1980; and his search for "the lost" relatives partly reflects his desire to undertake on his grandfather's behalf what Abraham himself had been unable to do. As the hero in David Grossman's Holocaust-based novel *See Under: Love* observes, love is a powerful motivator; it seems probable that Mendelsohn's love for his grandfather helped him to feel, and in a sense lay to rest, his grandfather's anguish and guilt at not having been able to rescue his own brother (Grossman, 1989).

But most of us do not have these living connections. For large numbers of ordinary Jews, the memories of family "left behind" are themselves lost. In addressing ourselves to our own feelings of loss in relation to the Holocaust, we tend to lack any meaningful sense of actual individuals killed, and the consequent feelings can be perplexing. Antonia describes it in this way:

> "I don't know why I watch them [every programme, every film] because I get upset. [...] But I still feel compelled to know what goes on. [...] [E]very now and again I think, it could have been us, but it wasn't. There is a definite distance, and I mean we have no relatives who died, not a single one."

Every loss has its own symbolic dimension. The death of a parent, for example, often evokes painful feelings associated with the loss of love, guidance, and protection; the loss through illness or accident of part of one's body impacts on one's sense of wholeness, independence, capacity to move and act. Exile is not simply the loss of a home country; it incorporates innumerable associations with that home—family, security, history, identity. In the absence of tangible connections with those who died in the Holocaust, it is in effect *only* the symbolic dimensions of loss we are left with; losses which may be inherently more difficult to mourn because they elude capture or naming in the way that Mendelsohn could eventually name and identify as individuals all his great-uncle's four daughters. By definition, symbolic losses act as powerful symbols in our own psyches, touching something not exactly the same as the external event but which does lie in our own experience; something that allows us to connect emotionally with the terrible losses of the Holocaust even though those particular losses are not directly our own.

Evoking what is present

For several of those I interviewed, it was images of the soon-to-die Jewish children that most deeply evoked grief and anguish. Victor, a man in his seventies, a father and grandfather, was not the only one who found himself so overcome at recalling "the children" that he could barely speak:

> "It's not the big numbers. For example, [one] summer, we went to various exhibitions. Auschwitz didn't do that to me; well, it did, but not as … there was one in which there was a film of people moving off to the ghetto. There was this film of children carrying their school chairs … It's moving me to tears now … […] I think it is because they're children and Jewish. I don't see myself but the children I know now …"

At this moment, he wiped his eyes and apologised for his tears.

Doris spoke of similar feelings, shared with her now-dead husband, who, like her, found the emotional experience hard to articulate:

> "I went to see […] the film *Shoah* and he said, 'You go on your own. […] [T]he worst thing', he said, 'I can't bear is the children, I can't sit through that […].' And then I get … when I … well, there's a block … I block out certain things because if you think of children, you can't … you can't bear it, I mean, this is not … this is not possible to block out."

Like Victor, Antonia also felt so overwhelmed by thoughts of the dead children that several times she had to stop speaking:

> "I think the children's house or whatever it's called in Yad Vashem's the worst. When you see all those camps …"

At this point she couldn't carry on and asked me to speak to her husband instead. Several times after she returned to the subject, always in similar terms:

> "I always go back to the children, how terrible to have a fate, you know … I just get emotional about …"
>
> "It upsets me whenever I think of those children […]".
>
> "It upsets me just to think about it in depth because of the children. Particularly because of the children."

All three of these speakers have one particular thing in common: their age. Amongst the people I interviewed, this small group comprised most of those in their seventies or eighties, and it was striking that none of the younger interviewees particularly singled out "the children" in this way. It seems highly likely that Victor's, Doris's (and her husband's), and Antonia's stage of life is closely connected to their symbolic associations with the loss of children in the Holocaust. But how?

Parents (and all these speakers are parents) usually have a powerful instinct to protect their children and will exercise all their strength and resources to do so. Even in the highly abnormal circumstances of the camps Ruth Kluger's mother had enough presence of mind and determination that she could exploit an opportunity in the selection process and thus save the daughter who, according to Kluger herself, should, by virtue of being only twelve years old, have been automatically selected for the gas chamber (Kluger, 2001, pp. 105–106). But a key factor involved in growing older is the diminution of one's strength and power, and an increase in the sense of one's own physical vulnerability. Looking at images of children known to be doomed can therefore be at one and the same time a painful *prompt* to protect, coupled with an even more painful recognition that one no longer has the power or strength to do this. It was, after all, children and the very elderly, those who had no value as slave labourers, whom the Nazis most readily disposed of. So for these three speakers at least, something of their own increasing vulnerability and their loss of protective capability is likely to underlie their deep sensitivity to images of doomed children.

Ageing itself is a poignant process, filled with its own losses, and one of the compensations is to take pleasure in the sight of and engagement with young lives; commonly one's own grandchildren. The very essence of life is its continuity, and a sense of generational continuity is one of the factors that allows people at the end of their lives to die with some degree of contentment. There is a subversive power in the images of Jewish children who were about to be intentionally killed; it inverts the normal order of life, and for people nearing the end of their own lives can unconsciously pose a disturbing question: can I count on anything of myself being left to the future? Perhaps this is why Victor saw the children in the film not as himself as a child, but as present children, with the future they represent that he will only be part of through them.

In *Poetry After Auschwitz*, Susan Gubar challenges the assertions of the first post-Holocaust generation of writers (including scholars such as Zygmunt Bauman, Saul Friedlander, and Berel Lang) who believed in various ways that the Holocaust, because of its uniqueness, was beyond the reach of any significant form of representation or interpretation: a position embodied in Theodor Adorno's famous dictum that "To write poetry after Auschwitz is barbaric" (Gubar, 2003, pp. 3–4).[2] In her monogram on the poetry of Kadya Molodowsky, Heather Valencia draws from Gubar's work to suggest that:

> a consensus now seems to be emerging that very little *comprehension* of the Holocaust can be transmitted through attempts at factual representation, and that poetry, the genre which is furthest distanced from 'factuality', may, paradoxically, be best suited to the task of confronting the Holocaust through the written and spoken word. As Susan Gubar recently put it, 'in an effort to signal the impossibility of a sensible story, the poet provides spurts of vision, moments of truth, baffling but nevertheless powerful pictures of scenes unassimilated into an explanatory plot.' James Young even asserts that '[r]ather than seeing metaphors as threatening to the facts of the Holocaust, we must recognise that they are our only access to the facts [...]'. Poetic images can facilitate insights and engage our emotional understanding in a way we would not otherwise experience. (Valencia, op. cit., pp. 9–10)

In other words, Gubar, Young, and Valencia propose that poetry, *because* of its power to use symbol, is a *more* powerful way of connecting to the Holocaust than efforts to try and reproduce factual events which are themselves dead along with those who experienced them. Thus while Victor, Doris, and Antonia struggle to articulate feelings that, as I have suggested, may arise in part from their stage in life, their feelings offer a window into one of the myriad aspects of the Holocaust which have a deep power to move. In any case, they are in good company, as Yiddish writer Aharon Zeitlin's moving post-Holocaust poem *Kinder fun Maidanek* indicates: a poem that whilst on one level tells simply of Zeitlin's grief at the physical loss of once-physical children, leaving him in his sleep-lost ("*shloflozer*") night only their names to recite, obliquely but subtly refers to other losses embodied by those same names:

Blimeshi, Toybeshi, Rivele.
Leyenyu. Feygenyu. Perele.
Khatskele. Motele. Kivele.
Hershele. Leybele. Berele.

Shayeshi. Khayeshi. Goldeshi.
Mendelekh. Gnendelekh. Mindelekh.
Kh'tseyl in der nakht in der shloflozer
nemen fun yidishe kinderlekh.

Nemen fun yidishe kinderlekh,
Rokhelekh, Raykhelekh, Nekhelekh,
Getselekh, Velvelekh, Vigderlekh,
Yankelekh, Yoynelekh, Mekhelekh.

Kopele, vu iz dayn kepele?
Vu iz dos likht fun dayn eygele?
Vu iz dayn hentele, Yentele?
Vu iz dayn fisele, Feygele?

Nemen—ot dos iz geblibn nor:
Dvoyrele—Dvoshele—Khayele,
Shmerele—Perele—Serele,
Shimele—Shiyele—Shayele.

Ver ken gefinen itst Moyshelen,
Shulikn, Shmulikn, Srulikn?
Got hot oyf zey nisht derbaremt zikh,
hot zey geshonken Amolekn.

Blimeshi—Toybeshi—Rivele,
Leyenyu—Feygenyu—Perele.
Khatskele—Motele—Kivele.
Hershele—Leybele—Berele.

Oys un nishto mer di Heshelekh,
Heshelekh, Peshelekh, Hindelekh.
Klangen, bloyz klangen, bloyz lidklangen—
nemen fun yidishe kinderlekh.

Vu iz dayn fisele, Zisele?
Tsipele, vu iz dayn tsepele?
Roykh bistu, Yenteles hentele!
Ash bistu, Kopeles kepele!

> ("Where is your little hat, Kopeleh? Where is the light from your little eyes? Where can I find you now, Moysheleh? Heshelech is no more; names are all that are left. Yenteleh's little hand is smoke; Kopeleh's little hat, ash.") (Zeitlin, 1947, quoted in Zucker, 1995, pp. 82–83)[3]

A distinctive characteristic of Yiddish, the language of the Ashkenazi ("Germanic") Jews, which was the principal language of the Jews of Eastern Europe until the war, is the use of double diminutives added to nouns by extra suffixes, as in -eleh, -elech, -iken, in the children's names. The effect of this in the poem is to emphasise the children's vulnerability and innocence that have also been lost. At the same time, the linguistic play on names and words (*Kopeleh-kepeleh, henteleh-Yenteleh*) evokes another lost world, one in which the Yiddish language, its cultural roots, and its own rich forms of expression have also been casualties. Not only are the children themselves lost; the oft-invoked Biblical figure of Rachel "weeping for her children because they are not"[4] can also be understood as weeping for the loss of a whole Jewish life that was wiped out from the parts of Europe where it once flourished.

Losing the past

My colleague K, who researches post-war Poland, believes that one of the legacies that continues to afflict ordinary Jews to this day is their failure to mourn "the loss of Yiddishkeit" that was a direct result of the Holocaust. Indeed, many writings about the legacy of the Holocaust reveal a pervasive nostalgia. In the epilogue to her study of a lesbian love affair in wartime Germany between Felice, a Jewish woman, and Lilly, the wife of a high-ranking Nazi, the writer Erica Fischer reflects this nostalgia in language that is certainly not unique to Jews but is particularly recognisable in post-Holocaust Jewish discourse:

> I feel closer to Felice. Felice, who is dead, is well known to me. I am familiar with her family and her childhood from what my mother has told me about her own childhood and youth in Warsaw. *It is a lost world that I long for*, even though I know I could not have tolerated its narrowness any more than Felice did. (Fischer, 1994, p. 271; my italics)

Similarly, Eva Hoffman's book *Shtetl*, a reconstruction of Jewish life and history in one small Polish town from mediaeval times until the Second World War, is filled with imagined descriptions of the communal life that was lost:

> What remains of the Jews of Poland? Mostly traces, echoes, and a few monuments; [...] There are a few thousand Jews left in Poland today, but the communities they inhabited, their characteristic culture and society, were all destroyed during World War II.
>
> [...] in a few places, modest monuments have been erected to those who perished. Relics, scattered and enigmatic, as of a lost ancient civilisation. But the pulsing Jewish world that was here, the small shops and stalls, the bustle of people, carts, horses, the sounds of Yiddish and Hebrew—these are no more. [...] That life can almost be intuited beyond the curtain of abrupt absence. We think we can almost cross the curtain; but we cannot. (Hoffman, 1998, pp. 1–2)

Like Hoffman, Eva Figes, a writer who came to Britain as a young girl with her family in 1939 as a refugee from Nazi Germany, writes about her personal loss of "that other world which had been so utterly destroyed": in her case, not the small-town world of the Yiddish-speaking, distinctively separate, Jewish-Polish *shtetl* or the lively Polish-Jewish mix of inter-war Warsaw, but the urbanised, cultured, assimilated middle-class world of the German-Jewish bourgeoisie (Figes, 2008, p. 8). I can also recognise in Hoffman's description of Polish *shtetl* life something very similar to evocations of the East End of London that my father and thousands of his generation grew up in. Descriptions—verbal and written—of that world are similar in tone and effect: the "pulsing" Jewish world, the "small shops and stalls", the "bustle", the "sounds of Yiddish", all of which belonged in retrospect as much to the world of the immigrant Jews of the late nineteenth and early twentieth centuries as they did to the Polish territories that so many of those Jews left. Of course the Jewish world in Poland itself did vanish as a direct result of the Holocaust; but the emotional form in which that world is recollected appears very close to a common human lament for a lost world.

In the expression of post-Holocaust Jewish nostalgia it is Poland that dominates the Jewish psychological landscape. Certainly it is not difficult to see why. Fully half the total loss of Jewish life in the Holocaust belonged to Poland alone: three million Polish Jews, equal to ninety per cent of the Jewish population of that country. Poland was also the country in which almost all the extermination camps were sited, a fact which has led Polish Jewish writer Stanislaw Krajewski to observe that "in the eyes of non-Polish Jews Poland is a Jewish cemetery" (Krajewski, 2005, p. 103). In fact, Krajewski, who describes himself as "a *Polish* Polish Jew" to signify that, unlike Jews of Polish descent living in other parts of the world, he has lived all his life in Poland and identifies with Poland as his home country, wrote his book *Poland and the Jews* as a counter-weight to a non-Polish Jewish fixation with Poland as the land of the Shoah, a land forever to be associated with death:

> I believe that Poland should be remembered primarily as the place of many centuries of the most important Jewish creativity, and not simply as the site of the tragic end. (Ibid., p. 26)

Jews outside Poland, however, are more likely to identify themselves with Hoffman's sense of aching loss than with Krajewski's desire to restore a rich Jewish past to its place in the living memory of Poland now:

> Because the extent of the loss was so great—so total—the act of remembering the vanished world has become fraught with painful and still acute emotions.[5] (Hoffman, op. cit., p. 1)

For Hoffman, the "act of remembering" Poland from the distance of living in the UK is inseparable from pain; for Krajewski, remembering Jewish experience in an earlier Poland forms *part* of his reality of living actively as a Jew in Poland today. It can be argued that while technically, as Polish-born Jews, both have a similar relationship to the Holocaust, Hoffman's loss as an emigrant Pole is greater because she has lost her living relationship to the country itself. Hence for ordinary Jews too, if K's view is accurate, loss as a feeling that becomes particularly attached to Poland has something to do with a history of separation and the impossibility of reconnection.

Neither Hoffman nor Krajewski is an "ordinary" Jew in my use of the term—their connection to family experience and the geographies of the Holocaust is too close. However, they implicitly articulate one of the dilemmas facing ordinary Jews in relation to Poland. Taken together, the two writers reflect how Jewish thinking tends to merge the loss *of* Polish-Jewish life with the millions of murders which took place *in* Poland in such a way as to render Poland so powerfully the central icon of Jewish loss that alternative ways of understanding feelings of loss themselves become lost in the shadow cast by this central *motif*. Teaching the Holocaust in Jewish education, for example, is very difficult to do without centralising Poland as simply a focus of disaster. Esther, a Sephardi Jew whose family derives from Bombay and Baghdad, saw how this impacted on her Indian-born cousin after her cousin began attending a Jewish school in London:

> "One of my cousins was brought up in Bombay [...]. Her parents [...] decided that for the future of their children they should move to England [...] [M]y niece, who was fourteen at the time, they put her in JFS [Jewish Free School] because she'd never had any Jewish education ... [She was] thrown in at the deep end ... I remember her coming to me: 'We've got to go'—and she still had an Indian accent—'We have to go to Poland!' I remember this very distinctly: 'Have you seen what happened?' Because she'd just learnt about it and she [...] really had [had] no idea [...] but she had this urgency that we had to go to Poland."

The domination by Poland in post-Holocaust "memory" can deeply upset Sephardi Jews who see their own losses, particularly the annihilation of the 500-year old Sephardi community in Salonika, marginalised or ignored. However, the Polish experience also dominates Jewish thinking to the extent that losses even amongst other Ashkenazi communities can get overlooked. A telling example is Romania. Romania, aligned for most of the war with the Axis powers[6] and happily compliant with German demands to deport Jews, lost the third-largest number of Jews of any country. More than a quarter of a million are estimated to have died, about eighty-three per cent of the country's pre-war Jewish population[7] (Hilberg, 1985). But how many ordinary Jews particularly notice Romania in the unending roll call of distressing statistics? Amongst all my interviewees, only one person even mentioned Romanian Jews, and that was to repeat a joke:

> "Apparently there was a joke going round Israel … something about, you can't swear at them for being a Jew, you can't swear at them for being Israeli, so you say that so-and-so Romanian."

Much closer to "ordinary" Jewish experience in the west, but no less paradoxical for these questions of loss, are the Netherlands. From the point of view of British Jews there is historically a close tie with Dutch Jews, since it was Jews from the well-established community in Amsterdam who in the seventeenth century became the first official Jews to resettle in England after the expulsion of 1290. To be a Dutch Jew can even be a source of status amongst Jews, according to Michelle:

> "On my mother's grandmother's side they were Dutch Jews, which I'm always quite proud of because I like thinking of myself as part-Dutch."

Yet amongst ordinary Jews there is no observable sense of loss or evocation of a past community or way of life in the Netherlands, despite the fact that seventy per cent of the 450-year old Dutch Jewish community—about 100,000 people—were killed; a detail which, if the Dutch exhibition in Auschwitz is anything to go by, is very disturbing for Dutch people themselves given the Netherlands' long reputation for religious toleration.[8]

The enormity of the numbers lost in the Holocaust and the sheer complexity of the whole thing are inherently so difficult to grasp, to imagine *what this means*, that in their own minds and hearts people will always give greater weight to some parts than to others. Krajewski discusses this point when he asks why it is Auschwitz, not Treblinka—a camp which functioned solely for the purpose of murdering Jews—which has become the symbol of the Holocaust. "Well," he says, "I feel there is no sense in posing such questions. Symbols of this kind are not devised intellectually, but appear independently of anyone's specific plans" (Krajewski, op. cit., p. 32). But he goes on to suggest that it was because people actually *survived* Auschwitz in some numbers—particularly writers such as Levi, Borowski, and Wiesel—that gives us each the means through which to connect with what happened.

Our way of relating to the Holocaust in all its manifestations therefore depends on the varied associations we carry. German Jews do not figure amongst the largest numbers of deaths mainly because so many managed to escape Germany before the major deportations began.[9] Whilst *they themselves* lost the substance of their former lives and subsequently also had to cope with learning of the fates of family members who for various reasons did not leave,[10] from the perspective of ordinary Jews, relating to this part of the Holocaust story is tied up with a different kind of loss: the loss of what was psychologically invested in German Jewry, and not only by German Jews themselves. During the nineteenth century, the Jews of Germany came to embody one of the dominant post-Enlightenment representations of Jewish life in Europe: urban, assimilated, materially successful, intellectually prominent, fully engaged with and fully identified with a country which was seen to be progressive, dynamic, and the home of high culture. For diaspora Jews, what happened in Germany is particularly disturbing: it renews a sense of insecurity; a loss of trust in progress, in the possibility of a rational, educated, and benign world. While in the wider, non-Jewish world, the fact that the Holocaust was devised and steered by Germany—supposedly the most cultured and advanced civilisation in Europe—is deeply troubling as a reflection of the hatred and destructivity lurking in even the most sophisticated society; for Jews the destruction of German Jewry by Germans is almost emblematic of Esther's "loss of hope". If it could happen in Germany, where can Jews live? As Bernice put it:

> "Jews in Europe and Germany had large numbers. They had been accepted, they were business, they were the musicians, they were

> the artists, they were established. They weren't a little clique who [...] [couldn't] do anything but be money lenders and rag collectors. In Venice, that's all they could be, in older times when there were restrictions ... [T]hat persecution then [was] because they were kept to be different, whereas here, these were people who were assimilating. [...] You know, 'I'm German, I'm not Jewish'—and yet it happened to them."

Poland represents something very different but at least as powerful in the minds of ordinary Jews. While many Sephardi Jews grieve as profoundly for the loss of life and of their own distinctive culture and history, as rich in language, song and food as any East European Jew harking back to the *shtetl*,[11] the fact remains that most ordinary Jews are descended from Eastern Europe, and in particular from the massive migrations westwards that took place at the end of the nineteenth and the beginning of the twentieth centuries. This demographic history shapes the context in which most ordinary Jews relate to Eastern Europe, and therefore, I suggest, is a key reason why loss and Poland are so centrally and inextricably linked in the post-Holocaust Jewish psychological landscape.

"I felt the impact of having to start a new life"

Between about 1885 and 1905, more than two million Jews[12] are estimated to have left the territories of Tsarist Russia to migrate west: the majority to the United States, but sizeable numbers to Britain as well as South America, South Africa, and Australia. Researcher Nicholas Evans calls this "a mass global phenomenon" created through large numbers of people migrating as individuals or in small groups, predominantly couples and families (Evans, 2005). Jewish emotional memory talks of these Jews as having fled from pogroms. While it is true that the big waves of emigration followed upsurges in pogroms, such vicious attacks were in reality confined to the southern parts of the Pale of Settlement in areas in or near to the Ukraine, in contrast to which large numbers of Jews came from the northern parts of the Pale; it is therefore probably the case that *fear* of pogroms rather than the actual experience was a principal trigger.[13] Evans and other historians point to the more powerful drivers behind the exodus: an 1882 Tsarist edict that imposed severe restrictions on where Jews could live and on economic opportunities for them within the Pale; the extreme poverty in which many Jews lived; and the new possibilities opened up in the west with the coming of the railways and cheap travel.

Whatever the reasons for this mass migration, one thing is clear: very few immigrants talked about their past. In interview after interview amongst ordinary Jews of Ashkenazi descent, the picture is almost identical:

HARRIET: "A lot of the tales that I have in my mother's family were not where they'd come from but of the arrival and settling in. They started off in the East End […] and they lived in the East End for years, so there are a lot of tales about that and moving on from there. That's really the history they talk about."

BERNICE: "When I did talk to my parents about … why don't you know more about their [the grandparents'] life, [my mother] said they were far too busy trying to put food on the table to talk about … They didn't want to talk about it, they'd left it, it wasn't happy. They'd left it because it […] wasn't a wonderful way of living and the life is better here. […] … [My mother] said, 'My parents were more concerned about putting food on the table and making sure we were all well […] … and if we talked about it [they] didn't want to talk about it.' Neither set of parents talked about their past."

LOUIS: "We don't know very much because nobody would ever talk about it. Three of the four of my grandparents came from Lithuania, the fourth came from somewhere else—White Russia I think."

PEARL: [My parents] were both from Russia [around the 1900s]. [T]hey never talked. We didn't know anything about … […] They didn't […] have energy or time to tell us anything. […] We didn't converse, we didn't hear stories. […] My mother was looking after nine of us, just trying in her poverty to feed us."

GIDEON: He really never talked about Lithuania at all, at all, there was just nothing."[14]

One part of the story is undoubtedly familiar: life was hard for the immigrants. If, as many did, they lacked valuable skills and couldn't communicate in any language other than Yiddish or Russian, surviving economically was a harsh struggle. One of my mother's grandfathers is recorded alternately as a "trouser presser" or a "slipper maker"—low-skilled, low-status, low-paid work—while his wife traded at a market stall until she was old. Families were large, and housing conditions often desperately overcrowded; illness and early death from conditions such as tuberculosis were not unknown; and there is clearly a lot of truth in Bernice's and Pearl's analyses that their (grand)parents simply had no *time* to talk of the past. But this can only be a partial explanation for the silences amongst the generation of immigrants. Silence is an emotional communication; people are silent when it is too difficult to speak.

Gideon's partial success in unravelling his father's own silence is an example of the pain that migrants' reluctance to speak could conceal. Gideon was over thirty before he discovered that his father had not, as Gideon always thought, been born in South Africa, but instead had been born in Lithuania and had come to South Africa at the age of ten. In persuading his father to talk, Gideon learnt something of the emotional story that was an integral part of his father's geographical migration: a story of parental abandonment which ultimately resulted in an irrevocable break in relationship between a son and his father:

> "My grandfather left Lithuania [...] promising to send money to bring his family across. They never heard from him again until my grandmother got fed up, collected the money [i.e., got the money together for the fare] and took the children and they went over to Johannesburg and found him shacked up with another woman. [...] One interpretation is that [their experience of extreme poverty in Lithuania] was one of those unpleasant things that [my father] just wanted to leave behind. [...] [But] my dad never spoke to his father [again] after he was aged fourteen. He arrived in South Africa when he was about ten, so I can only speculate that it was related to the fact that they'd been left behind [...]."

The specifics of Gideon's father's story may be relatively unusual, but ordinary Jews are not often in a position to know. Many more may lack facts but possess (or be possessed by) an elusive feeling, which itself can have a haunted quality. Harriet's great-grandparents arrived in Britain in the 1880s. When she visited Ellis Island in New York, she was deeply affected by seeing the evidence of what her own family could have gone through in their journey westwards:

> "[W]hen I visited Ellis Island [...] I found [it] extremely moving. There were definitely ghosts there, it was quite an extraordinary place. A lot of pictures of the families who came there, obviously a lot of them were Jewish, and [...] that really brought home the huge upheaval that had come into so many people's lives, escaping from all different sorts of ... That was quite a wake-up. [...] It brought the emotional impact ... I [got] quite upset about it [...]. I [felt] the impact of having to start a new life and not knowing how you were going to be treated and what it was going to be like, and [...] that was what hit me, I saw it as quite upsetting [...]."

Various things, I think, inhibited the immigrants' desire or ability to talk about their pasts, to bring their past, as it were, *with* them and keep it alive as a memory in the new family. One is the likelihood that it was simply too painful to speak about the life and the people they had left behind. A second was the pressure to get on and succeed; to have made the journey—in some cases their sacrifice—worthwhile. Living in a psychological environment in which almost everyone was under the same pressure, who were they to talk to? Third is the cultural shift that every immigrant family goes through, and the resulting gap—of language, of values—that invariably opens up between the immigrants themselves and the next generation, compounding ambivalent feelings around loss of the old ways. And finally, there is the timing of the Holocaust itself. At the very point at which some of the immigrants may have been able to relax from their own labours, to be heartened by the sight of their children "doing well", and possibly to respond to their grandchildren's curiosity about the past, what they had left behind itself was destroyed.

On the basis of relatively recent research, it is certainly possible to surmise that it was too painful for the immigrants to speak. Studies indicate that permanent migration to another country inherently has a huge impact on migrants' psychological well-being, at least for a period. In the 1970s, mental health care professionals began to recognise that migrants and refugees registered a much higher prevalence of mental health breakdown than indigenous communities; and increasingly saw parallels between the "culture shock" of migration and the experience of bereavement.

Permanent migration from one country to another and from one *culture* to another is an experience which presents individual migrants with enormous psychological challenges. Garza-Guerrero has described "cultural shock" as "a stressful, anxiety-provoking situation, a violent encounter—one which puts the newcomer's personality functioning to the test", and as an experience that "is accompanied by a process of mourning brought about by the individual's gigantic loss of a variety of his love objects in the abandoned culture [...]: family, friends, language, music, food and culturally determined values, customs and attitudes", the combination of which "causes a serious threat to the newcomer's identity" (Garza-Guerrero, 1974, p. 410). Garza-Guerrero sees the initial experience of moving to a new culture as "one of puzzlement [characterised by] anxiety, sadness, hostility, desperation, a yearning to recover what was lost [...]—reminiscent of the mourning related to the death of a loved [one]", an experience which is then often expressed in "an idealisation of [the] original country" (ibid., pp. 418, 420). In a paper entitled "Migration as part of life experience" June Huntingdon, a voluntary migrant from the UK to Australia, wrote, of her own experience, that even in the most auspicious of circumstances, the process of migration is difficult:

> fluency in the English language, security of employment at a level commensurate with the migrant's knowledge and skills, and [...] entry into the [new] society via marriage to a native son, cannot ensure settlement, nor can they ensure a positive and pain-free transition from one society to another. (Huntingdon, 1981, p. 1)

She continues,

> Migration alters perhaps more than any other experience our outer reality and imposes on us [...] a discrepancy between our inner and outer worlds and the task of realigning inner and outer if we are to adapt and survive with any degree of physical and mental health. (Ibid., p. 2)

Huntingdon goes on to describe with great feeling the complexity of changes which are experienced as shocks by a migrant individual: the changes of physical reality imposed by "climate, topography, flora, fauna, seasons, diurnal light"; changes in social status and role; the disorientation that arises from the loss of a social world based on and expressing unconscious assumptions about the world: a "taken-for-granted construction of reality;" and the loss of "the loved and familiar". In addition to this, Dinesh Bhugra and Matthew Becker suggest that many migrants also suffer "feelings of guilt over abandoning culture and homeland" (Bhugra & Becker, 2005, p. 3).

It is true that the social environment into which many Jews arrived in the 1890s and 1900s did not entirely involve loss of a culturally familiar environment, as may be the case, for example, with present-day refugees and asylum-seekers. Jewish organisations were well-established, and the descriptions of East End life in London (or Lower East Side life in New York) reflect the lively existence of familiar social norms: language, food, synagogues, newspapers, and theatre. Nevertheless, even if their cultural transition was eased somewhat, Jewish migrants in their hundreds of thousands *must* have gone through huge emotional pressures in their shift from east to west. The loss of intimates—family and friends—would be permanent. As the major migrations happened before the days of telephones, they would never hear their loved ones' voices again. While the move held out hope of a better future and there was certainly a greater freedom of *opportunity*, many immigrants clearly endured poverty at least as bad as previously; and for many the shift from small towns and villages to the densely populated urban environments of London, Manchester, or New York offered little opportunity to escape to countryside. For women the shift may even have been worse: undergoing repeated childbirth, and the daily pressures of feeding (and worrying about) a growing brood of children in restricted space, without the support of mothers or sisters unless these family members had also migrated, were unlikely to have been easy. My aunt, the youngest of my grandparents' seven children, found it impossible to ask her mother about "the old country". If she did ask, she says, "Mum would say *'der haym'* and burst into tears." Pearl, whose immigrant parents ended up with nine children to feed and clothe, is awe-struck at what the generation of immigrants took on:

> "When you think of the enormity of people who couldn't speak the language, coming with young children, probably no money, how did they do it? How did they cope?"

In the dominant rags-to-riches stories of Jewish success, relatively little attention has been paid to the emotional consequences of the huge upheaval that most of our relatively recent ancestors went through. In a later generation and in rather different circumstances, Olivia, whose Iraqi-born grandmother emigrated to England with her children after the Iraqi revolution, observes with hindsight that her grandmother clearly experienced feelings of loss for her life in Iraq but could only communicate these indirectly:

> "Loss [...] wasn't expressed [directly], [...] it was more sublimated [...]. [O]ne way in which loss was dealt with [was through] the projection of this [i.e., Iraqi-Jewish] culture, or [its] preservation, into the future. The other way was straightforward nostalgia, so suddenly all the bad things fell out of the picture and life in the East was perfect, wonderful. 'We had such a fantastic life.' [...] [T]hat was a way of dealing with loss—canonising it. [...]"

Olivia certainly felt the impact of this on herself, in a powerful pressure to conform:

> "There was a huge pressure to be Iraqi-identified, to stay Iraqi and to behave in an Iraqi way [...] so that it would continue",

and while she resisted this pressure, she believes that later generations cannot avoid bearing an emotional legacy:

> "The incredible legacy that families suffer[ed] [...] a couple of generations ago [and] they foist on to the children, good or bad."

Olivia is here referring to what psychologists describe as a "transgenerational legacy", an unconsciously driven pattern of behaviour in families, which I referred to earlier, in Chapter One. Numerous studies, from Fraiberg, Adelson, and Shapiro (1980) to Coles (2011), have shown how the traumas of earlier generations can feed into later generations. Coles refers to these traumas as ones of "loss and abandonment" (Coles, 2011, p. xvii). Typically such traumas manifest at the time and (if not adequately grieved) subsequently in patterns of silent and withdrawn behaviour.[15]

Literature on transgenerational legacies is now extensive, and valuable for clinical work in the consulting room. My concern here is to suggest that the upheaval involved in migration has had ramifications well beyond the immediate lives of the migrants, and that amongst "ordinary" Jews this has had both personal and cultural repercussions. Our immigrant predecessors lost their families of origin; this cannot fail to have been enormously painful, equivalent to an unfinished grief, and—tellingly—predominantly expressed in silence. Harriet's unexpectedly deep upset at seeing the photographic material in the museum on Ellis Island suggests something of an "inheritance of loss" in process.[16]

There is an important distinction between loss as an *event* and loss as a felt *experience*, although of course the two are intimately connected. The loss of "*der haym*" was an event for the migrants, not for their children. However, the unspoken strength of feeling associated for the migrants with this event must have impacted on their children, and transgenerational studies suggest that this could continue into later generations. While Hoffman's and Figes' writings tell us something very directly of the emotional wrench experienced by migrants and their often painful longing for "the lost world", the ways in which such experiences are spoken about—or *not* spoken about—shape the kinds of bonds that develop between parents and children, in turn influencing the ways in which the next generation forms its own emotional responses to other events. When feelings of loss about the Holocaust, an event which ordinary Jews never actually experienced, become focused on Poland as a particularly powerful symbol, ordinary Jews are in one sense living out of an historic loss within their own families which was never properly grieved about. The centring of Poland in the foreground of "ordinary Jewish" post-Holocaust grief reflects a need in a later generation for a tangible object to grieve about, one that might unconsciously fill the emotionally empty space of the ungrieved "*haym*" which my, and hundreds of thousands, of grandparents, could not speak about.

There is another crucially important aspect to this dimension of loss. Weine and colleagues found that "when refugee families live with memories of traumas and losses, the family itself becomes a very important context for narrating memories" (Weine et al., 2004, p. 158). One function of such narration is to keep *alive* the life lived before, with all its quirks, sorrows, and richness. In not speaking about their lives before migration, it was not only the migrants themselves whose past life became frozen (a kind of death). Parental (or grandparental) narration is an extraordinarily powerful means of connecting later generations to earlier ones. Family, ethnic, and community identity are constantly shaped in the process of telling who was who and who did what, when, and where. "Belonging" is not simply a question of group membership *now* but involves a sense of positioning both in history and in geography. It is an instinctive process which is observable in the questioning by young children: "Where was I then? Who was with me? Who was that person in relation to me?" The immigrants' silence wholly interrupted this ebb-and-flow of meaning and relationships across time and space. Perhaps the first generation, focused on establishing membership and a future in the new country, did not notice or did not mind too much that they had little sense of "where they had come from"; but in the aftermath of the Holocaust, such things matter hugely. Within at most two generations of the mass migration, the Jewish world of Eastern Europe disappeared almost without trace, rendering permanent and absolute the loss of a tangible, personal connection to these *particular* "lands of our forebears": a geography where most Jewish families had lived for almost 600 years. There is no "homecoming" possible, not now, not ever. The Holocaust made complete a loss of personal history that began with our grandparents' or great-grandparents' departure from Eastern Europe. "Poland" becomes forever fixed: in imagination as the epitome of a traditional, small-town, deeply religious, Yiddish, seemingly unchanged, Jewish "*haym*"; and in horror as the graveyard of Jewish life. It is this double effect of a lost past, coupled with the irrevocable finality imposed by the Holocaust, that gives such a potent charge to "ordinary Jewish" centralising of Poland and the old Yiddish heartlands of Eastern Europe in the annals of Holocaust loss.

It is impossible to explore fully here all the ways in which the losses associated with the Holocaust present themselves to ordinary Jews: the loss of "security, of people, of civilized ideas, of hope" that Esther talked about. What I have tried to do in this chapter is to suggest, partly as examples and partly because they are genuine experiences in their own right, what may lie beneath some of the felt losses that people talked about. If, as K thinks, there has been a collective failure to grieve, it is, surely, when we know more accurately *what* we each grieve for that mourning becomes possible.

In the next chapter I focus on anger. Anger is a natural—some would say inevitable—reaction to loss, especially when a loss is so complex, so multi-faceted and so overwhelming. Jews are undeniably angry about the Holocaust. Not only is this about the actuality of the losses; though in the words of the Passover service this alone "would have been enough."[17] It also concerns the raw wound inflicted on the Jewish psyche, on Jews' sense of a rightful and worthy place in the world, by the Nazis' total onslaught not just on Jewish lives but on every aspect of

Jewish life and Jewish dignity. The anger that so many ordinary Jews feel relates to an experience of fundamental violation perpetrated, in some sense, against all Jews. In the next chapter I explore different dimensions of the anger which ordinary Jews feel in relation to the Holocaust; and I suggest that a unifying theme underlying disparate triggers for anger is a sense that in violating a long-held expectation as to the nature of Jewish people's relationship with a Europe in which they had lived for so long, something akin to an implicit contract was shattered.

CHAPTER THREE

The broken contract

"Anger", Harry wrote to me, "[is] a constant."

> "There are so many feelings crowding in on each other, it is not easy to express them in words. However, the more I have thought about it, the more I have come to understand that my feelings of anger are a constant … Anger is always to the fore. I am angry that the Holocaust happened. I am angry that a group of amoral murderous thugs took upon themselves the decision who should live and who should die. I am angry that very few individuals and not a single nation came to our rescue. I am angry that we could not help ourselves. I am just angry."

It is easy enough to understand why Jews should be angry about the Holocaust, but the feeling itself is not an easy one to have. Far from being an emotion easy to accept, anger's frequent association with aggression, violence, hatred, and destructiveness gives it disturbing and frightening qualities. Moreover, in the context of the Holocaust, the absence of an obvious target for one's rage complicates the *bearing* of this feeling immensely. Who is Harry to direct his anger at now? What can he hope for?

We all learn about anger in infancy. For an infant, being angry with a primary caregiver is a risky business. Parents faced with a baby's screaming rage do not always respond optimally; hence some of our most complicated relational exchanges with the outer world in later life derive from the early mechanisms we develop to deal with an inevitable frustration and disappointment that the world does not necessarily act the way we want it to. As Melanie Klein indicated, our growth as adults is profoundly shaped by our early-learnt capacity to deal with disappointment.

Throughout life, anger presents human beings with particular challenges because its core function is twofold. We need anger as a way of learning how to stand up for ourselves, both in relation to the outer world and internally in our way of self-relating. At the same time, in expressing to the outside world what we want and don't want, anger also seeks a response; in this it is an inherently relational form of self-expression. Failures of response will always leave us in some kind of predicament involving issues of impotence and self-esteem, which are likely to reinforce painful experiences of loss: loss of an actual relationship; loss of an imagined state-of-relationship between ourselves and another; loss of self-value in how we view ourselves. More than any other of the feelings associated with trauma, anger forces us into psychological dilemmas of frustration and choice. Fear of undesirable outcomes if we express our anger collides with fear over our felt helplessness if nothing useful happens as a result of expressing it. Anger breeds anger when doors appear to be closed and we do not know what to do. "I am angry that very few individuals and not a single nation came to our rescue."

In the spectrum of ordinary Jews' emotional reactions to the Holocaust, loss is comparatively straightforward. After all, no one other than a Holocaust denier can refuse to recognise that in the Holocaust massive losses were involved. But to be *angry* about the Holocaust is another matter. Who, now, to be angry with? To what end? As Harry reveals, there can be "too many" feelings "crowding in on each other". What to do with them all? We can find ourselves caught between a frustrated desire to do *something* and an anguish that if we give up, something that matters very much has been diminished.

It is inevitable that ordinary Jews will in some way feel very angry about the Holocaust. The Holocaust was a massive attack on Jews at every level—on individuals, families, whole communities, whole populations; on the overall size of a globally small population; on the continuity of Jewish life in Europe; on Jewish self-esteem and self-image. In fact, *not* to be angry at such a comprehensive onslaught would be abnormal. But people's feelings of anger vary, as does the focus of their anger. Once again, there is complicated territory to navigate. People relate personally to the Holocaust, and that personal reaction is partly driven by feelings aroused by their own life experiences: in this, once more, the Holocaust evokes personal life issues which have no connection with the Holocaust. At the same time, every Jew *was* targeted in the Holocaust, therefore by extension every Jew in his or her own mind *is* targeted by what the Holocaust represents: an unremitting assault on the value and entitlement of being Jewish. All Jews are personally implicated in this. Therefore while what is personally aroused in individuals is not derived from personal experience of the Holocaust, there is a level at which Jews undoubtedly share an angry response, complicated further by anxious uncertainty over "what to do". In this chapter I suggest that one way of understanding how the Holocaust has impacted so profoundly at a shared and meta-level of Jewish experience is to see the Holocaust as embodying a broken psychological contract.

"It's completely overwhelming, the rage I feel"

For Diana, who worked for years in the field of Holocaust education, there is no question but that there is an explicit connection between her personal experiences in her family and her later feelings of rage and impotence aroused not only by the Holocaust but by any "abuse of power, racism, genocide". She describes how powerfully affected she has been in her life and in her work by her experience of a disjunct between her parents' avowed politics focused on the world outside, and what actually took place within her family. Her rage is associated with abuses of power:

> "[…] There are dynamics in the family that I can remember and still carry on to a certain extent, which are to do with bullying and powerlessness and humiliation, and exclusion and jealousy […]. […] [T]he politics of [our] home […] were about … *tikkun olam* …, to

make the world a better place. My parents were both so involved [...] that it was inevitable that we'd all end up with those sorts of politics."

Although she does not actually say so, it is perfectly possible to imagine that, brought up in a family with several siblings, where the focus was so powerfully directed to putting right the world outside, injustices and inequalities inside her family may well have gone ignored. She herself cannot ignore the intensity of her own feelings, and explicitly connects her particular engagement with the external world to this more inner experience:

> "[...] For sure they're linked ... It's very powerful, it's completely overwhelming, the feeling that I have around bullying, the rage I feel, which is sometimes constructive and sometimes ... impotent."

After many years of researching and teaching about the effects of the mass destructivity of Nazism, and in keeping with her parents' teaching, she turned her attention towards building collaborative social action through supporting people's courage and confidence. Underlying her plans for her future work was a strong desire to ensure that political forms of exploitation and abuse are not forgotten, and this seemed to be driven by terror as well as rage:

> "I work [now on] building people's collective responsibility, to see themselves as possible agents of change. So for example, if they see bullying, or any issue that concerns them [...] they can feel a sense of responsibility and ability to ... their communities for the common good. [...] Nothing terrifies me more than people who speak out to defend other people being killed themselves, [...] the idea of a society where people are afraid to ... Bad things will always happen but if people feel able to speak out against them and to join other people, in theory they're always more powerful in bigger numbers.
>
> I [want to work] with people who are campaigning about Darfur. Who can name all the places where there's abuse of power, racism, genocide? It just happens that that genocide [Darfur], it enrages me how that's happening ... I'm not sure a lot of that's been informed by doing the work on the Holocaust, but I know that we were brought up as a family to think about politics in that way."

For Diana, the associations are clear. Her personal experiences seem to have intensified in her a common annihilatory terror, and this means she is particularly sensitive to genuine annihilatory threats in the outside world. The impact of her family has been a major factor in an emotional drive "to make the world a better place", as though in that way, at least, she can experience herself as powerful and influential. For others, though, the links are not always immediately obvious; they may find themselves, as Diana also describes, alternating between feeling quite detached from Holocaust material, and being overwhelmed by it:

> "I was surprised how most of the time I managed to talk to people about the Holocaust or read information or watch a film [...] there's almost like a detachment. I just kept it in my head rather than it penetrating feelings. And then sometimes some material or testimony just consumed me."

Ruth, too, alludes to a similar shift between detachment and overwhelm. At first, she feels angry about the Holocaust in a rather impersonal and general way:

> "It's related to a compassion anger. When I see survivors, I suppose something, some visual stimulus, seeing somebody's face, watching something on TV, listening to something on the radio or watching a film, *The Pianist* for example, with the Holocaust theme ... an anger on their behalf. It's not such a personal issue for me, more a diffuse anger that it happened."

When she starts to focus explicitly on the people who had "stood by" and not protested, her anger becomes very strong:

> "I think ... when I'm directly reading or looking at material, material is being fed into my consciousness, yes ... it's an appalled disgust—how could so many people have stood by and not done more to protest?"

Then her sense of outrage ("appalled disgust") that "more was not done" shifts to the present and arouses feelings of powerlessness: an anguish that she is (and always was) powerless to rescue those who suffered:

> "If I see something on TV, old newsreel, documentary ... archival material, yes, it's the sense that I wish I could rescue these people, I could pluck them from out of my TV screen and do something to save them."

It is significant that Ruth is speaking as though what she watches on the TV or on film is still happening. Even though she knows quite well that the events of the Holocaust are in the past, emotionally she still experiences something reflected by it in the present. This would seem to connect back to theory about trauma, for it is a feature of trauma that past events continue to be experienced *as though they are still happening*. Ruth does not describe herself as traumatised "by" the Holocaust, but in a certain way she is living in her own life with a kind of trauma that evokes in her a desire to save. In fact, there is a personal dimension to Ruth's feelings of powerlessness, a dimension that paradoxically emphasises the real power of our own feelings to "understand" something of the experience of events that happen to others. Ruth is someone whose personal history has already sensitised her to feeling powerless. As a teenager her parents were both chronically ill, and her father died when she was fifteen. She has known from a young age what it means to stand by helplessly angry and watch someone who matters sicken and die; her testimony thus poignantly reflects how personal experience provides the emotional context through which we relate to and interpret external events, no matter how long ago or where they occur.

At this point, something needs to be said concerning *witnessing*. In *Fantasies of Witnessing*, Weissman (2004) suggests that efforts to recreate Holocaust-like experiences in such a way as to enable an "immediate" emotional "knowledge" of it are essentially "fantasies" which distract from the critical historical task of studying and understanding the Holocaust as a phenomenon of time and place. However, there is a way in which readers and viewers of the extensive written accounts by survivors and of the photographic evidence and newsreels reproduced in numerous documentaries and museums, are, in practice, in a position of "witnessing". Whilst not actually witnessing the events as they occurred, what consumers of Holocaust material read or view *seems* as though it is happening now, because in a sense for that person it *is* happening now. In the here-and-now experience, the viewer is reduced to being a helpless bystander: one, moreover, who helplessly watches something being done to someone who, in an internal process of identification, could be themselves or someone they love. Time frames temporarily collapse; what is being read or observed has a powerful emotional impact in the present; and part of that emotional response is anger.

"A little painter from Austria ..."

Anger in its spontaneous expression is a normal attempt to change a painful situation; to get something remedial *done*. One of the painful inheritances that ordinary Jews carry in relation to the Holocaust is that nothing now *can* be done about what happened. (Whether or not nothing could be done at the time is another matter.) So anger is in part a response to an embedded sense of impotence or helplessness. Harry, for example, is both "angry that we could not help ourselves" and angry that so few others helped. This is not only a comment on the utter powerlessness of the situation that European Jews were then in, but an indirect expression of his own terror at the thought of being in such a paralysing position: helpless to help and helpless to be helped. Victor makes the point even more explicitly. Reconnecting with elements of the Holocaust, whether through visits to Poland or through seeing photographs, evokes in him both anger and frustration:

> "I'm pretty sure [my anger is greater now] [...]. Especially when we went to Poland. Whenever I see some kind of (heavy?) manifestation now, I feel great anger. [...] There's a photo I've seen once of Jews in their synagogue being made to listen to a Nazi reading something—with bare hands. All these things make me so angry; frustrated anger, you know."

Psychologically, it is extremely important for people in their own lives to discover how they can triumph over the terror of feeling small and helpless: to know that they are able to take action, to feel themselves as potent individuals rather than "passive objects" to whom things "happen". Images of the Holocaust act as potent stimuli, evoking those times in all our lives when we were precisely in the position of being small, dependent, and helpless, and this is one reason why for ordinary Jews, remembering the Holocaust evokes such powerful feelings of rage.

For some ordinary Jews, rage seems to hit up against the sheer impossibility of understanding. "Incomprehension" was a word that arose frequently in my interviews. Most interviewees (and one must assume, therefore, most ordinary Jews)[1] struggle with sheer bafflement as to how "this monstrous crime" could have taken place. Pearl and Bernice both focus their anger initially on Hitler. For each, there is a terrifying and sickening mystery as to how an individual like Hitler managed to wield so much power and influence in the pursuit of horror and murder:

PEARL: "[It] makes me feel sick. How do human beings get … […] … into doing these … doing the bidding of that lunatic! A lunatic! Who was a failed painter and then chose to … oh, how does this happen? What do sociologists say about matters of that kind? How can they find reasons for peoples' behaviour? And he's not the … I mean he is perhaps the worst, but they keep talking about Stalin. How could he influence millions of people?"

BERNICE: "A little painter from Austria … How he got believed … that's incomprehensible to me. How that man carried … people got carried away by him, how? How people just didn't think it through or they just thought it was going to be best for them? And to hell with everybody else?"

While an obvious target, albeit one rendered even more frustrating because he is now dead and beyond the reach of anger, the figure of Hitler provides a personification of the whole Holocaust. Without Hitler as the focal point of quasi-messianic hysteria and brutal paranoia, the Holocaust would almost certainly never have happened. In representing an event of such enormous and difficult-to-comprehend complexity, his figure can also "stand in place" for the complex feelings the cataclysm itself evokes. For in a complex, inner reality, Pearl and Bernice's anger is not *just* at Hitler, the Nazis, and Germans but at *others* (a world, and one, moreover, which includes themselves) who cannot provide an explanation for this terrible event. Behind their anger and incomprehension, too, lurks fear; and within this, fear not just of the possible event and its terrible consequences, but fear of their own impotence: for if we cannot understand how and why the Holocaust arose, it could happen again and we would still be powerless to stop it.[2]

Amongst psychoanalysts, anger is understood as having a direct relationship to loss. Bowlby, who studied loss in clinical situations over many years, saw anger as a normal and predictable reaction to an experience of intolerable pain (Bowlby, 1973, ch. 17). Any unbearable loss generates anger. Whether it is the infant's terror of abandonment when his mother "goes away", the seeming futility of life when someone centrally important dies, or the loss of one's own previous self through illness or injury, anger at what has happened and at its painfully felt consequences exist out of an overwhelming need to seek relief from the pain. Speaking on BBC radio, Jim Swire, whose daughter Flora was one of those murdered in the Lockerbie bomb attack, spoke of how "fighting [driven by anger] is a way of protecting oneself from the pain of bereavement in shocking circumstances" (Swire, 2010). At the same time, anger is also associated with fear. Deep pain associated with loss can itself feel frightening in its endlessness and in one's helplessness to stop it, while it is often also accompanied by other fears: fear of rejection, fear of helplessness, fear of the consequences of being angry.

I will look in more depth at issues of fear in relation to the Holocaust in the next chapter. Here I want to emphasise that one of the functions of anger is *to defend* not only against the pain of loss but against terrible feelings of fear and powerlessness. Anger, at least, offers hope, and against situations of despair, hope for the future is a crucial motivation to continue living. Anger becomes a hopeful counter-weight to feelings and experiences of helplessness.

"Israel seems to be the one thing ..."

It is in this context that Victor reflects on one reason why the establishment of the State of Israel quickly became a powerful symbolic force in the Jewish psyche. Victor was seven years old and living in suburban London when the war broke out. He lived through its six years hearing "all sorts of bits on the radio about mistreatment of Jews, it said no more than that, so that you knew something horrible was happening to Jews." He found himself during these childhood years in the position of being, via the radio, the recipient of "bits" of information that clearly related to his own identity. At the same time he was exposed to his own family's inability to talk about it, and one wonders what a child in his position (he was an only child) could make of this experience other than to feel in some way silenced and helpless:

> "I can't remember parents or family discussing it much as a Jewish thing. They obviously discussed the war, but ... it's strange ... And

> this includes when I went to stay for a short while with relatives in Newcastle, who were very Jewish in the sense of being quite *frum*,[3] and many of them overseas born. I don't remember people speaking about it or voicing thoughts about it, except thoughts about the war in general."

In 1945, Victor was thirteen and began learning, as did all Jews and most of the developed world, about what had happened to Jews in Europe. Predictably, his reactions were initially of horror and then of anger:

> "What were the emotions? […] A horror. […] When you saw the newsreels, it was unbelievable. […] But certainly my feeling was anger. I don't know if it was accompanied by a feeling of vulnerability at this stage—'it could happen to us'."

By this time, Victor was "beginning to have the inklings of Zionism, in that our place was in [that] country, which was then Palestine," and early in the 1950s he "made *aliyah*"[4] to the newly established State of Israel. This was partly out of a hope to experience himself as "belonging"; it was also, he believes, the only way then available for Jews to channel their anger over what had happened into hope for another future:

> "It just seemed to make logical sense: if we don't belong here, this [Israel] must be where Jews belong. So I joined Habonim[5] at a young age and … made *aliyah*. […] I very much belonged in Israel at that time. […][6]
>
> I think we do have a common thing of anger, which relates of course to our relationship with Israel, because Israel seems to be one thing through which we could channel our anger …"

In the post-Holocaust psychological Jewish landscape, the role of Israel must have a chapter in its own right. There I will consider how Israel has become the repository for all sorts of dislocated feelings Jews hold in the aftermath of the Holocaust: for example, anger at centuries of oppression and persecution which could never be safely expressed at the time and which are now affected by the realpolitik of the Middle East. Such feelings complicate and leave unresolved important questions concerning Jewish life in, and Jewish relating to, a non-Jewish post-Holocaust world. Here I want to concentrate on the phenomenon of anger as it affects ordinary Jews when it is not simply translated to the context of the Middle East.

As it happens, Victor did not stay in Israel. He came back to London when his father died and re-established his life in Britain. His feelings about Israel have become more ambivalent as the years have gone by. At the same time, he reflects on the fact that his anger in relation to the Holocaust has grown even stronger; perhaps because he no longer has the same outlet for his anger and frustration that Israel once offered him but must continue to feel some degree of pain and helpless anger, such as that caused by his inability to stop Holocaust deniers from questioning the very existence of the Holocaust:

> "Maybe [it's] because I'm an older person. Maybe […] part of it [then] was modified because it was just something which had come out of a war. Lots of people had been killed, and things like that. So maybe that modified the horror; certainly it was a youngster's understanding. […] But [my] anger is greater now […]. It's important that I'm much angrier now. I can appreciate the value of life and what it means to people to be a parent. That's one of the issues. I'm sure that part of it is the whole Holocaust-denial bit, which makes it a big issue—how can people say those things?"

Anger is a call to action. Helpless impotence sets in when no action is possible, for whatever reason. One condition in which action is not possible is when there is no clear thing—or person—to focus on, a difficulty which will occur when what is going on, or what is felt to be going on, is too complicated or confusing to grasp.

One complication affecting our Holocaust-related anger is the way we have become accustomed to using the term "the Holocaust" as a form of shorthand. In some ways the term has become quite problematic as other groups and nations adopt it to describe their own collective sufferings, not necessarily at the hands of the Nazis.[7] It is, for example, easy to get distracted into feeling angry with those (academics or otherwise) who appear to be trying to take over or obscure *"our"* Holocaust,[8] as though in so doing all become guilty of some form of Holocaust denial.[9] At issue here, especially when we have not lost or had close family affected by those events in Europe, is not just *what* happened—though that in itself is a sizeable subject—but what all the different, confusing, complicated elements leave us with; what that catch-all phrase "the Holocaust" actually involved. What in practice ordinary Jews mean by "the Holocaust" was the deliberate programme of mass murder perpetrated by the Nazi regime against the Jews. What, emotionally, we include in it is something much larger: involving collaboration, betrayal, indifference, comprehensive dispossession, abandonment, denial, denigration, distortion, and humiliation. In some ways more than the actual deaths, it is this complexity of associations with the Holocaust that sticks with us; and such complexity is itself deeply confusing. It is probably for this reason that references to, or ideas about, the Holocaust often become restricted to single or relatively simple concepts or images: such as Hitler as the source and cause; Auschwitz as the representative symbol of death; or statistics ("the six million"). In *The Lost*, Mendelsohn (2006) shows how disturbing it is when this history is only transmitted in vague generalities, and what a relief it is to be able to grasp something of a whole story. In his long search for details about his grandfather's lost family, Mendelsohn sought to grasp something more explicit about the fate of his relatives, and so provide a meaningful focus for his family's feelings about those who had been murdered. When he finally saw the box-like hole beneath the floor where his great-uncle and cousin had spent their last months, he had not just a tangible but a symbolically meaningful focus to attach his family's loss to and to cry over; once he had this, the family could fully grasp its loss and live with the knowledge.

"I suddenly got very angry"

Ordinary Jews, unlike the children of survivors who can in theory learn specifics from their parents, frequently live with only partially informed generalities about the Holocaust. Anger can equally be directed at everybody, or at a vague nobody. Harry, it can be seen, is trying to express as succinctly as possible his anger about *everything* to do with the Holocaust. He tells us that there are many specifics to be angry *about* and many people to be angry *with*, but he still does not know which way to turn: in the end all he can do is simply feel: "I am just angry." When Ruth first learnt about the Holocaust she felt angry but, with "nobody" obvious to focus this on, kept looking for "somebody" to hold responsible. Her first conscious memory of being angry about the Holocaust came when she was studying history at school at the same time as the TV series *The World at War* (1973–74) was being screened:

> "I remember as a schoolgirl at secondary school studying history and reading … information about the Second World War. We were required to study a certain amount in preparation for the Highers[10] exam. [I remember] reading about the Holocaust as a footnote only [in her textbook]. [That was] a turning point for me because I had experienced watching *The World at War* on TV, often as a backdrop to doing homework on a Sunday afternoon, and I'd become very aware of the awfulness, the hideousness of that period. I was beginning to identify more strongly as a Jewish person during my teenage years. It was the contrast between becoming much more conscious of the issue at home … this programme being repeatedly shown and … the marginal treatment that it received academically … that … stuck in my mind as an important issue."

This massive discrepancy between the way the Holocaust was presented within her history curriculum and what she was learning through the media provoked Ruth's anger, but she was unsure who to direct it at:

> "I got quite angry. I wasn't angry with the teacher, I was angry with … the curriculum, the book publisher or something … the editor. […] … The editor, the publisher, somebody had … passed this as acceptable material for school age children studying history for the sake of a Higher. […]"

Confusion can only reinforce a sense of helplessness. The consequence of this is that ordinary Jews may feel stuck with a powerful anger without a clear focus for action. Arriving relatively late in life at a strong emotional connection with the Holocaust, Doris seems to have caught up with it all at once. She catches herself back from calling it "the greatest crime in history" (although many Jews, flooded with such an intense level of rage, may want to); what is important to see is how much she is grappling with, and how impossible this makes it for her to know what action she might want to take by way of reaching some kind of resolution:

> "The Holocaust is the greatest … this unique crime in history and … when I talk about Palestinians or Arabs in connection with it … I mean, the Nazis were the ones who *did* it, but it's today that they

> are putting on soaps based on *The Protocols of the Elders of Zion*, and there is an anti-Semitic … television channel in the Lebanon […]. [I]t goes back thousands of years, all of it, […] in this country and the forced conversions in Spain and so on.
>
> […] If there was anything [that brought the Holocaust particularly into her consciousness], it was the Munich Olympics in 1972. […] What absolutely really got me [was], there we are at the Olympics, the whole of the Israeli team, they went on with the bloody games! […] They couldn't care less, they couldn't care less. And then I started reading stuff … and I read a lot […] about what was actually happening during the war, very well documented stuff about Roosevelt and Churchill not allowing Jews in even though in America they hadn't even filled the German quota … I started reading … about what had really being going on. […] [I suddenly got] very angry, very … … without any problems about being angry at all."

Thus far, I have focused on anger as a response to feelings of helplessness and impotence, a response amplified by, and in, confusion. I think that, in a way, this dynamic runs throughout the whole experience of ordinary Jewish, Holocaust-related anger. For example, Sonia, like Victor, sees that many Jews avoid talking about the Holocaust; unlike Victor, she becomes particularly angry about this:

> "I get very angry when people think it's time to move on, this happened […] two or three generations ago; even Jewish people […] saying, you know, 'Why are we still talking about the Holocaust? Everyone's sick of talking about the Holocaust.' This is only seventy years ago! These terrible things happened to millions of people only that length of time ago. In a continuum of things, it's nothing … it's yesterday."

Like Victor, Sonia knows something close at hand about feeling frustrated and powerless in the face of family silence. Much the youngest of several children, at the time of our interview her family was badly split. In the wake of her father's death her siblings were at loggerheads and her brothers had not spoken to each other for some years. Her anger with (Jewish) people who *avoid talking* about the difficult subject of the Holocaust is likely to be partly provoked by her anger at this much more personal situation.

Silence is in itself a powerful communication.[11] On the whole, people opt not to speak (or even not *to think*—thinking itself being an internal communication) on certain questions when those issues are too difficult, too challenging, or too disturbing to be spoken or thought about. As Orlando Figes showed, silence was unarguably a survival strategy in the Soviet Union under Stalin. The Holocaust is an intensely disturbing subject, particularly for Jews, who cannot avoid being personally implicated in the fact that the Nazi programme of genocide was so explicitly geared towards Jews in total and thus towards every Jew as an individual.[12] Many difficult feelings are disturbed—horror, disgust, fear, shame, violent reactions—and Jews cannot fail to find the whole subject, and their feelings, confusing and hard to speak or even think about. But the disturbed feelings exist whether spoken about or not; and in the complex way in which it is perfectly possible to possess one feeling *about* another feeling, the very fact of possessing disturbed feelings which cannot be spoken about must generate anger. In this sense, ordinary Jews may collectively share a sense of enormous anger simply *because* the subject of the Holocaust exists, and is so unavoidable.

Angry about the loss

When Bowlby observed that there is an intimate relationship between anger and loss, he was, of course, doing so in the context of studying how infants and young children responded to the material loss (whether temporarily or continuously) of their primary carer. For the very young child whose world is composed of life-giving material experiences (touch, sound, warmth, food), loss is a material event. It is as we grow up, and especially through acquiring language and ideas, that loss can take on symbolic dimensions: dimensions which may well be tied back to earlier material experience but which also exist in their own right. For ordinary Jews, whose ancestors had been living safely (or relatively safely) for at least a generation in Britain or the USA or Australia during the 1930s and '40s, and for whom there was no direct material loss—of home, of way of life, of known family or friends—anger cannot realistically be associated with a direct experience of exceptionally painful loss as it undoubtedly has been for Jim Swire in losing his daughter to terrorists. But anger is no less real or meaningful for being related to symbolic experience ("we can never go back to this home of our imaginations"); it is simply more difficult to explain. Harry's and

Doris's attempts to describe a range of thoughts which trigger their anger indicate that it derives its strength less from immediately tangible *things* than from *states of experience*. Harry thinks of being the target of other people's murderous intent; he feels the terrible abandonment by the world at large, and Jews' (therefore his own) helplessness to change what happened. Doris feels rage at being considered unimportant, of no consequence. These kinds of states, described by psychoanalysts as primitive states,[13] hold a peculiar intensity, an intensity which acquires its strength from the seeming impossibility of pointing to (or finding a language for) a tangible *thing* or *person* to name as the source of one's rage. This is the "everybody" and "nobody" experience I referred to earlier. It is a state, I think, that arises from trying to find meaning for one's feelings in external material causation, when in fact the grief (hence anger) is connected with something more difficult to describe, more symbolically representative of a once-tangible experience.

In Chapter Two, Sephardi-born Esther, whose family history means that she is unrelated to the late-nineteenth century Ashkenazi history of mass migration, talked of her own sense of loss. She explicitly understood loss as having significant metaphysical associations:

> "[It's] a loss of security [...]. A loss of the ideas in the civilisation that went with it. [...] It's a concrete loss of who was lost, but it's also loss of hope."

"Loss of hope" is an idea which featured highly in Bowlby's studies of loss, anger, and depression. Bowlby associated loss of hope with what he called "the anger of despair". In numerous papers he drew attention to "the frequency with which anger is aroused after a loss, not only in children but in adults also". He surmised that the normal function of anger aroused after a painful loss (such as when a parent or parent-figure goes away temporarily) is to prevent such a loss from recurring (Bowlby, 1973, p. 286). Even when a loss is permanent, such as after a bereavement, anger can still be related to hope: in the early stages of grieving after a bereavement, when the bereaved person cannot really believe that the loss is permanent, anger directed against the lost person is linked to an unconscious hope of recovery.[14] However, Bowlby also observed that other kinds of loss, especially ones which are prolonged or repeated or repeatedly associated with a certain kind of threat, generate a more confused and conflicted anger. This form of anger is associated with the fear of alienating those who are also needed; it generates deep insecurity, an insecurity which can either be internalised and repressed or turn violently outwards; and it completely changes the nature of the affectional bond from one which is well-rooted and capable of surviving the ups and downs of relational experience, to one which is accompanied by "a deep-running resentment, held in check only partially by an anxious, uncertain affection." This idea on Bowlby's part has an important bearing on what I will consider in the last part of this chapter: that is, Jewish relating to the non-Jewish world, and in particular to Europe.

Bowlby studied infants, but he noticed a strong correlation with later adult behaviour. Bowlby saw that an infant's despairing anger reflects his or her experience of the threat of abandonment. It does not require a huge leap of imagination (as Harry and Doris both emphasise) to see the way in which Jews were left to their fate during the war as abandonment on a terrifying scale (Bowlby, ibid., pp. 288–289).

I have taken Esther's "loss of hope" as an illustration not only of Bowlby's ideas of the relationship between loss and anger, but also of the intangible associations with loss to which anger also becomes a reaction. Even though the positioning of the Holocaust in the public psyche has materially changed in that it has a far more central position than before (Ruth would have less cause now to be angry about the school history curriculum, and Doris less need to feel that what happens to Jews is ignored), there is in effect still an accumulation of metaphysical losses, each and all of which might well result in a continued feeling of incoherent and unresponded-to rage. For example, to Esther's list of losses might be added what I call "the loss of innocence". We no longer have the option of living in a psychological world in which the Holocaust has not happened. We know, to great cost and consternation, what humanity is capable of. Of course, non-Jews as well as Jews share this horror; but for Jews there is an added twist, for has not this unlooked-for knowledge been gained at their expense? Any Holocaust survivor might, with complete justification, have said to someone who did not endure ghettos and camps, "You don't know what it was like." Similarly, any Jew might hold a feeling that people *not* born into a community with this history, with its web of personal connections, "don't know what it's like" to carry an unbreakable association with being targeted for "licensed mass murder".[15] And while it is true that no one can actually know the physical or psychological experience of another, this does not defray a feeling of angry frustration amongst ordinary Jews that they bear a particular burden in carrying this particular legacy.

I called this chapter "The broken contract" for a particular reason. It is obvious that the intense associations that ordinary Jews make with the Holocaust—being targeted; loss of hope; loss of innocence; its unavoidability as a subject in Jewish life; despair—all converge to make the Holocaust something that Jews must be angry, even rage, about. However, underlying this is an intense frustration, not to say anguish, that something can never be put right: in other words, that something has been irreparably broken. One of the most prominent of post-Holocaust Jewish theologians, Emil Fackenheim (1982), communicated this idea through his use of the word *rupture*, meaning a profound breaking, through which he sought to capture his personal desolation. To Fackenheim, this rupture was both of faith and in the history and experience of Jews.[16] Not only did the Holocaust catastrophically interrupt Jewish sense of the continuity of God's presence in Jewish life ("Jews who re-enact God's saving presence at the Red Sea must now remember the Holocaust—a time when God failed to save"), but "Jewish life [itself was] ruptured by the Holocaust" (Braiterman, 1998, pp. 141, 150).

For the children of survivors such as Finkelstein and Karpf, or the children of pre-war exiles, such as Amos Oz, whose mother was one of many thousands who later committed suicide following the devastating losses in their families, this sense of something irreparably broken is most manifest in that it cannot be put right in the lives of individuals (their parents).[17] But even amongst ordinary Jews, something associates with a *history* that cannot be put right. Whether it is our faith in God, the devastating end of Jewish life in large parts of Europe, or something else, *something* has been broken.

"Betrayal because they were Jews. Only because they were Jews"

In Chapter One, I observed that a central component of trauma concerns experiences in which implicit assumptions or *givens* of human experience have been violated: that is, that normal expectations (whether conscious or unconscious) which we each of us implicitly and necessarily carry from birth in relation to the world around, such as expectations that our parents (or parental figures) will be present and will care for us, have been seriously breached or even destroyed. Such violations constitute an experience of betrayal; a word which carries important connotations with a violation of trust, confidence, and faith. The experience of betrayal is profoundly disorienting (as trauma indeed is), leaving the psyche, if not quite fragmented, then in important ways lacking bearings or securities: in a certain kind of way, homeless.

Although the word "betrayal" does not always explicitly appear, in a sense it lies at the heart of ordinary Jewish anger in relation to the Holocaust. Bernice is one who does use the word, in speaking of Jews killed by Poles:

> "I've heard about what happened and the betrayal of people, our people [...] who came back and were then murdered. [...] Their betrayal of them ... that their neighbours would murder them, just because ... because they were Jews.[18] It's only because they were Jews.
>
> [...T]hey were all betrayed. They were betrayed by their neighbours, by everyone. Those who were hiding were betrayed, a lot of them. A lot weren't and that's how they survived. But there is a betrayal, that a whole nation can turn upon people."

An experience of being violated penetrates deeply into the human heart. At its root, it tells of an experience that one's own self has been cast aside, has no value. Leah and Simon both have had particular experiences that lead them, in the maelstrom of post-Holocaust reaction, to feel angry with other Jews. Their respective anger turns around what they each experience as an undermining of, an attack on, a key part of their identity: Leah as a mother; Simon as a gay man. Leah is the mother of a child whom she unwittingly exposed to the violent attentions of a Holocaust survivor. She is still deeply affected by the memory of this experience and is profoundly angry with the way in which members of her ultra-orthodox community even today go into denial:

> "The rabbis have changed their stance now. They're much more on top of the issues and ... they're much more willing to [...] go to the social services, but this was [some years ago]. [...] The thing that I felt particularly angry about was not the Rabonim [...] but other ... one particular person, prominent in the community, who [...] was endorsing that parents should send children to this childminder [despite being told what was happening]. [...] In fact I know, whenever a case of abuse comes up in the community, there'll be respectable

> pillars of the community who say, 'Oh, this is a respectable member of the community who couldn't do anything like that, and the people who are complaining of abuse are unbalanced'. [...] That's a common reaction ... It's a wish to maintain the perfect image of the ... *frum* community and of the orthodox Jewish lifestyle. If you are *frum* you can't do anything wrong. And there are no problems that need to be addressed."

Simon is angry with Jews who describe the Holocaust in purely Judaeocentric terms: that is, that the Holocaust was *only* and *entirely* to do with Jews. As a gay man he sees the Nazis' murderous regime from two perspectives. He experiences Jewish people's implicit dismissal of what also happened to homosexuals under the Nazis as even more of a denial than the converse (homosexual people's ignoring the specificity of Jewish suffering), possibly because in the intimacy of his own family he had for a long time to conceal his gay identity:

> "I get very angry with them [such Jews] all, very angry. [...] [I]t's so wrong and so manipulative. I also get irritated, not to the same extent, by ... gay people for instance, who glibly invoke the Holocaust and imply that everyone was treated exactly the same, which also wasn't true. I think the level of ignorance about the Holocaust generally, including amongst many Jews, but certainly amongst some non-Jews, is woeful. But I get much more angry when I hear Jews talking as though we're the only ones who suffered, and even if we weren't the only ones who suffered, we're the only ones whose suffering really counted [...]".

One can also hear feelings of betrayal in Doris's fury at "those who went on with the bloody games! [...], [who] couldn't care less, they couldn't care less", and in Harry's anger that "not a single nation came to our rescue." Pearl is furious with God: the God who let His people down, as well as those who have taught for so long that God exists:

> "If I think of anything, I think of the so-called 'God' who chose the Jews, for what? For suffering? [H]ow can I believe in a God that allows His people and others, not just His people, to be burnt or gassed ... [when] He's supposed to be a miracle worker? [...] I was given [...] Richard Dawkins' book *The God Delusion*, which is for me difficult

> to read but I didn't need to be convinced that all that we read about and all that we've been brought up on is a myth. [...] How could anybody not be angry with God, if there is a God: where was He? [...] ... never mind that people did this, but if there's a God, He allowed this to happen. [...] [I want to] explode with anger."

Claud, descended from a line of Sephardi-Arab Jews so old and so well-established that they can claim to be "Jewish aristocracy", regards the Holocaust with a deep pessimism reflecting betrayal of hope in the very idea of human progress:

> "It profoundly depresses me, in that it revealed what human beings like ourselves are fully capable of doing without too much effort. They murder and they do unspeakable things; [...] that is profoundly depressing because it's all around us, it hasn't gone away. [...] The only thing one can learn from what went on in Europe is that this is a very real possibility in our time, in our days, in our children's days, and I find that very depressing."

The possibility that the Holocaust constitutes, theologically, a betrayal by God of "His people" (or, perhaps more precisely, an abdication from His perceived role as protector of His people) has haunted Jewish (in particular) theological writing concerning the Holocaust for over forty years.[19] Arguments rage over the significance of the Holocaust for this "special relationship". As Braiterman puts it:

> The Holocaust has only intensified extant problems with the image of a covenant-people. Does God love Israel? And if indeed God had chosen Israel (or if Israel had chosen God), why should contemporary Jews continue to accept this designation? It is no longer evident why a people should hold to a covenant whose terms have included recurring patterns of marginalisation, vilification, persecution, exile and (in the twentieth century) systematic genocide. [...] Catastrophic suffering may not logically preclude the image of a covenant-people, but it threatens to make the very notion unbearable. (Braiterman, op. cit., pp. 27–28)

While, like Pearl, some people rage in bewilderment against God as well as with Hitler and his acolytes, ordinary Jews tend to leave theological or spiritual wrestlings to the rabbis. Nevertheless, a central theme within rabbinical reflection has an important relevance to a shared Jewish sense of this-worldly betrayal. This is the notion of *the contract*:

> The notion of covenant introduces a third and unpredictable element into the relation between God and human persons. Law becomes a mediating power with its own jurisdiction. […] Israel and God are co-partners. (Ibid., p. 32)

For the past thirty years, psychoanalytic thinking has developed around a core premise that human beings are fundamentally *relational* and *relationship-seeking*. The seeking of relationship is understood as an infant's primary impulse, and, as infants progressively test out their individuality in relation to the world beyond their immediate selves, as a dynamic which forms the bedrock of subsequent development. As individuals, we come to live in both an inner and an outer world of relationships with those around us and/or in our memories. It follows that, as groups or communities, people collectively also live in some kind of shared relational field with their surrounding society. Thus as individuals and as members of a group we are in a constant relational interaction with the world around, an interaction formed as much by people's internal *perceptions* of the relationship as it is by actual contact. Indeed, at the heart of the Jewish religion is the notion of a relationship with God, a relationship which is simultaneously individual (each individual must pray and observe the *mitzvoth*, or commandments) and collective (the community as a whole is held responsible for its actions). To an important degree, this relational process develops around certain expectations and obligations that are either implicit or have evolved over time: an infant implicitly (and necessarily) expects his parent to care for him; social expectations of governments or communities develop as a result of experience, and so on. Such expectations form part of an unspoken psychological contract.

As minority communities living in Europe and beyond for two thousand years, Jews have had to live within the parameters of some kind of implicit contract with the world around them. The conditions for Jews to live as minorities required an acceptance of the laws and norms of the dominant societies. Historian and rabbi Marc Saperstein, for example, observes that:

> "in the middle ages, the worst that the king would do would be to decide to expel the Jews. It was recognised throughout the Middle Ages that the king had a right to do this: that we lived here at the good graces of the king, not as a matter or right." (Saperstein, January 2007, personal communication)

Christopher Browning also comments that:

> Europe's Jews survived this escalating [...] persecution [in the late Middle Ages] because the Church, while sanctioning it, also set limits to it. (Browning, 2004, p. 4)

The concept of law is central to Jewish tradition. Torah, Talmud, Mishnah, and countless rabbinic commentaries through the ages have revolved around the pivotal premise that the law (i.e., God's law) and observation of the law are immutable guiding principles governing not only people's relationship to God but to each other. So central is this concept of the law in Jewish thinking that, as Braiterman describes, God Himself can even be brought to account under the terms of His own law by dissatisfied rabbis:

> Like Job, other rabbis express complaint with the way God orders the world against the righteous. [...] Unlike Job, the rabbis seldom protest on the basis of personal torment or even in their own voice. They enlist biblical personae to justify a suffering community before God. [...] God is once again put on trial on account of the innocent. And remarkably, God accepts their judgement and repents! (Braiterman, op. cit., p. 50)

It can be construed from this that it is an unconscious given in Jewish thinking that human law, too, matters; we may not like the law; insofar as it relates to us it may be unjust; but it has to be respected. This premise was not essentially shattered during the two millennia of diaspora existence. For the most part, even allowing for periodic outbreaks of persecutory violence or expulsions, Jews had a certain place in the societies where they lived. Even if their status was heavily circumscribed by the local laws, there *were* laws. Like Browning, Saperstein notes that for the first thousand years of the diaspora, Jews were actually protected by Church law, outbreaks of violence or attempts to stir up hatred frequently being met by Papal condemnation.[20] Even after the position of Jews in Christian Europe began to change after the First Crusade, attacks and persecutions were consistent neither geographically nor through time. It was therefore reasonably safe for Jews to assume that, oppressed and disparaged as they often were, there were legal frameworks[21] within which they could live, work, and even prosper; and that even if those changed from time to time, they did not change everywhere and completely. Jews became accustomed to thinking of themselves as a minority that, provided they complied with the restrictions imposed on them, could continue living with fluctuating degrees of molestation. In this way there built up a psychological contract which in general terms lasted until the twentieth century.

The singularity of the Nazi regime in this respect was to pervert the basic concept of law. The world created by the Nazis was not one in which law was *absent* (it was the breakdown of regulation and control which led to the chaos that was Belsen), but one in which the very purpose of law has been violated. Far from being a regulatory framework designed to organise the terms (however unequal) on which people cohabited, Nazi logic led to a position in which regulation was meaningless. When a group of people is deemed, purely because of who they are, as having no place in life, the normal law of human affairs ceases to exist. The shock left by the Holocaust therefore partly takes its force from a complete violation of the basic premise of Jewish life and Jewish belief: a premise which substantially had not changed for two thousand years. Emotionally and psychologically, the effect has been to sweep the ground from under our feet. Saperstein describes what happened like this:

> "But now [...] the elements at the top of the political hierarchy become the enemy, and all of the resources of a modern bureaucratic state are mobilised for the purpose of destroying a population. That is a fundamental change from the past, and there was no tradition that helped to guide what we should do under these circumstances. Jewish political strategy had always been to try to build contacts, access in the court, because that was the source of protection, and to some extent with the Pope as well. ... And finally the policy of total mass murder—that is also a fundamental break ... no political authority and no religious leader ever in the previous periods said, this should be our goal to kill every

> Jewish man and women and child. There were ways in which the Nazi policy gave the impression that what they were doing was an ultra-conservative turning back the clock to the medieval position. That was the impression in the 1930s, that they were undoing emancipation, they were bringing back the toleration and protection of Jews in second class status, no longer citizens, and then later on in ghettos wearing a Jewish badge … all of those elements that seemed as if it was simply a return to the medieval state. What [Jews] didn't appreciate was that those were only the externals, that there was really something radically new that was under foot." (Saperstein, January 2007, personal communication)

Law is fundamentally a regulator of human affairs, and when the very basis of law and custom is perverted in this way, it leads to a massive disorientation. Jewish participation in society pre-the Nazi era may have been conditional, but the possibility of participation on some terms existed. The Nazi programme of genocide removed that very possibility. No compromise or sacrifice could help; as Claud states, this is "profoundly depressing".

Claud may not exactly have meant it like this, but there is a link between something which is "profoundly depressing" and anger; or more precisely between depression, and anger which cannot be expressed. Here I come to what was, or might have been, unconsciously built into the psychological contract under which Jews lived: in other words, what Jews compromised for themselves over the centuries so that they could live, and which acts as a subtext in our experience of collective anger.

In psychotherapeutic thinking, anger which is internalised frequently manifests in the form of depression. Busch, for example, writes:

> A series of psychoanalytic theorists and clinicians have suggested that conflicts about anger play a central role in the development of depression. Research data have supported the notion that patients struggle with the experience and expression of angry feelings. Anger in people with depression often stems from […] a sensitivity to perceived or actual loss or rejection. These angry reactions cause intrapsychic conflicts […] [which] lead to anger being directed inwards […] creating a vicious cycle. (Busch, 2009, pp. 271–278)[22]

What I wonder here is the degree to which the conditions of Jewish life in Europe tacitly required Jews to restrict normal and spontaneous expressions of anger at their situation and at the experiences to which they were periodically or routinely exposed. As I noted in Chapter Two, there seems to be an epidemiological association between Jews and depression. I connected the manifestation of depression in unusually high levels amongst Jews to the still relatively recent (one century-old) history of exile and migration away from Eastern Europe; but this may not be the only reason.

Jews and Jewish communities had to make many compromises in order to survive during the two thousand years of diaspora settlement. Some of these concerned outward agreement with the laws and decrees of the ruler; others involved a more internal process. For whatever else was or wasn't possible for Jews, it certainly would not have been easy, if ever possible, for Jewish communities to protest at their status. Even in the highly stratified structures of earlier societies, where before the late eighteenth century no concept of social equality existed, it was still possible for indigenous communities to protest against oppressive rule (as Jews themselves had done under Roman rule in Palestine). For Jews, protest against repression without an accepted right to be there would be a risky strategy. It is thus well possible to imagine that, over the centuries, Jews and Jewish social structures developed a pattern of inhibiting expressions of anger against their experience of repression and marginalisation. Shakespeare (no Jew himself, obviously) understood this, and his capacity to sympathise with Shylock's situation is what gives *The Merchant of Venice* such a poignant edge for Jewish audiences. Shylock is full of anger at his contemptuous treatment by the Venetian Christians, and although the play is classified in collected editions as a comedy, to Jewish eyes it is a tragic warning of the dangers of getting carried away with wrathful vengeance against those dominant in society:

> You call me misbeliever, cut-throat dog,
> And spit upon my Jewish gabardine,
> And all for use of that which is mine own.
> Well, then, it now appears you need my help:
> Go to, then; you come to me, and you say
> 'Shylock, we would have moneys:' you say so;

> You, that did void your rheum upon my beard,
> And foot me as you spurn a stranger cur
> Over your threshold: moneys is your suit.
> What should I say to you? Should I not say
> "Hath a dog money? Is it possible
> A cur can lend three thousand ducats?" or
> Shall I bend low and in a bondman's key,
> With bated breath and whispering humbleness,
> Say this,—
> "Fair sir, you spit on me on Wednesday last;
> You spurn'd me such a day; another time
> You call'd me dog; and for these courtesies
> I'll lend you thus much moneys"?

We can, perhaps, understand Shylock as the product of Shakespeare's imaginings of what much-maligned Jews *would* have felt (murderous rage) when exposed to the relentless contempt which Shylock rails against. It is, amongst other things, a play about marginalisation and the unequal weighting of the law; a law which, nonetheless, existed and could be lived within up to a point as long as its basic premise was accepted. It is also a play about betrayal: what tips Shylock over into actively pursuing his blood-revenge against Antonio is the bitter betrayal of him by his daughter, who not only robs him of his money and his cherished memento of his dead wife, but steals from him his standing and dignity as a father, cruelly exposing him to the derision of the Christians around. The scenes are full of despair and painful humiliation:

> TUBAL: One of them showed me a ring that he had of your daughter for a monkey.
>
> SHYLOCK: [...] it was my turquoise; I had it of Leah when I was a bachelor: I would not have given it for a wilderness of monkeys.

Clive Lawton, a prominent member of modern orthodoxy and a leading figure in the establishment of Holocaust education in the UK, observes that through the radical shift in post-Enlightenment thinking and the resulting development of the concepts of citizen equality and civic rights, a major change in European Jewish expectations and self-understanding developed over the course of the nineteenth century:

> "We have always had the narrative that Jews are in exile. We're in exile because we're being punished, and we're being punished because we did not live up to God's highest expectations of us. That's in the liturgy. That's not the same as suffering dreadfully. The only suffering for Jews is not to be in the land of Israel with our own Temple. That's the punishment. You don't have to be beaten up and at the bottom of the heap to be punished. [...] Once Jews started to say, 'We know we've been suffering all the time; what's the nature of the suffering? Not living in the land of Israel/having the Temple?—what's that got to do with it? It's because they don't let us have our rights', they reinterpret the definition of suffering as meaning being exiled from contemporary civil life, like not being able to go to university. That wasn't what Jews were talking about when they were talking about the suffering of the Jews in the fourteenth century." (Lawton, October 2006, personal communication)

Lawton thinks that this fundamentally altered the psychological basis on which Jews constructed their life in Europe. If he is right, it will have set up new contractual expectations, and for the first time have permitted Jews to *feel* and to *express* their anger at their situation.[23] Maureen Kendler, head of education at the London School of Jewish Studies, observes that in Britain in the 1920s, this anger manifested in the work of a group of Whitechapel artists such as Mark Gertler. "It was expressionist art, often immigrant art: very angry, anti-establishment, challenging": a marked contrast to the conservative, quasi-Dickensian literature of the children of an earlier migrant generation, often desperate "to be English" and to conform (Kendler, November 2009, personal communication).

At the heart, I think, of the deep anger which so many ordinary Jews feel and express in relation to the Holocaust is a complexity of interwoven elements: the shattering of a basic framework in which social presence and social interaction, however conditional, took place; a deep sense of betrayal of what had been understood as some kind of norm; and a rupturing, not only of God's presence in Jewish life and of Jewish life itself as Fackenheim saw it, but of a long and complex relationship in and with Europe. Until the late nineteenth century, most Jewish life *was* in Europe. Not only has Jewish history substantially been formed *by* Europe, but Jews themselves are a significant and formative part *of* European history: a history in which Jewish presence not only contributed significantly to developments in European life, but where Jewish experience reflected the shifting patterns and ideas, the multiple languages and cultures of Europe itself. The Holocaust radically shook the terms on which Jews thought they engaged with Europe. In the process it complicated Jews' whole concept of their relationship with the world around: it generated heightened anxiety, it undermined even an ambivalent "affectional bond" with Europe and Europeans, and it aroused what Bowlby might have called an "insecure attachment". By shattering a base that was assumed in some sense to be secure, the Holocaust dealt a major psychological blow, forcing a crisis in Jewish identity and Jewish relationship with the world; a crisis which the establishment of Israel has distracted from, but by no means resolved.

CHAPTER FOUR

"It's all very frightening"

Fear is an intrinsic part of the human condition, and is an emotive force essential for survival. Functionally, fear alerts us to the presence of danger and triggers the crucial primitive reactions of freezing, fighting, or fleeing. We need our adrenalin-fuelled alarm bells so as to take care of our own safety and the safety of those who matter to us. Not all dangers are the same, of course: some require split-second decisions, others allow time for more measured responses. Nevertheless, recognising the presence and significance of fear is key whenever danger threatens. In certain circumstances, acting on fear can literally be a lifesaver.

But fear can also be irrational, arising even when there is no visible threat. In certain conditions or situations, human beings are prone to feel and act as though at any moment danger was about to strike, even when objectively there is nothing to worry about. Deeply traumatised people commonly feel this way. Present events, whether personally experienced or not, whether dramatic or apparently innocuous, can trigger a disproportionate, even extreme, reaction. Such reactions, which to the puzzled outsider themselves may appear unsettling and scary, reflect the way in which terrifying experiences in someone's earlier life can be re-experienced as though still happening and still as dangerous. In such conditions a quite unconscious equation is made between *what was* and *what is now*. Lemma and Levy, for example, record how, on 11 September 2001, a psychotherapist working with traumatised patients in a London clinic encountered one patient who particularly exemplified the way in which past traumas can spill over into the present:

> He was filled with panic, convinced that this apocalypse in the US was imminent in the UK. He felt terrified that he would die or be horribly injured. He did not know how to manage his fear. All he knew was that he hated Arabs, hated Muslims, hated refugees [...]. [F]or this patient (with a history of severe violence and trauma), [...] thinking or knowing about the September 11 assault was immediately collapsed in his mind with being attacked. There was little separation between the event *actually* happening to him and a mental representation of his fear or anxiety that it *might* happen. (Lemma & Levy, 2004, p. 2)

Time seems to stand still when, like this patient, people are caught in an inner world haunted by images of perpetual danger. In such a world, time has itself become frozen in an embedded experience in which what *was*, still *is*, ever present and always now.

A continued relationship with fear is a recognised feature of trauma. In consequence, many ordinary Jews draw on the language of trauma, particularly the trauma embodied in the Holocaust, as a way of explaining certain feelings of fear generated in the here-and-now. There is a simple, if only partly conscious, equation that goes something like this: "The Holocaust was a trauma for us. It proves that we can never take where we are for granted. We must always be alert—ready, if necessary, to leave. Above all, we must always have our own country (Israel) available to us." Thus Michelle believes that her parents, along with many Jews in her parents' generation, feel a guilty obligation to Israel "because of what happened":

> "My parents do have an obligation to Israel [...] and I think it's linked to the Holocaust and maybe the guilt of surviving. [...] [Q]uestioning Israel is almost like adding to the Holocaust. [...] In my view, they've got this idea of Israel as this safe haven for Jews, and Jews will always need a safe haven because of what happened before."

For her part, Leah observes how fear is transmitted between generations beyond any rational experience of here-and-now conditions. She points to the way in which children in present-day ultra-orthodox communities, despite being born and brought up in Britain, are frightened of dogs, apparently as an instinctive consequence of Jewish experiences under the Nazis:

> "Dogs ... children were terrified of dogs. [...] it just passes down, the terror of dogs. My husband has been to Poland several times and he says the dogs in Poland ... he's not surprised anybody's terrified there, they're horrendous. But I think the terror, one would assume, comes from the way the Nazis used dogs to hunt Jewish people down."

At the same time, Leah is aware that existing cultural norms, and the way in which these are taught and transmitted to the next generation, have a bearing on this phenomenon of, as it were, "inherited" fear:

> "You know, in Jewish culture there's a lot of ... folk-type beliefs which generally cast dogs in bad light ... you know, black dog and the *treife*[1] animal [...]."

Leah thus reflects an inadvertent psychological dilemma facing the parents and teachers of these present-day children: a dilemma which arises from the imperative of choosing which interpretation of the past to hand on to children. In this instance the choice, conscious or otherwise, lies between seeing the cause of the children's fear as inevitable and therefore unchangeable ("because of what happened"), or as an inheritance which could be changed if the parents themselves became less terrified.

"I want to be open about being Jewish, but it's difficult"

For ordinary Jews contemplating their feelings about the Holocaust, their fears contain a puzzling illogicality. Like Jacobson's Maxie Glick, ordinary Jews living in the diaspora have been "born safely, at a lucky time and in an unthreatening part of the world, to parents who loved and protected [me]" (Jacobson, 2006, p. 5). They, too, can think of themselves as children of peace and refuge; and in relation to their lives in the countries of the diaspora, they usually do. Yet lurking below the surface is an easily triggered anxiety: one invariably focused around an insecurity as to whether, as Jews, we are liked, welcomed, wanted; or whether we are simply being tolerated "for now". Michelle, born in the mid-fifties, and Sonia, a child of the late seventies, even while each is aware that anxieties can be irrational, even obsessive, also reflect latent worries as to whether they can even be seen, let alone seen with acceptance, *as Jews*:

MICHELLE: "I sometimes think the older generation exaggerate, but that's how they feel. Maybe it's not an exaggeration. I've an aunt, we have funny conversations, she's very elderly but very live-wire. We were talking about somebody and she said, 'Is he anti?' I said, 'Anti-what?' and she said, 'You know, anti-Semitic.' She just uses 'anti'. It's the way she sees it. Her kids were brought up to think that you can't necessarily trust someone who's not Jewish not to be 'anti', because she thinks everyone is 'anti' apart from the few that aren't. I don't see the world as quite like that. ... [But] it feels almost like a vulnerability that you could be open to, yourself. I talk a lot about being Jewish, and there are people at work who are interested in religion and like to talk about things in the staffroom, and sometimes I regret that and wonder, 'Is it safe? Do they really like Jewish people?' [...] I had an instance last year when a friend said something that really upset me, and we fell out. I took it as being anti-Semitic."

SONIA: "When I was growing up my mum ... seemed to be quite well-tuned into hiding the identity. [...] I went to a school that was predominantly a Christian school ..., [...] [and] if anything ever came up about somebody saying something about me being Jewish, it was like, 'What did they say?' And then I ... there'd be ... an immediate defensive position was taken, and I grew up and adopted it. [...] My father was very much for 'be who you are', and he didn't seem to have that same wall of defence built round him as my mother. [...] My mum was much more distrusting of other people ... [...]

My father [...] was involved with the Association for Jewish Ex-servicemen and he was chairman for a couple of years [...]. At one point he had some literature coming to us for ... some computer software that was being used for the charity that got delivered to my parents' house. Instead of just telling the software people to send it to AJEX, A-J-E-X, we're a charity, here's the charity number, it was coming to the door with Association of Jewish Ex-servicemen

> and Women, (x) branch! And my mother [...] was just *wincing* every time it came through the door. We'd been outed as the Jews that live at number seven. ... It goes so deep and .... on one hand it seems ridiculous that .... it was ... almost like an obsession. [...]
>
> I want to be open about it like my father was, but I sometimes find in certain situations it's difficult to say, 'Hello, I'm Jewish.' The people in my university group don't know I'm Jewish. Even friends from my university don't know I'm Jewish and I find that ... I just can't ... there's something from childhood that I find difficult to shake off. [...] I do find that ... some people have a problem with it, so it's a natural instinct to keep it out of the equation and opt for a simple life. It's difficult. You don't know what people's prejudices are. [...] There's whole areas of my life that don't know I'm Jewish."

Clearly present in both narratives is a *motif* seldom far from ordinary Jewish thinking. Fear of anti-Semitism is a big preoccupation for Jews. Implicitly or explicitly, certain questions continue to haunt them: does anti-Semitism exist? How much of there is it? How dangerous is it? How much should we fear it? Michelle's question, "Do they really like Jews?" has a more dangerous counterpart: if "they" do not *like* us, do they, in fact, hate us? And if they hate us, to what lengths will they go? Such questions continue to bubble away, sometimes obviously so, sometimes less clearly; and because there is no obvious answer, they have a significant impact on the way Jews perceive, and often react to, the world outside.

"It's hard for people to conceive of an anti-Semitism that isn't genocidal"

Without an obvious answer, one outcome of all these questions is to induce a continued state of fear. Anti-Semitism exists in the general context that irrational prejudice exists and probably always will in some contexts, for as long as human beings continue to be subject to their own ill-understood psychological drives. As a focus for irrational prejudice, Jews certainly carry a particularly poisoned burden, for various reasons: the fact of having been a distinct minority in Europe for so long and therefore a ready target; the longevity and continuity of anti-Jewish sentiment; the supposed justifications for anti-Semitism, whether backed up by theological or racial arguments, and so on. Backed into a long-standing corner, we frequently find ourselves at a loss when it comes to challenging the dangerous and specious arguments behind anti-Semitism, and if we lack a countervailing challenge it can only add to our fear. In its most pernicious form, anti-Semitism is a delusion in the sense that it derives from fantasies as to Jews' supposed power, control, and collective evil intentions, to the extent that it was perfectly possible during the 1930s and '40s for Jews to be viewed simultaneously as steering both capitalist and communist world control.[2] Deluded fantasies about oneself invariably hurt; and in certain conditions can clearly become a real threat. But if we do not know how to answer anti-Semitism we remain in turn subject to it: protesting, but prone to fall back into helpless worry that, in the end, there is nothing we can do about it.

In *Trials of the Diaspora*, Anthony Julius traces the history of anti-Semitism specifically in England. In defining anti-Semitism, he draws important distinctions between different kinds of "enmity" towards Jews, asserting that it is possible to oppose, or be hostile to Jews, without being anti-Semitic:

> Jews have enemies in much the same way that non-Jews do—that is, they experience enmities neither caused nor sustained by Jew-hatred. Not every hostile encounter is a consequence of anti-Semitism. (Julius, 2010, p. 3)

Julius distinguishes between different kinds of "enemies" of Jews. He describes one group as "rational enemies", a second as "opportunistic enemies", and a third as "irrational" enemies of Jews. Only the third category, according to Julius, can properly be considered as anti-Semitic, although, he warns, the boundaries between categories can be "porous".

For Julius, "rational enemies" may in an objective sense be justified in their opposition to Jews in that they may have perfectly legitimate reasons for opposing Jews and Jewish interests:

> Jews have additional enemies [...] to whom their Jewish character *is* relevant, because these enemies find themselves in conflict with a genuine Jewish project or stance. [...] '[E]nemy' may in many cases safely be exchanged for 'adversary' or 'opponent'—the opposition

> need not be coloured by hatred or malice. Judaism is the principal Jewish 'project', so to speak, and Christian anti-Judaism therefore need not be anti-Semitic. For example, the Christian conviction that Jews ought to convert, because adherence to Judaism bars the Jew from salvation, is not in itself anti-Semitic. [...] [In addition] [i]t would be a mistake in analysis to regard confrontations with Zionism and Israel as taking place between Jews and anti-Semites alone [...] because real interests were and in certain respects continue to be at stake. (Ibid., pp. 3–4)

By contrast, "opportunistic enemies" are, he believes, emotionally neutral. They may have no particular dislike of or hostility to Jews: they simply exploit them and their weakness:

> They arm themselves, so to speak, with anti-Semitism, the better to pursue their Jewish victims or adversaries. But they are not infected by any special animus towards Jews [...]. They merely take advantage of opportunities created for them by anti-Semites. [...] They may be teenage children—street gangs glad of the chance to bully and to harass. [...] They may be Jews themselves—preying dockside on newly arrived immigrants, using their knowledge of Yiddish to win over and then defraud their victims. [...] They are also wartime profiteers preying on vulnerable Jews [...]. (Ibid., p. 4)

"Irrational enemies", however, differ entirely. Their enmity, Julius asserts, is rooted in no genuinely arguable cause and is far from simple self-serving, but is derived from imaginary grievances and a paranoid malevolence given entirely and specifically to Jews who are seen as the cause of all ills:

> Jews have enemies to whom their Jewish character is determinative, but whose enmity does *not* derive from opposition to any genuine Jewish project or stance. The hatred of these enemies mostly derives from imaginary grievances, imputed to an imaginary collective entity, 'the Jews' or 'Judaism' [...]. Their enmity is determined not by Jewish *projects* but by their own *projections*. Jews become the bearers of these irrational projections. These are the anti-Semites, the irrational enemies of the Jews; grievances or complaints are pretexts for defamation and persecution. (Ibid., p. 5)

Drawing these distinctions is central to Julius' purpose: not only to trace the fluctuating character and expression of English anti-Semitism over the centuries but to argue that anti-Semitic tropes of the irrational kind have a continued presence in the present day. Julius is probably led in part by a desire to help Jews see the world in more proportionate terms, though not necessarily for its own sake: he wants Jews to be able to organise their challenges to the more dangerous forms of anti-Semitism more effectively. Julius' own categories are not watertight: as he points out, rational enmity is often infected by irrationality. So, too, rational assessments of the threat of anti-Semitism can be completely clouded by panic. The following exchange between husband and wife Claud and Antonia illustrates the way in which, lacking workable definitions, Jews may not realistically be able to assess the seriousness of any particular threat. Some react to all expressions of enmity—even minor ones—towards people who are Jewish as though all were expressions of the most toxic anti-Semitism. Others go in the opposite direction:

ANTONIA: "… little things which happen. [Our grandchildren] go on a school bus, a JFS, and somebody gets on and there's trouble, you know? And it's very minor. Or else the kid is there with his mobile and somebody says, 'I want it', you know? Little threats like that, but some people get really roughed up, really roughed up."

CLAUD: "But … that's not to do with Jewish …"

ANTONIA: "It is because they are Jews and they're wearing *kippot*[3] and they're wearing that uniform."

CLAUD: "Nah […]"

ANTONIA: "The yobs are after them because they're Jews […]"

CLAUD: "I think they're after any middle class children."

ANTONIA: "No, they're after Jews actually."

CLAUD: "Okay."

ANTONIA: "They're vulnerable, they're vulnerable, definitely more vulnerable."

While "the yobs" in the episode described by Antonia clearly fall into Julius' category of "opportunistic enemies," it is apparent that husband and wife, who stand in exactly the same kinship to the event, cannot help each other relate to it in a way that resolves Antonia's ingrained fear or Claud's resistance to taking this fear on. The conflict between them is characteristic of the terms of debate amongst Jews as to the threat of anti-Semitism and the question of fear. In a certain way, we all stand in a conflicted relationship with fear: on the one hand we cling to beliefs that we are right to fear what we fear, while in other circumstances we persuade ourselves that there is nothing to be afraid of. Both these reactions can exist *despite* objective evidence. We not only have to relate to external events which may or may not give us genuine reason to be afraid; we also have to relate to the way in which fear is already established in our emotional vocabulary and inner world with a fixed quality of its own, restricting our emotional room for manoeuvre to a choice between embracing or resisting it. What the Holocaust seems to have done is reinforce for many Jews one side of this dilemma: that is, a predisposition to believe that the non-Jewish world is innately dangerous and therefore a source of perpetual fear. In the face of felt threat, more rational distinctions, such as Julius makes, fall by the wayside. As Tony Lerman, a long-time observer of the British Jewish scene, puts it, for Jews in the post-Holocaust era anti-Semitism has insidiously become equated with genocide:

> "It's very hard, isn't it, for [Jewish] people to conceive of an anti-Semitism that isn't genocidal? [...] You only have to see a swastika daubed on ... and already the link is being made between that event or incident [...] and a pretty quick road towards the complete destruction of Jews." (Lerman, December 2009, personal communication)

The Holocaust thus plays into an existing psychic structure in which fear already exists. But the Holocaust is not one single, isolated, easily-describable event. On the contrary, it was a vast and complex phenomenon, spanning countries, cultures, different people, different histories, and time. Our capacity to become fearful "because of what happened" is repeatedly activated in many forms. For Jews specifically, knowledge of what happened impacts imaginatively on ordinary, embedded, primitive anxieties and experiences concerning survival, love, hate, helplessness, and so on. For one thing, the Nazi regime massively expanded both the geographic and conceptual territory in which anti-Semitic violence was played out. Not only was Nazi violence pursued throughout Europe, effectively trapping its victims in circumstances in which they could do little or nothing to save themselves; it also took a form which was unprecedented in its relentlessness and systematic nature. Gideon compares this in feeling to having the unstoppable and awful quality of a Greek tragedy:

> "There were all these people, men and women [...] ordinary men and women, girls and boys, living a normal life [...] but then taken to the slaughter [...]. [Jews] being hemmed in on all sides, losing any means of escape, and ... seeing your destiny in Greek tragedy sense—I'm going to die in the fire or in the gas chamber. Try to fight it but having no means to avoid ending up there. [...] The magnitude of [all] that took long years to sink in."

Almost anyone can identify with such feelings of doomed helplessness, often constructed in dreams of juggernauts bearing down, or of fleeing from some invisible assailant. The light of day helps us place dreams in some kind of rational perspective, but in contemplating the Holocaust ordinary Jews feel imaginatively caught up in a nightmare from which they fear there is no escape even in the form of answers to the agonised question, "How did it happen?" Julius's distinctions, and the endless quest by historians and other researchers to understand exactly how it did happen, seem irrelevant. There is insufficient light of day to banish this darkness. The Holocaust therefore continues to exert a powerful pull over our fears because it can tap into the worst horrors of imagination, as though our imagined experiences were actual ones that we ourselves had physically lived through.

A less obvious dimension of fear which the Holocaust activates concerns what it arouses of how we feel about ourselves. The idea of the Holocaust, and the continuity of our relationship to anti-Semitism, in themselves evoke in us contradictory impulses. In the face of anti-Semitism, we want to stand up and protest about our treatment; we also, as Michelle and Sonia observe, want to stay hidden from potentially hostile gaze. This creates another internal conflict, which we do not know how to resolve. Unresolved conflicts have a tendency to paralyse; this particular one also prompts disquieting feelings about ourselves as a result of our very inaction, the supposed weakness of our arguments, our desire to stay hidden. We are, I think, haunted by a pervasive anxiety not just about anti-Semites and the power of their irrational hatred, but about ourselves, our weakness, our failure to stand up in our own defence, the reasons that we are disliked; an anxiety potentially linked to an equally irrational fear that we may also somehow have brought disaster upon ourselves. It is, for example, a constant *motif* in the Old Testament that disobedience to God's commands risks punishment. Judaism (whence Christianity) contains a fundamental preoccupation with the polarities of love and hate (usually represented as God's anger), faithfulness and disobedience, reward and punishment. Whether one understands this as a theological figure per se or as a psychological anxiety projected into theological form, it acts as an important backdrop in Jewish discourse.[4]

Gideon reflects a not-uncommon concern amongst some Jews with the separatist tendencies Jews have, and the implicit elitist messages this may transmit to the wider world:

> "I don't think that anti-Semitism has got to be there all the time or as deep as it was in Europe in the nineteenth century. I think particularly the Jews in Moslem Spain acted very sensibly. [….] [T]here is an Ashkenazi orthodox notion […] that the Jews have to be completely separate—separate in customs, separate in clothing, separate in everything; and that's really the problem. They want to believe that they're keepers of tradition. […] [T]he orthodox Jews of today—the Ashkenazi orthodox—are the keepers of the ritual of sixteenth and seventeenth century Poland. […] They're certainly not the keepers of the tradition of two thousand years ago. […] If you look at *Mishnah*, it is so evident that a lot of what the community was concerned about at the time was keeping the peace with the non-Jews. It was a matter of how to be a good human being […] together with being Jewish, not because you're Jewish. These two things are absolutely crucial."

Here Gideon is touching on issues of guilt and shame linked to identity: an intrinsic human concern that revolves around a core question: "What does it mean to be who I am?" Psychologically, fear is related to guilt (the subject of my next chapter) in the sense that in everyone's primitive psyche fear at what the world does or may do "to me" is accompanied by an unconscious fear—hence guilt—that I may have myself caused the terrifying thing to happen in the first place. This is a reaction recognisable in instances of traumatic fear. Guilt at having been in the wrong place at the wrong time, of having done something in particular, or conversely for having failed to do something necessary, are common, if irrational, aspects of traumatic fear. One effect is to produce a need "to get away" from such feelings (that is, a need for psychological flight), together with a longing to be safe and protected from the distress caused. Without refuge, the combination of anxious, guilty feelings will become circuitous, relentless, and in its own way, persecutory. If felt consciously at all, it will typically be expressed in relation to the external world, whose every action is interpreted through the internal experience of an unceasing conflict. Thus Sonia's assertion that "on one level we are always persecuted", has a genuine psychological reality in Jews' internal world. Jews *are* persecuted by their own fear, to an extent irrespective of what the outside world does. Since the external world also does itself behave in complex, irrational, and unpredictable ways, this unresolved conflict potentially traps us in a constant pessimistic relationship with that world: a relationship in which we may well anticipate or experience ourselves as frightened, without resources, and permanently at risk of attack. Our desire for psychological flight converts into an anxiety about physical flight, and our consequent need is for a safe home. And that, unfortunately, is where, in the real world, the Holocaust succeeded in raising the stakes, hence our fear, to unprecedented levels.

Nowhere to go

Not far below the surface of Jewish thinking, seemingly handed down over countless generations, is the notion that we must always be ready to leave. Clive Lawton puts this into a theological frame, observing that:

> "In classical Jewish thought, you should never feel established wherever you are, because you're always in exile and you're always waiting, ready for the Messiah to arrive and to go back to the land of Israel. So there's this tradition that you don't fully decorate your house; you leave a corner of it unplastered or undecorated because you never fully settle there." (Lawton, October 2006, personal communication)

This theological teaching, that we are only where we are temporarily, is clearly a symbolic representation of life itself. All of us inhabit life temporarily, and since we do not know when death will strike must be ready to leave at any time. Whether symbolic or actual, however, dominant discourse amongst ordinary Jews is not one in which "leaving" is a theological matter. For them, it is almost invariably tied with ideas of *having* to leave: having to leave out of fear for one's security, possessions, one's very life. Thus Naomi Alderman explained to a small group one evening how in her view this is built into the fabric of the Jewish psyche. "If you had to leave," she asked us, "where would you go?" Without hesitation, we each summoned up aunts in Canada, cousins in America, old friends in other parts of the world to whom we could turn if ("heaven forbid") we found ourselves having to flee where we lived and seek refuge elsewhere. "You see," she said, "when I ask non-Jews that question, they look puzzled; they don't get why I'm asking it. Jews don't need to think twice about it" (Alderman, January 2007, personal communication).

What Naomi Alderman alludes to in this dinner-table conversation is a certain kind of psychological reality. Jews do not need to think twice about the putative question, "Where would you go?" because it is a question around which the Jewish psychological world is spontaneously oriented. Our ancestors all came from somewhere else, often within living memory and usually for good reasons. Since there are numerous examples throughout Europe of places where even centuries of settled existence have been abruptly or devastatingly terminated and Jews forced to move somewhere else, there is a defensible proposition that the accumulation of such experience creates a constant background alertness. Victor certainly thinks so:

> "Well, I know [that there have been] periods when Jews have been in positions of privilege. I suppose you can talk about Britain being one of those periods more recently. We've done very well. I accept that, but nonetheless, I think there probably has always been an undertow of vulnerability all the time. Thinking of my father … He was well-established … pretty much a normal London life, [but] always talked about the possibility of having to move away."

In some quarters, the ever-present possibility of having to move away has materially influenced the occupations and securities that Jews have sought to build up. During broadcaster Dennis Marks's research for a BBC programme on the state of the Yiddish language in the twenty-first century, he found the diamond trading area of Manhattan still centrally important in the economic life of orthodox Jews. When he asked one trader, Moishe Moysbacher, about the connection between Jews of predominantly Eastern European origin and the diamond business, Moysbacher's response referred straight back to Jewish experience in Europe:

> "Historically Jews were persecuted in all countries. Opportunity was not available to them, so they had no choice. I think it was more out of necessity than out of choice. […] [T]he diamond business [was seen as] particularly safe … because … Jewish people historically would never know when they had to run. There was a knock on the door, you had to go out the back door … run out. […] [Y]ou would take whatever your possessions were. You didn't need a moving truck to take your diamonds, you just put them in your pocket and run. They were very easily transportable. […] That's probably why they ended up in the diamond business as opposed, say, to the cement business." (Moysbacher, cited by Marks, 2009)

This particular way of seeing the world presumes an inevitability of exile: not the theological exile of separation from God, Israel, or the messianic state of perfection, but material exile and loss. And we certainly have plenty of forced exiles to look back at. From the first exile to Babylon and the later scattering (dispersal) of Jews from Palestine throughout the world,[5] to expulsion from England, France, and Spain in the Middle Ages, then to persecution and oppression in Eastern Europe from the mid-seventeenth century onwards, we are not short of historic reference points that back up a notion that ours is an inescapable history of upheaval and fear. Such a psychological framework creates not only a desire for a place of *physical* refuge, but one of emotional safety, too: intrinsically a more difficult place to reach, as the emotional legacy suffered by Holocaust survivors so heartbreakingly tells.

But this ostensible history is only a partial reading. For every expulsion, attack, or oppression leading to emigration, there are other, more optimistic, stories. Clive Lawton points out that after the massacre of Jews in York in 1190,

> "[after that] huge trauma, Jews did leave York. By 1205, fifteen years later, the Jewish community of York was more numerous and more prosperous than it had been before 1190. Within less than a generation, fifteen years after people they knew had been killed, they had returned. [… Yet when] I went to University in York, […]

> lots of people said to me, 'How could you? Don't you know about the massacre? Jews aren't supposed to live there.' Seven hundred years later, in this modern historical mode, we're saying, 'You can't live there, this place is steeped in blood'." (Lawton, October 2006, personal communication)

And, in more immediate times, he observes that:

> "Straight after the war Polish Jewry attempted to re-establish itself. [...] There was certainly over quarter of a million and possibly half a million Jews returned or re-emerged in Poland. It was only then that the Stalinist purges and the imposition of Communism finally drove them out. The resilience of Jewish communities to return gets lost in a concertina-ing of history." (Ibid.)

These are stories of return; of resilience; of the ability to pick up the pieces and carry on. But there are still other kinds of story. In Esther's family, there is less a sense of *having to move from*, but rather *choosing to move to*:

> "It was trade but it was also safety. [My grandfather] had come from Baghdad to Manchester [in the 1920s], then [...] went back to Iran ... [...] In the thirties he was travelling round Europe. [... T]hey liked Berlin, which was funny, but when he heard that a war was coming, he wanted to be in England which he felt was a safe haven. [... So it] was safety but it was [also] financial. You know, in the twenties he'd already moved from Baghdad to Manchester anyway, to build up this textiles business. He knew that that's where he could thrive. [...] It was definitely a pull factor rather than a push factor. And on my father's side basically the pull had been to India, again for ... that had been my great-grandfather ... again for commercial reasons. And yes, no persecution at all, everyone was very happy there [...]."

Something that gets lost sight of in the familiar narrative that "we must always be ready to flee" is that, by and large, even when there were good reasons *to* flee, there were also opportunities and resources to draw on. Until the Holocaust, for every expulsion there was somewhere else to go: from England in 1290 to southern France; from the Rhineland in the twelfth and thirteenth centuries to Poland; from Spain in 1492 and Portugal in 1497 again to France, to North Africa, the Middle East, and the Netherlands; from the pogroms of the mid-seventeenth century Polish-Ukrainian borders back west, to Alsace, the Netherlands, and England. The dinner table conversation I referred to earlier inadvertently reflects another side to the "need to leave": that is, not only is there some*where* else to go, there is very often some*one* else to go to. When my paternal grandfather Abraham, a cabinet-maker, arrived in London in 1903, he was following his uncle who had already established a furniture-making business there. Siblings, aunts, uncles, cousins, friends of friends: for most of our scattered history, there have been resources we could use, and an ability to use them. Without exception, those of us who are descended from the East European migrants of the late nineteenth and early twentieth centuries descend from those very abilities. Our history is not only one of persecution, exile, and loss, but one also of opportunity and resourcefulness.

The Holocaust ended both this pattern and the unconscious expectation, a certain psychological security, that went with it. As the war progressed, options for Jews to escape the disaster in Europe closed down. German and Austrian Jews who fled to France during the 1930s were trapped after 1940. Polish Jews who moved into Soviet-occupied Poland in 1939 were caught by the Nazi invasion of 1941. Italian and Greek Jews, relatively protected until 1943, and Hungarian Jews until 1944, overnight found themselves exposed with nowhere to escape from the mass deportations. What Browning describes as Europe's pre-twentieth century "permeable boundaries [which] allowed expelled Jews to escape and settle elsewhere" by 1944 had closed into a trap from which there was virtually no escape possible (Browning, 2004, p. 4). Resources and resourcefulness gave way to almost complete helplessness.

"Helpless to prevent the assault"

In Chapter Three, I discussed the way in which the helplessness that ordinary Jews feel when confronted with images of the Holocaust acts as a stimulus to their anger at the Holocaust. But helplessness is more fundamentally tied to experiences of fear, whilst anger acts as an attempt to triumph over fear by seeking some potential for action. Lemma and Levy describe the relationship between trauma, helplessness, and fear, when in certain kinds of situation one's inability to act results in being dominated by helpless fear:

> According to Freud, trauma is associated with what he termed "annihilatory anxiety", or more simply, a fear of death, either in relation to the self or someone close to the self. Freud (1920) saw this anxiety as a core, universal fear, present in all humans. [...] If, in addition to near death, there is also an experience of helplessness and passivity, then the chances of a post-traumatic stress reaction are considerable.
>
> Let us take, for example, a man and his child, who are accosted by a group of thugs while walking home. He and his child are threatened with death. If there is the possibility, he can grab his child and run away from this danger. He can also fight his way out of their predicament [...]. Either way, his body gears him into the position for a fight/flight response. The fight/flight response is a survival impulse, which bypasses thought and intent and automatically prepares the body to respond to a threat on its life. [...]
>
> If, however, the man has a gun to his head and sees his child in a similar position, then the options for flight or fight are removed. Instead the two of them are forced into a passive compliance with their attackers. They face death, and are helpless to prevent the assault. In this instance, the fight/flight response is inhibited and prevented from protecting the individual.
>
> The inhibition of the fight/flight response does not, however, inhibit the massive anxiety [... which is] aroused by the experience. (Lemma & Levy, 2004, p. 8)

One does not need to have suffered the kind of traumatic experience Lemma and Levy posit above in order to understand what feeling helpless means. All human beings can identify with being helpless and at the mercy of someone more powerful, and the associated fear that comes with that, if only because all humans have endured the helplessness of being a baby, utterly dependent on someone else for succour and support. Even though mothers seldom explicitly attack their infants to cause the deepest degrees of infant trauma, infants inevitably undergo some degree of abandonment, an experience which, according to the French psychoanalyst Jacques Lacan, is essential if they are to acquire new resources and learn ways of overcoming their helplessness.[6] There is a finely tuned balance in the saga of human development: "just enough" frustration forces development; too much generates paralysing anxiety and terrifying rage. Like Harriet, every Jew, depending on their own individual experiences, will resonate more or less strongly with the potent images and thoughts of abandonment, of having "nowhere else to go" generated by the Holocaust.

> "[It's deeply frightening]. It was just so horrific. Somebody else controlling your life so much; one you're imprisoned, two, when are you going to die? So little control over that. You can just identify with that."

Abandonment in infancy, however temporary (it is still keenly felt) is associated with an absence of secure holding (physical holding by the motherer).[7] Symbolically, this "loss of holding" becomes equated with the loss of home, since in a real way infants know the physicality of their mother's warm body, voice and arms *as* "home". Loss of this secure holding—literally an expulsion from paradise—is extremely painful, and it becomes immensely important for human beings to develop through their lives an equivalent security that acts as a psychological "home".[8] This is what Frankl (1946) alluded to when he found that what enabled him to survive in the camps was realising that he retained his freedom "to choose [his] attitude in any given set of circumstances"; for this meant that he possessed one secure psychological "home" that the camp regime could never take away from him.

The actuality of the Holocaust, which simultaneously closed off options for escape and rendered people helpless, has had, I think, two effects in terms of fear for ordinary Jews. One is to distort our sense of our own history, emphasising a history of danger, flight, and exile, and marginalising that of opportunity and resource.[9] The other is that it not only triggers but magnifies a normally occurring experience of fear as a component of abandonment, helplessness, anger, and guilt. These feelings are themselves so difficult to deal with that we seek in fantasy a place of refuge, a safe home, where we no longer have to feel them. The terror of being *psychologically* trapped in our own fears finds a ready echo in the images of ghettos, cattle trucks, and closed borders. It fuels a desire for safety: an actual place, an "Israel", where we can head if and when all else fails; or an over-arching authority, some "One" to hold it all together, to make the world not just physically but psychologically safe; as members of a group discussion expressed it:

> "Whether you understand it or not, you find it keeps on happening, so that's … that's the more frightening […] You look at the Holocaust regime and then you look at … you've Rwanda, it doesn't matter, does it? It's almost academic, isn't it? Why it happened, why these things happen?"

> "When I look at the bigger picture […] people [together] can't be trusted to act in … a normal way. There has to be something like the UN for what it's worth, there needs to be a community force that's going to police—I hate to use that word—to … to look after the world."[10]

There is another deep-seated dimension to this question of our post-Holocaust, ordinary Jewish fear from which we may yearn to be safe. It emerged sometimes subtly and sometimes strikingly in interviews. It concerns the way we see ourselves and our fear of seeing ourselves in a hideous light. Whether or not people are consciously aware of this, it is very difficult to protect ourselves from the images of Jews produced and replicated by the Nazis themselves and then through Holocaust "memory", and these malignant images go to a very primitive level of our psyche.

"I just knew that I was a Jewish girl growing up, I must look awful"

In Sonia's and Michelle's earlier descriptions of their responses to the world, certain things can be seen. One is that neither of them asserts that the people they move amongst *are* anti-Semitic; rather, they are saying that they *do not know*, and it is this uncertainty that weakens their trust and causes them to worry. The other is a subtle, but significant distinction. They are not in practice wondering "Do these people like *me*?", but "Do they like *Jews*?" By implication, the question of being liked has become one of "Can these people like me *when I am Jewish*?" In other words, personal significance or value in their own minds has become subverted by anxiety about a faceless labelling under which "I as a Jew" takes priority over "I as a unique human being". This sense of a marginalised self is intrinsically a vulnerability in relation to any form of discrimination, positive or negative (although more obviously damaging when negative), whether based on race, religion, gender, or any other kind of significant difference. But it has a peculiar potency for Jews. Something that sits at the core of our identity comes back, even in a benevolent society such as Britain, in a hostile or distorted form *"just enough"*, as Julius puts it, to promote some degree of fragility as to who and what we are:

> [O]ne could not grow up as a Jew, living in part among Jews, without some sense of anti-Semitism. For Anglo-Jewry in general, it is the background noise against which we make our lives. Almost always barely audible, one then must strain to detect it—though very occasionally it irrupts into a dissonant, heart-stopping din. The question of the extent of my experience of anti-Semitism, then, is perhaps best answered thus: *just enough*. That is, just enough for it to inform my understanding of the subject, but not so much as to overwhelm me. (Julius, 2010, p. xvii)

Israeli-born Gideon was shocked by an experience of blatant anti-Semitism:

> "One of the big shocks I've had here […] is when there was a knock on the door, and I opened it and there was a BetterWare man with a delivery. I said, 'We haven't ordered anything, and he said, 'Yes you have'. He gave me the stuff, it was something like £29.90p, and I gave him £30 and waited for the change. I waited and waited, and reluctantly, in the end, he pulled out 10p and then said, '… for the Jewboy.' I was so shocked. I had never actually come across face-to-face bare anti-Semitism. I didn't know what to say, and he was well out of sight before I could gather my thoughts. That one man was enough to spur …. I had heard that there was anti-Semitism in Scotland but I'd never come across it."

Most Jews can attest to some similar, usually passing, incident of anti-Semitism. From Olivia's:

> "I've met English people who just don't like Jews and you can tell. They just … alter, ever so slightly, if they find out you're Jewish"

to Victor's:

> "[I]t's quite some time since I experienced it [anti-Semitism] directly. A queue in the swimming pool, it must be about five years ago, there

> was this .... guy who was always getting out of hand ... He said something about it's good the Jews get blown up in Israel. I think that's the last time that I experienced it. I remember hearing a slightly anti-Semitic joke",

such incidents, perturbing, even shocking, are part of the warp-and-weft of living in a society where *others* may be disturbed *about us*. People have different degrees of resilience to such experiences. In part this can be put down to variations in people's sense of belonging or adaptation to the particular strand of British society which they occupy. Howard, unlike Olivia, Victor, or Gideon, comes from a family long-settled in Britain. He notices what others might think of as potentially dangerous anti-Semitic outbursts, but is not frightened by them:

> "I never had that experience of not belonging. [...] My family's been well established in different places [in Britain] [for 200 years], and is thoroughly British. [...] It makes me appallingly incapable of spotting anti-Semitism. [...] A few weeks ago some yobs drove past me as I was walking to *shul*, and yelled out 'Jew'. I shouted back, 'Right!' Now, someone else would be reporting this to the CST.[11] It just seems to me to be an act of stupidity on their [the yobs'] part. I'm just not good at seeing it. I think that some Jews are very good at seeing it."

In general, however, there seems to be "just enough" experience of prejudiced behaviour or opinions to perpetuate amongst Jews in some form an ongoing background anxiety: "If 'they' do not *like* us, do they, in fact, hate us? And if they hate us, to what lengths will they go?"

One of the most insidious aspects of prejudice[12] is the way that it proffers distorted pictures of who we are. Seeing ourselves, or imagining ourselves seen, in the eyes of others in a distorted way is always disturbing and therefore always likely to produce anxiety if not, in some instances, more violent reactions. At the very least, this experience of a distorted self-image questions our sense of who we are; and in forcing us to doubt ourselves, our acceptability and our love-ability, it attacks our sense of belonging in the world and our unquestioning belief in our inalienable right to be here.

In the psychoanalytic world, "how we are seen" has come to occupy a central role in the crucial question of the development of Self. Winnicott and others have discussed how, from birth onwards, we come to experience and "know" ourselves through an interactive process from our earliest days with an Other, usually mother, through whose face and in whose eyes we see ourselves as lively, co-creative individuals, or conversely (if the mother is depressed or angry) as dulled, separated, and anxious ones. Kenneth Wright, for example, writes:

> The face as mirror—Winnicott offers a rich new metaphor for exploring the meaning and function of the face. The face reflects and what it reflects back is the other person. The baby looks in the mother's face and sees a reflection of himself. Of course, the baby does see the mother's smiling face, but this, which is in reality her response to his smiles, reflects back to him his own aliveness: "The mother is looking at the baby and what she looks like is related to what she sees there." (Wright, 1991, pp. 11–12)[13]

In contrast:

> What happens, however, if the mother's face does not respond in this way—if, for example, she is depressed, with a masklike face, or if her smiles are brittle with the rigidity of her own defences? "In such a case", says Winnicott, "what does the baby see?" He looks and does *not* see himself, but the mother's face. The mother's face is not then a mirror: "perception takes the place of that which might have been the beginning of a significant exchange with the world." (Ibid., p. 13)

Wright goes on to speculate that:

> the fixed face of the unresponsive mother could equally be experienced as a reflection, but a distorting one [...]. [E]ven in adult life, it is hard to free ourselves completely from the feeling that we are the "cause" of expression we see in the faces of those near us. This brings us back to the idea of [...] true or false reflections. (Ibid., p. 14)

He quotes Lacan, who:

> seems to see this as the start of a dissociation between our own experience of ourselves and our image for others, which increases with time and extends into all our relations with others. The looking glass lies; [...] because we believe its lies, we lose touch with our

> real selves [...] and eventually try to live out the images that have been bestowed upon us by others. (Ibid., p. 15)

From a psychoanalytic perspective, therefore, all human beings have a tendency to be vulnerable to distorted perceptions of themselves in the outside world, and the degree or severity of our vulnerability derives from the robustness and sensitivity of our early infant experiences of carer responses to us. If a relaxed carer-infant interaction is so key to our later adult selves, perhaps Jewish sensitivity to, and anxiety about, anti-Semitism is not *just* a product of external enmities but is also a consequence of the emotional impact on child-bearing Jewish women of the mass migrations of the 1890s and 1900s, which I discussed in Chapter Two. The pain of permanently leaving "*der haym*" and everyone associated with care and familiarity has depressive consequences, particularly for those vulnerable to the emotional turbulence of subsequently giving birth. A depressed, withdrawn mother creates a baby at some level fearful of its own self. There is plenty to suggest that depression associated with migration and passed on in some form to at least the next generation forms an underlay of shared emotional inheritance amongst Jews.

More pertinent, however, is that we are all susceptible, partly for reasons grounded in infancy, to being affected by actual, or what we perceive as, malignant or distorted images of ourselves. If we cannot be relaxed and secure in who we are, we are likely to become anxious. Gideon describes it in terms of worry:

> "Over the years coming away from Israel was a very healthy experience in the sense that I stopped being so worried about being Jewish [...]. I don't think I'm alone in that."

However, it is Doris who provides a particularly telling commentary on the relationship between fear and self-image associated with being Jewish. She describes herself in the present-day as "terrified" of anti-Semitism, and particularly of Arab and Moslem anti-Semitism which she equates with the Final Solution:

> "They [Arab Moslems] took over the Final Solution in a sense. [...] When I talk about Palestinians or Arabs in connection with it, it's ... I mean the Nazis were the ones who did it, but it's today that they [...] the Egyptians or Lebanese [...] are putting on soaps based on *The Protocols of the Elders of Zion* [...]. ... It's seamless, the whole

> thing is … it suddenly became immensely threatening, this sense of anti-Semitism, and through that […] not only the Holocaust but two thousand years of persecution suddenly became immensely emotional for me. These days I feel extremely terrified … I know I've got an … I'm defensive about it […]. I don't think I'm over sensitive about it, I …. I don't know."

Doris's terror can be best understood as a delayed reaction to an upbringing in which her Jewish identity was placed under great pressure. A present-day Moslem anti-Semitism which perpetuates horrible distortions of Jews links back psychologically to the unusual circumstances of her childhood, when she was persistently exposed to a hostility towards, and a devaluing of, Jews and being Jewish.

Doris's mother died when Doris and her sister were children. Their father then employed a non-Jewish housekeeper to care for them. It was a distinctly unwise choice, for this housekeeper had hostile and anti-Semitic views which she expressed openly to the two girls. The experience deeply marked Doris in her growing years; in effect, she has never quite recovered from a severe wound to her self-regard not only to being Jewish but to being a Jewish *girl*, born of a daily experience of anti-Semitism inside the walls of their own home:

> "My sister and I came back [from seeing the post-war films about the camps], … we were in a terrible state and this housekeeper, Mrs. [M], said, 'It was a punishment on Jews because they had not accepted Jesus.' […] So for my sister and me, the whole thing, anti-Semitism and the Holocaust, it is very traumatic, you know? Because we grew up with this, we had it. […] There was no protection and […] … that affected both of us deeply. […] I just knew that I was a Jewish girl growing up, I must look awful […]. It really emotionally crippled me for decades. I had to sort of rescue myself. It took decades, and it took psychotherapy [to help her recover]."

This experience of a hostile, if non-family, "Other" inside what should be the sanctuary of the home sat in the context of an even more painful experience, one which complicated at a more fundamental level Doris's normal need to feel good about her Jewish identity. Doris's mother had died after an operation went wrong:

> "She had a mastoid in one ear. She had two operations and it went wrong. It so happens that her parents wanted her to go into the Jewish

> hospital in the East End which then existed, and my father didn't. […] She went to the Jewish Hospital and she died there. I can hear my father saying to different people, 'If my wife hadn't gone into that hospital, she'd be alive today.' It's all connected. It was very nasty. Of course, I didn't react at the time, as children … don't react as much as people think. They just take what is as given, don't they? […] [But] it would have reinforced the sort of, 'Jewish is not very nice', or 'It's not very … there's something about being Jewish,' you see? Something wrong but you can't do anything about it. […] When I look back it makes me very angry … with my father."

Effectively, Doris felt robbed by her father, both through his hostility born of the distress of his wife's death and through his action in introducing someone anti-Semitic into the household, of the opportunity to grow up feeling good about being Jewish. Once adult, she joined the Communist Party, which she saw as "by definition anti-racist, it cannot be anti-Semitic", and this was clearly in part an effort to feel safe: "I never experienced any anti-Semitism in the Communist Party, and I did feel pretty safe there … safe from racism." It was only in the aftermath of the Munich Olympics, some years after leaving the Communist Party, that she reconnected emotionally with being Jewish, the history of the Holocaust, and the situation in the Middle East. Angry and outraged as she is over her childhood conditions, the current external situation seems to provide her with a focus for the terror she once felt, growing up in a bereft household where she had no protection against attacks on an intrinsic part of her identity.

Doris shows us how disturbing it is to look into the face of a hostile Other and see distortions of who we are. It is frightening, not only because it directly puts us at risk if the Other acts on what we perceive to be his hostility, but because it disarms us in our very need to stand up for ourselves: to assert the "all-rightness" of who we are and to *feel* the integrity and validity of our real selves. Fear of anti-Semitism and of the possible consequences of anti-Semitism, the stakes of which have been terrifyingly raised by the spectre of genocide, is not only a reaction to the imputed strength of the hostile Other; it is also a fear about ourselves: as writer Howard Jacobson put it, an "underlying fearfulness" [about being Jewish] "that is its own form of anti-Semitism" (Jacobson, 2011).

Post-Holocaust ordinary Jewish fear therefore takes its strength, I suggest, from several interwoven sources which are psychological at least as much as they are actual. Hatred, of course, puts our physical survival at risk, and we may justifiably be fearful of that. But fear also points to our sense of helplessness: helplessness in the face of the frightening nightmares evoked by Holocaust imagery; helplessness to resolve or find refuge from our contradictory and conflicting reactions to those nightmares; our feared helplessness to find "good answers" to those who may hate us; helplessness because we cannot easily tell who hates us and who doesn't, and we therefore have to be fearful of making the wrong judgement call. Over and above this, I think, we fear that *being* seen means *to be seen* in a way that is inherently hostile and therefore dangerous, and we cannot entirely free ourselves from the lurking fear that there is "something wrong [about being Jewish]."

In my next chapter, I turn to the theme of guilt and its associated affect, shame. As with fear, I explore how ordinary Jewish emotional reactions to the Holocaust have been deeply coloured by toxic images under whose shadow we still live. I also consider how ordinary Jews, particularly in Britain, brought up well away from the territories of the Holocaust, may in the wake of the Holocaust have marginalised the experience they, along with all other Britons in the years 1939–1945, did share: the direct impact of the war itself.

CHAPTER FIVE

Guilt—or shame?

In his last book, *The Drowned and the Saved*, Primo Levi soberly observed that, "that many, (including me) experienced 'shame', that is, a feeling of guilt during the imprisonment and afterwards is an ascertained fact confirmed by numerous testimonies. It may seem absurd, but it does exist" (Levi, 1989, p. 54).

Jewish "guilt" in relation to the Holocaust has always had a perverse irrationality about it. The very idea that any people should feel guilty for being victims of such a massive crime is, as Primo Levi observed, absurd. Yet it is well-established that amongst many survivors, deep feelings of guilt were paramount. In *From Guilt to Shame* Ruth Leys cites at least four of the most prominent survivor-writers, each of whom described unequivocally their terrible feelings of guilt at having survived when so many others died (Leys, 2007, pp. 4–5).[1] Formulating the concept of "survivor guilt" was an early outcome of post-war efforts to deal clinically with traumatised survivors. For clinicians struggling to treat survivor-patients carrying such immense trauma, it was crucial to understand the dynamics involved in survivors' guilt feelings; clinicians therefore drew on various psychoanalytic theories, most notably "identification with the aggressor", in order to create some kind of coherent framework within which to approach treatment.[2] However, Leys also points out that this particular theoretical formulation provoked powerful emotional and philosophical reactions in a wider audience. Not least was an almost outraged reaction by writers such as Lawrence Langer and Giorgio Agamben to the implication that victims of the camps could in any degree be considered complicit in what had happened there, given that they had been surviving against all odds in a reality that was ultimately utterly "incomprehensible and unredeemable" (ibid., p. 6).

For many writers and academics, discomfort with the difficult implications of "survivor guilt" led to a significant shift in the way post-traumatic experience has been latterly discussed. The once puzzling and troubling concept has now been replaced by the idea of shame as "the emotion that for many investigators most defines the condition of post-traumatic stress" (ibid., p. 6). In her analysis of this change, Leys observes that:

> the general privilege they [Langer and Agamben] accord to shame over guilt can be situated in the context of a broad shift that has recently occurred in the medical and psychiatric sciences, literary criticism, and even philosophy, away from the 'moral' concept of guilt in favour of the ethically different or 'free' concept of shame (ibid., p. 7)

and, she continues:

> [they—i.e. numerous cited writers] posit […] a clear differentiation between guilt and shame in order to make use of shame theory for various philosophical, post-psychoanalytic, postmodernist and political projects and critiques. (Ibid., p. 8)

Leys devotes the rest of her book to tracing the evolution of these two conceptual interpretations of post-Holocaust survivor trauma, a conflict which she sees as reflecting a not only unresolved, but in her view unresolvable, tension between two theories of trauma. For Leys, the displacement of guilt by shame in the diagnostic criteria associated with post-traumatic stress reflects a cultural shift (one which she particularly identifies as American) away from questions of ethics and moral value towards ones of identity and personal being; a shift which she sees as inherently unsustainable given that events such as the Holocaust pose inescapable—even if unanswerable—moral questions. But Leys' book is not an analysis as such of the post-Holocaust legacy: it is, as she puts it, "rather a work of intellectual history" in which she endeavours to evaluate at a more philosophical level some of what is at stake in how a nation formulates, changes, and promotes its view of itself.[3]

I have begun this chapter in this way for several reasons. One is that, depending on which clinical material you read, there are well-founded arguments for the proposition that guilt and shame are equally part of the human condition and, therefore, both implicated in conditions of trauma. Even in the earliest literature that has come down to us, guilt and shame are both present in human history, whether implicitly or explicitly denoted. The second, however, concerns a paradox in my own research. While several of my, ordinary Jewish, interviewees talked about feelings of guilt arising in relation to the Holocaust, apart from some passing references almost no one mentioned shame as an emotion consciously experienced in this context, and in one or two cases, the idea was even actively discounted. There was, however, one notable exception who saw shame as central to his, and Jewish people's, traumatic experience. In addition, in certain literature relating to the post-Holocaust legacy—particularly for the children of survivors—"shame" is referred to frequently, and in such a way as to indicate that it provides a central dimension not only of survivors' actual Holocaust experiences but of the transgenerational experiences of their children. The generally accepted thesis about shame is that it is inherently associated with a powerful need to hide; I therefore suggest that this is precisely why in this context of ordinary Jews' "Holocaust inheritance", shame, even if invisible and unmentioned, is still present. Whether we descend from survivors or not, the Holocaust as we receive it contains material and imagery that are intrinsically shaming to Jews, and this echoes the central position that many clinicians believe shame holds in human trauma.

Guilt and shame are affects commonly linked in discussions of the "bad" feelings human beings own. The shorthand difference usually drawn between them is that guilt is associated with what one has *done*, that is, actions one has committed, while shame more fundamentally concerns *who or what one is*. The internal dynamics, however, are more complex. For example, guilt may arise not only in relation to actual actions (or inactions) which are manifest in the outside world, but to the inner world of one's feelings: feelings which one is not "supposed" to own. Thus Anne Karpf, daughter of two Holocaust survivors, writes of feeling "draped in guilt" over the rage, hatred, and envy she felt towards her parents, whose suffering dominated her childhood and seemed to make it impossible for her to feel her actual feelings and to lead her own life:

> Lugubriousness was among the proscribed sentiments—along with sadness, rage and depression. 'Depressed, what's depressed?' my father would ironically ask if my sister reported one of her schoolfriends to be low […]. 'Her life isn't endangered, she has enough to eat'. (Karpf, 1997, p. 10)
>
> When my sister or I ventured criticism of my mother […] our protective father would invariably pitch in with a 'Remember what she's been through'. […] Our lives were heavily symbolic: we were meant to tip the family scales towards happiness. (Ibid., pp. 38–39)
>
> Hating one's parents is a necessary stage of childhood […] [But] [h]ow could you hate those who'd already been hated so much? (Ibid., p. 38)

No matter how much Karpf tried to "compensate" her parents for her unforgiveable feelings, for example by buying them "hugely extravagant gifts, to the limit of my finances", it "never seemed to [be] enough":

> When I left [work] at the end of the day, I'd often find myself draped in guilt. […] It seemed wrong to have time without burdens, freedom without limitation. […] As for leaving home, I couldn't imagine it happening […]. (Ibid., p. 53)
>
> I'd always envied my parents their suffering. This was so obviously shocking that I couldn't have admitted it, had I even been conscious of it. It didn't mean that I underestimated the horror of the war, or that I masochistically sought out pain, only that their terrible experiences seemed to diminish—even to taunt—anything bad which happened to us. In its drama, enormity and significance, their war could never be matched. (Ibid., p. 126)

The intrinsic difference between these two extremely difficult psychological states, guilt and shame, may be understood in this way. Guilt is a relational feeling: that is, it is a feeling which primarily arises in relation to another or others, whether through an action one has performed (or failed to perform) towards another or others, or over feelings one harbours towards someone. Psychoanalysts consider that guilt arises at a stage in infancy by when the infant has learnt to distinguish between himself and the outside world (initially personified in the shape of his mother(er)). Rage, which an infant feels when his mother(er) fails to meet his needs in the right way at the right moment, becomes associated not only with fear but with guilt at feeling such anger towards the one who cares. Shame, by contrast, is a self-directed feeling; it is a feeling *about oneself*: that one is unworthy, contemptible, even hideous. Many writers consider that in certain forms shame arises at an even earlier, pre-relational, stage in the infant's life, at such an unconscious period as to be one of the formative factors in making it so difficult to own, much less discuss. "This type of shame is unimaginable and nameless, beyond speech", says Mary Ayers: a description that itself powerfully echoes survivors' almost incommunicable experience of the camps (Ayers, 2003, p. 12). Shame involves a putative "other" "in whose eyes" one is seen; but unlike guilt (for which theoretically one can atone), its essence is that the detestable "self" that is oneself can never be put right. Thus in the ancient Greek myth of Oedipus, Oedipus' immediate reaction to learning the horrifying truth that he has killed his own father and married his mother is to put out his own eyes: so that he will never again have to look at his own reflection and see the shameful creature that he is.

Distinct as they are, guilt and shame are inexorably linked. Guilt at having done something cannot easily be separated from a sense of shame at being the kind of person who would commit such an action or actions. For Levi, Steinberg, and other survivors, guilt and shame were all part of the one experience of being an inmate in a *Lager*, required to do and to witness appalling acts, and at the same time to experience themselves as dehumanised beings, without worth or value. Steinberg was to write in later life:

> I lived and am still living in humiliation, I have never managed to wipe my image clean. I am still the passive witness of Philippe's death, the person who slapped the old Jew, the boy hiding out in the latrines, the toady who fawned on brutes and murderers to make sure of his extra helpings of soup (Steinberg, 2001, p. 162)

while Levi observed that in every case it was after liberation, with its concomitant return to something approaching a normal human existence, that survivors could look back *at themselves* with intense shame at the degraded self that had endured and survived:

> Coming out of the darkness, one suffered because of the reacquired consciousness of having been diminished. Not by our will, cowardice or fault, yet nevertheless we had lived for months and years at an animal level. (Levi, 1989, p. 56)

Whilst for very many Jews who endured the Holocaust, guilt—or guilt feelings—were inescapable; and whilst even for people in the next generation, like Karpf, who were caught up in the aftermath of their parents' experiences, so that for Karpf managing her own life in relation to that of her parents' caused her intense feelings of guilt; for ordinary Jews the question of guilt is a more elliptical one. Why should ordinary Jews feel guilt or shame in respect of the Holocaust? Yet consciously or unconsciously, these feelings seem to be present; and, difficult as they are to contemplate, they deserve attention.

"There is this obligation"

Of all the emotions that could reflect some kind of indirect collective trauma amongst ordinary Jews to the Holocaust, guilt is one where there is likely to be the sharpest divide between Jews alive then (at the time of the war), and Jews born since. Jews alive at the end of the war (and there are still a good number now in their eighties and nineties) would have found it very hard to escape feelings of guilt and responsibility, no matter how obscure, towards the millions who had died. If not their own feelings of guilt, they may well have found it difficult to avoid being affected by their adult parents' similar feelings. Bernice describes a not-untypical conversation of the kind that could well have taken place in many Jewish homes during the 1960s between the post-war generation and their parents:

> "I know I spoke to my parents about it and saying, 'You were Jews in England, what were you doing?' And they said, 'There was … at the time, I don't think there was anything we *could* do.'"

Was it an obscure sense of guilt that led Bernice some years later to becoming the secretary of a London synagogue that consisted almost entirely of German Jews, a fact which is directly connected in her own narrative: as though she unconsciously took on a sense of obligation to do *something* in the face of her parents' helplessness to do "anything"?

> "And then in later years, working with [German Jews] and learning what really did happen to people … because we had no involvement in it."

Even today, some two generations later, it is possible to discern in the testimony of young ordinary Jews certain feelings which can be linked to those of guilt. There is a sense in which feelings of guilt, of blame, of culpability, of responsibility, however obscurely these feelings may be felt, have become part of a collective "unspoken", ambiguously transmitted from one generation to the next, and resulting in a vague or even explicit sense of obligation towards some "one" or some "thing". Michelle describes it in this way:

> "The way I see it is that my parents do [feel] an obligation to Israel—I think they do—and I personally think it's linked to the Holocaust and maybe the guilt of surviving",

while Harriet fought against her parents' expectation that she should have nothing to do with Germany:

> "I remember getting very frustrated with … my parents … […]: you know, 'You can't hate Germany forever, you've got to give new Germans a chance to live their lives. You can't blame every German in the world for being German.' I think that generation felt that obligation to […] in no way […] relate to Germany."

To understand these feelings of guilt, one has partly to look back to the actual events of the 1930s as they affected ordinary Jews living outside Europe. During the 1930s, Jews in Britain, and no doubt in America and elsewhere, were, as Victor describes, well aware that:

> "Jews were having a rough time in Germany. […] I can remember various incidents … you just knew that it was bad. My most prominent memory is, I think it was Tisha b'Av[4] 1938, we went to *shul,* which wasn't a usual thing for my father to do […] for a service for

> intercession [...] for Jews in Germany. I know this for a fact because I've recently found the order of service."

Such awareness would have been sharply heightened by the huge increase in flight by Austrian Jews after the Anschluss and by German Jews after Kristallnacht in November 1938. Large numbers were received in Britain; somewhat fewer (proportionately) in the United States, which in 1939 earned the unenviable—and, to Pearl, shameful—accolade of refusing to admit a shipful of German Jewish refugees seeking asylum, thus resulting in their being transported back to Europe just in time for the war:[5]

> "we must have become aware somehow that the Jews were having a helluva time ... and a lot were escaping. Then ... we began to hear about ... [...] when the ship got turned. [...] [T]hat was a shameful time. Shameful time for America [...] that awful thing happening."

Doris is particularly eloquent on the impact of being faced with numbers of German Jewish refugees. In a theme echoed by Eva Figes concerning the reception of German Jews in Palestine after the war, Doris recalls resentful and hostile attitudes amongst some British Jews towards the incomers:

> "[W]hen refugees were coming over from about 1936, '37, a lot of British Jews were antagonistic. [...] It used to be said, refugees bring ... they bring anti-Semitism in their suitcases. You can't imagine ... I used to hear stuff about German refugees being said by even my grandparents and their friends. [...]'Why are you making things worse for us? What's going on in Germany, it's for German Jews to deal with, not to be brought into Britain'. [...]
>
> Also [deep sigh], you see [...] what actually happened was, Hitler wouldn't let Jews bring out any money—I don't know how much, a pound or something. So what they did was, they spent money for instance on very good overcoats. Consequently, whenever you saw refugees it seemed they were wearing incredibly posh clothes, very expensive clothes. And I remember this very well, at my grandparents' house, people saying, 'You should have seen them, the overcoats they had on. I wish I could afford an overcoat like that'."[6]

Doris still feels guilty over her own reactions. Her feelings of guilt take several forms, but foreground is guilt over the way she related to Jewish individuals who came her way. Having known German Jewish refugee girls at her school in London:

> "I feel guilty now. I don't think any of us Jewish girls, British Jewish girls, were particularly understanding about the plight of these other girls. It sounds awful, doesn't it?"

It is now almost impossible for people to separate out in their minds *what came after* 1939 with *what went before*; that is, to distinguish the massacres, the mass killings and gassings, from the more historically "familiar", even if frenzied, attacks on Jews in Germany in the early years of Nazism. Retrospectively, we tend to collapse the Holocaust into a single, undifferentiated event. With hindsight, Jews can take on feelings of responsibility and guilt for events they could not possibly have envisaged at the time. Doris shows clearly that in the 1930s, Jews were not necessarily sympathetic to the plight of German Jews, a fact which would have been painfully difficult for British and other Jews to accommodate after the full horrors of the Holocaust became known:

> "A's parents had the sense to come over in 1933 and they brought everything with them, so she was all right. [...] They had [had] a clock and watch factory in Germany and they were quite well off, and because they were knowledgeable about these things they did the sensible thing, I suppose, if you had a lot of money, they bought a farm. You can't imagine the envy and hostility that created in our house ... 'They're all right, you know, they're all right'... [...] There wasn't any sense of 'Poor things, they had to leave' [...].
>
> A used to come to school and I was envious, too. She used to have chicken sandwiches and I only had sardine sandwiches. It may sound a small thing but to this day, I find chicken sandwiches a beautiful luxury. ... We all of us thought A was showing off in having chicken sandwiches. She was a refugee ... [but] we didn't sympathise."

Doris's words reflect that even though Jews worldwide are remarkably close-knit, sharp differences and divergences still exist. Jews have lived in very different cultures and over the centuries have become culturally distinct, not only in language but in class, economic and social position, as well as in religious and political affiliations. Envy and enmity arise as naturally between Jews as amongst any people, and these less salubrious feelings jockey for position with beliefs about loyalty and mutual responsibility. Clearly, not all Jews in those countries which received Jews fleeing Germany were wholehearted in their welcome. On the contrary, it is more than likely that members of "recipient" communities found themselves juggling with a set of complex and conflicting emotions towards the refugees: a sense of community responsibility and an impulse to help; fear at the implications for themselves of such an influx; even anger at the refugees for being in such a situation, a feeling that often surfaces in the guise of contempt.

In Britain, successive waves of immigration by Jews from Europe since the late seventeenth century seem always to have raised anxiety levels amongst the existing Jewish population. As communities with a precarious sense of security and aware of themselves as outsiders and aliens in the perception of the dominant population, they often viewed with disquiet the influx of large numbers of other Jews. Such tensions had been apparent in the late nineteenth century. It was not purely out of altruism and community solidarity that the-then Jewish Board of Guardians acted to help the thousands of East European Jews arriving in London in the 1880s and 1900s: it was also an attempt to make the incomers less threatening to themselves. Anne Karpf quotes a *Jewish Chronicle* leader of 1881:

> They come mostly from Poland; they, as it were, bring Poland with them, and they retain Poland while they stop here. This is most undesirable: it is more than a misfortune, it is a calamity. We cannot afford to 'let them slide'. Our outside world is not capable of making minute discrimination between Jew and Jew and forms its opinion of Jews in general as much, if not more, from them than from the Anglicised portion of the community. We are then responsible for them. (Cited in Karpf, 1997, p. 172)[7]

Karpf speculates on the "guilt and discomfort" British Jews must have felt after the war when faced with survivors and aware of how little they themselves had "done" to help by exerting pressure on the British government at a time when it may have made some difference. Doris's testimony, however, suggests another take on such guilty reactions: that after the war Jews felt a strong underlying guilt not only because of what they had "not done", but because of how they had also felt and thought about those "other" Jews:

> "… it's very bad that people need to feel that they are safe if they are superior to somebody else; and [my grandparents] needed to feel superior. […] [I]t's this need to build up a sense of being safe with a group, but that necessitates having another—an Other".[8]

Jews are reluctant to talk about the divides amongst themselves, but these are real. Feelings amongst British Jews in the 1930s about the "Otherness" of German Jews derive from a gulf that grew up between German and Polish-Russian Jews during the nineteenth century. In this period, German Jews, freed by emancipation from the mediaeval restrictions attached to their position in society and hugely energised by the intellectual possibilities opened up by the Enlightenment,[9] assimilated rapidly into German culture. At the same time, Polish-Russian Jews, tied to the neo-feudal structure of Tsarist Russia, laboured on, mostly in poverty and superstition, living an enforced separate existence in small towns and villages: a life which was, for lack of any alternative, still heavily defined by the traditions and restrictions of Orthodox Judaism. Thus, two images of Jews, two competing ways of life and philosophy, became dominant amongst Ashkenazi Jews: the highly cultured, ambitious, and assimilated German Jews who produced many of the intellectual giants of the twentieth century;[10] and the "new arrivals" in Britain and America: the petty tradespeople, unskilled labourers, at best skilled artisans, who settled in the impoverished urban areas of the West and clung on hard to their *shtetl* loyalties.[11]

It is easy to see how, for Jews in the 1920s, still struggling to establish a secure position in British and American society, feelings about German Jews may have been deeply mixed. Admiration and awe of German Jews who had so signally "made it" are likely to have concealed deeper feelings of envy: feelings which clearly emerge in Doris's narrative. Envy of what? German Jews' wealth and position, their intellectual and cultural achievements, their ability to liberate themselves from the petty tyrannies of *shtetl* life—all of these will have been deeply provocative to the former Russian-Polish Jews. Even today there are certain echoes of such feelings, albeit expressed in religious terms, as Sonia indicates:

> "Some people say that [...] the Holocaust [...] was a punishment to the Jews at a time when people were breaking the Sabbath en masse. There's apparently video footage of Jews going to work on a Saturday and this was all rife at the time that the Holocaust happened and [...] ... there is a religious argument that had we been behaving ourselves [...] ... we could have been spared this."

In some schools of psychotherapy, envy is considered the most dangerous of human emotions: dangerous because in being usually so shamefully hidden, it has enormous destructive power. Psychoanalysts speak of "envious attacks" which always have the possibility of taking place between people: attacks which in Kleinian terms an infant, envious of what Melanie Klein called "the good breast", might unleash on his mother, but which parents can also visit on their own children when they nurture a secret envy of their children's opportunities and potential. Pearl is someone who seems to have been on the receiving end of such an envious attack from her mother when, offered the chance at the age of thirteen of a scholarship to a grammar school, she felt obliged to turn it down:

> "I sat the exam and [I asked my mother], can I go [to the interview]? [...] ... she sort of shrugged her shoulders while she was washing the dishes and said, 'Get it first'. [...] No enthusiasm, no encouragement. [...] When I went for this interview [...] there's everybody [else] sitting with their mother. ... This was a terrible blow [that she was there on her own]. [...] I was one of [only] two [from her school who got the interview] and I got a place. [But] she wasn't into education [...] for anybody. [... So] I chose to leave school because [...] [my brothers] didn't have that opportunity."

Envy of this kind, the envy of people who have done, or who may do, "better" than you, who appear to have more, whether materially or intellectually, is a poisonous feeling, and one which in the aftermath of the Holocaust will have been impossible for Jews to own that they held against those very German Jews whose presence in Germany had inspired such murderous envy amongst Germans themselves. A shared, if unspoken, sense of guilt is likely to have been one consequence haunting that generation and fuelling a need to make reparation "somewhere". To Michelle, this took the form for her parents of having "this sort of obligation [...] to Israel."

"I don't think any of us could do enough"

Alfred Garwood is a British psychoanalyst and the child of Holocaust survivor parents. In a paper published in 1996, he linked what he called the "unhealed wound" of "survivor guilt" to the experience of powerlessness (Garwood, 1996, p. 243). In this paper, Garwood traces the exact conditions under which Jews in Europe were forced to live (and die), and from which many, if not most, survivors would have come. These conditions "of systematic terrorisation", he says, were calculated to reduce Jews to a state of abject powerlessness, constantly threatened with annihilation:

> These carefully planned and developed programmes of systematic terrorisation, ghettoisation and concentration camp internment—intended to impoverish, humiliate, deceive and enslave—made the Jews feel they were in part responsible for their own fate They were led to believe that if they obeyed, worked and were useful, they could buy a little more time and survive. The true purpose of these systems was to ensure that virtually no Jew had enough food, luck or resourcefulness to escape death. To have survived despite all this, the survivors were made to feel they had had more than their fair share of luck, resourcefulness or food. Thus they were made to feel [...] that the price of their survival was the death of their loved ones and fellow Jews. (Ibid., p. 246)

Garwood considers that in these circumstances, "*self blame* and consequential guilt were almost inevitable":

> It is my view that '*survivor self blame*' had the [...] principal function of reducing the pain and anguish of intolerable powerlessness in the face of annihilation risk and overwhelming loss. Being forced to be totally passive and helpless in the face of the Holocaust was perhaps the most devastating experience for the survivor. (Ibid.)

In Garwood's thinking, self-blame and guilt are intimately connected. It is his contention that for survivors, self-blame (and its corollary of guilt) forms a barrier against feeling feelings which would otherwise be intolerable: the painful losses of loved ones, coupled with the memory of "the overwhelming feelings of powerlessness and annihilation fears that were experienced at the time": a combination that, for many survivors, worked against the psychologically essential tasks of mourning and grief. Garwood links this to early infant states in which, he says, an infant's "early experience of annihilation threat and helplessness produces what may be described as primal agony, which [...] becomes hidden by infant amnesia." For Garwood, this acts as an essential background against which an individual's drive for action, sexual maturity, and procreation takes place, psychically masking a primitive terror of impotence and annihilation through a very different experience of potency. Guilt, for Garwood, masks helplessness. In similar vein, Felicity de Zulueta cites Fairbairn's concept of guilt being used as a "moral defence":

> by blaming himself for what happened, the victim thus acquires some sense of control over his life rather than feeling totally helpless. The need to feel guilty rather than an impotent victim of destiny betrays how deeply we need to protect ourselves from feeling totally helpless, a state tantamount to psychological annihilation. (de Zulueta, 2006, p. 26)

In Chapter Three, I discussed the relationship of the quite-evident anger which most ordinary Jews feel about the Holocaust to the experience of helplessness and powerlessness. If Garwood's as well as de Zulueta's thesis holds, guilt is also part of this equation. Garwood is compelling in communicating the primitive "agony" that will have been exposed in survivors' real-life experiences of ghetto and death-camp terror:

> The power and effect in later life of this neonatal experience have been underestimated. Permanent loss, bereavement, is a psychic trauma which forces us to confront our mortality and thus resurrects these earliest instinctual annihilation anxieties. This gives grief its extraordinary psychic power. Thus loss, powerlessness and annihilation anxiety are instinctually and psychically linked. [...] Self-blame and consequential guilt, though still causing great psychic pain, are less emotionally painful, anxiety-provoking and overwhelming than powerlessness. They create a self-empowering

> omnipotent phantasy which presupposes responsibility and the power, ability and possibility to exercise it. (Garwood, 1996, p. 247)

Certain schools of psychotherapy consider that guilt is retroflected anger: that is, anger that is directed back against oneself when it is not possible to express it (or act on it) outwardly. It must be assumed that all survivors experienced intense rage over what they had gone through and what they had lost, though this seldom appears in survivor narratives. Amongst ordinary Jews, anger can be more freely felt and expressed; but there is a dilemma: anger towards whom? And to what end? The expectation that something ought to be able to be *done* can easily slide into a helpless, anxious guilt: *what* can be done?

Garwood talks about the extreme difficulty, for anyone who did not directly experience the Holocaust, of grasping its impact on those who did:

> The experiences of the survivors are unimaginable. Even if the survivor's suffering is graphically described, the listener's self-protective conscious and unconscious defences prevent them subjecting themselves to that degree of suffering. (Ibid., p. 244)

Ordinary Jews in the post-war generation in most countries where survivors and displaced Jews went to live after the war were in an ambivalent position. They could, if they chose to and if a survivor wanted to speak, listen; yet, as Garwood suggests, they will also have experienced an instinctive concern to protect themselves from hearing about material which must stir up intense anxiety. Steinberg, for one, describes people's reactions to him on his return to France graphically:

> The family and friends I came home to stopped up their ears. Those who could avoid me fled. (Steinberg, 2001, p. 158)

Feelings of anger about what they heard would leave ordinary Jews in a state of powerless inaction to make anything better; while their "self-protective conscious and unconscious defences" against being exposed to any more would lead them to abandon the sufferer. In both cases, some degree of guilt would be bound to ensue.

I think it is some kind of paralysis of guilt that partly answers Weissman's question, "Why?" (which I discussed in the Introduction). What fuels people's "fantasies of witnessing", their apparently illogical desire to "get close" to what happened to Jews in the war, as though they could vicariously experience it? The illusion of action, the fantasy that one can act to do "something" even when meaningful or reparative action is patently impossible, defends one against a guilt-inducing paralysis. A number of my interviewees spoke of being haunted by a question along the lines of "What would I have done?" or "What would I do?"

GIDEON: "Sometimes when I get very upset about things which happen here I think, 'What would I do if there was strong anti-Semitism [...] in Britain, what would I do—would I go on the rampage?'"

RICHARD: "One of the questions I ask myself again and again is, 'What would I have done in 1933?' Would I have closed my eyes, would I have wanted to believe? Or would I have said, 'Fuck this, I'm out'? I don't know [...]. Do I [also] have some guilt about being untouched by it?"

PEARL: "I can see it so clearly in my mind. [...] I can see them getting on ... being pushed on to this horrible train, and did they know? They didn't show in their faces at that time. And did they know when they were told to have a shower? I could live that with them. But ... I don't know how I would ... well, I would have just done as I was told. I was always an obedient child."

MEMBER OF GROUP DISCUSSION: "I don't think anyone is sure what they would have done if they were in the position of their parents or grandparents in the ghettos or in the work camps."

Such wonderings reflect, I suggest, a real effort to engage with feelings of guilt through identifying with the victims; but in so doing, they simultaneously bring people up against their own powerlessness. It is noteworthy that each of these self-challenges is couched in terms of "doing": that is, that they presuppose for the thinker some possibility of action. "What would I have *done*?" It is almost impossible to place oneself imaginatively in the position of total powerlessness: the "primal agony" of which Garwood speaks is simply too terrifying to re-experience, however unconsciously. Only Pearl identifies with a passive acceptance; but Pearl's own life has been completely overshadowed by the depressive impact of her early feelings of guilt and powerlessness, so she is in a good position to recognise its deadly effect:

> "I was so guilty, well ... that [I]'d lived. [My mother] actually told me she [...] tried to get rid of me. [...] To be told that you might have been destroyed ... I don't know what effect that had on me, I really don't know. [...] She ... used to say in Yiddish, 'You call this a life?!' [...] I did my utmost to help her. That's what seemed so important. [...] I had no thought of being able to help in any other way but physical, you know? Mainly shlepping, as my friends would say, shlepping the shopping. [...] I don't think any of us did enough for Mama, but I don't think any of us could do enough for Mama.
>
> I [went] to see my first psychiatrist because I was unwell and nobody could figure out why. [...] One of the first things he said [was], 'You've got to stop being your mother's good little girl'. [...]
>
> I've often thought about suicide. [...] I would imagine that I am a depressive and I am on anti-depressants. [...] I have this terrible guilt. [...] I suppose it's lived with me ever since ... well, I probably felt guilty at being born [...]. My mother had such a burdensome ... life that ... I couldn't blame her for not wanting any more children ... [But it] wasn't a clever thing to do, to tell me."

To speak of ordinary Jews' feelings of guilt in these bleak terms—envy, resentment, desperation to avoid feelings of powerlessness—is to make no moral judgement. Rather it is a comment on the intolerability of what any Jew faces when thinking about the Holocaust. If any single thing separates survivors from ordinary Jews, it is the fact that survivors had to find ways of tolerating the intolerable. Ordinary Jews have a degree more choice over how much of this intolerable experience to confront; while non-Jews who have no connection to the Holocaust's perpetration have greater freedom still. All the Jews I interviewed, even when their family background meant they had no association whatsoever to Europe, acknowledged some feeling of connectedness to the Holocaust. If some Jews "can't go near it", it is because the confusion of personal experiences and communal identifications that it touches is too great for most "ordinary" people to bear. We may simply feel guilty for our sense of betrayal.

One thing that connects these different aspects of guilt—whether envy or the paralysing terror of powerlessness—is that both have the characteristic of being unspeakable. If shame demands invisibility, guilt cannot be spoken. We suffer in silence, afraid of being condemned should we speak out about our actions, our failures, or our inner feelings. Many survivors never spoke about their experiences. Those who did do so needed courage and commitment, as Ruth saw:

> "I read in the *Jewish Telegraph* that a few years ago he [Reverend Levy][12] wrote that he had felt a compelling need to talk about his past ... [... partly] for the sake of history and future educational needs. But the more he did this, the more the nightmares affected him."

In the last part of this section on guilt I turn to certain events that particularly affected British Jews. Although these are a relatively small part of this very large Jewish story, they have a significance in their own right. They poignantly illustrate how the over-arching story of, and reaction to, the Holocaust could impact on the individual lives of ordinary Jews through complicating personal grief and guilt. The way in which such experiences work in the depths of our psyche also suggests a more shared motif amongst ordinary Jews: one which, whether we are consciously aware of it or not, is likely to stir disquieting feelings of guilt.

"All so sad ..."

When the war broke out in 1939, my father and each of his three brothers were almost immediately involved. My father and his second oldest brother joined the army; the third brother was deployed into intelligence; and the oldest, who had followed in the family tradition of cabinet-making, was assigned to a reserved occupation constructing and repairing aircraft. He was dispatched to Filton on the outskirts of Bristol; consequently he, his wife, and their two young children rented a house nearby in the small, safer, historic city of Bath.

In 1940 the Blitz began and my uncle suggested to his, by then elderly, parents that they should send the two youngest of the family, both sisters, away from London to Bath so as to be safe from air raids. Cissie, aged twenty-two, and Rita, seventeen, both went to stay in a hostel; after a while they moved out to digs with different families.

On 26 April 1942, the Luftwaffe bombed Bath. As an "open" city, Bath had no air-raid defences and was completely exposed. Many died and there was extensive destruction, but my uncle, his family, and both my aunts all lived. Deeply alarmed, my uncle tried to persuade the two sisters to go and stay with him and his family in case of further attack, as there was an air raid shelter outside their house. Rita, the youngest, did so, but Cissie stayed in her own digs as she was expecting her digs-mate to return from London and couldn't get word to her. The Luftwaffe returned on 27 April; the house in which Cissie was staying took a direct hit, and Cissie, her friend Kitty, and the entire family whose lodgers they were, were all killed. Rita describes how:

> "the following morning, my brother went to Wells Street and was gone for ages. When he returned, his face was ashen, and his hands were raw from trying to remove the pile of debris that was all that was left of the house."

Three decades later, my uncle hanged himself.

Until I spoke to Faye, I had thought that this was simply a private event in my family: tragic and haunting, but with no wider ramifications. Quite how the subject came up in my conversation with Faye, I have no recollection: but to our mutual, and considerable, surprise her family contained an almost identical story: a young aunt, a bombing, a death, a subsequent suicide:

> "My mum was evacuated with her only sister in 1939 but came back to London in 1940 as they were so unhappy. My mum was fourteen and her sister eight. In 1940 my mum's sister was killed in a raid at home in the East End of London. She was with the cleaning lady (who survived). My mum and grandmother were not there. It was never really spoken about.
>
> My grandmother died by [...] taking an overdose [...] in 1963. On the rare occasions my mother has spoken about it she was very bitter. She felt her grandmother blamed my grandmother. There was certainly the feeling that my grandmother [the mother of the child who died] did not get the comfort she deserved from her family after this tragedy. All so sad ..."

In World War Two Europe, Britain was unique in being at the frontline of the war whilst never occupied. The war was partly fought out in mutual destruction through bombing raids, and civilian casualty rates were exceedingly high. Ordinary British Jews, no less than the general population, died: deaths less comprehensively horrifying than the systematic programmes of degradation and horror to which European Jews were subjected, but deaths nonetheless.[13] And all painful, traumatic losses need to be mourned.

To write about these events as I have ("my uncle hanged himself") may provoke a puzzled, even an outraged, question: "What is the relevance of this to the Holocaust?" That is partly the point: for the Holocaust tends to overshadow "more ordinary" Jewish experience to such an extent that the latter can almost become delegitimised.[14] My aunt and Faye's were ordinary war victims: victims of Hitler, but not of the Holocaust, yet their deaths still had a huge impact on our respective families, most particularly on the individuals who felt most responsible for what had happened. Faye is of the view that these isolated but by no means uncommon "ordinary" war casualty deaths embody a way in which the Holocaust actively impacted on ordinary Jewish people and families hundreds of miles away. It is perfectly possible to envisage the scenario. Two ordinary deaths in air raids, two years apart, in different places. Two families devastated. But the war was not over and air raids—and deaths—continued, right up until the end of the war.[15] The time to grieve fully would be afterwards. But even before "after" had begun, Belsen was liberated and the harsh, dreadful news began to arrive. Millions of Jews had been wiped out, in conditions too horrible to contemplate. The impulse to pour out grief, rage, guilt, at the painful loss of two loved daughters and sisters would, in Faye's view, have been stifled, if not by an explicit injunction, certainly an internalised one. The "smallness" of such families' own losses would have paled into insignificance in the face of the enormity of the Holocaust. To speak of their own feelings of guilt over their personal loss would be to risk incurring another guilt at speaking of something ostensibly so small in comparison with something so large. "It was never really spoken about." For two particular individuals, burdened by their feelings of responsibility, the consequences of such suppression were personally disastrous.

There is another relevance. Premature and sudden death, especially ones which take place in violent and horrible circumstances, tend to "freeze" the lost ones in the psychic landscape of those who live on, so that those who died become fixed in memory more for how they died than for how they lived. I know this about my aunt. At the age of five, I knew her mainly as the one who was "killed in an air raid", and she stayed this way in family memory for nearly five decades until a series of accidental events prompted Rita to recall her—to bring her back to life—as a personality in her own right: "the only child of a large family who was not the least bit academic [...]; the qualities she had were kindness, sweetness, generosity, and a heart of gold." To forget the life and living qualities of someone, or a community of people, that they lived before their awful death, and only to remember how they died, is a form of double killing; unconsciously, that becomes a complicit action for which we may well feel guilty. The paradoxical "identification with the aggressor", even when consciously we tend to see ourselves (if anything) as identified with the victims, has a certain reality: our preoccupation with the manner in which people died threatens to render invisible, to continue to kill, what they meant in life.

Ordinary Jews have a dilemma here. So near-total was the Nazis' programme of annihilation, additionally complicated by the post-war politics of Communism in Eastern Europe, that re-engagement with the lives European Jews lived before the war has seemed next to impossible. We do not quite know whom or what we are to remember, or how. Efforts are increasingly made to recover names or to reconstruct histories,[16] and this at least opens up the possibility of mourning for, appreciating of, who and what was lost.[17] Without this, we run the risk of fixing ourselves in a permanent state of inveighing about "the Holocaust", its perpetrators and colluders, whilst consigning to the dustbin of history not only the individuals whom we never knew who actually died, but the living, changing history of our common heritage.

"Shame is inherent in the formation of self"

> Shame is a normal, probably universal, human phenomenon, where one's own experience (inner) and the Other's view (outer) invariably meet. (Wright, 1991, p. 29)

Modern psychotherapeutic writing tends towards the idea that shame is at the heart of trauma. This idea derives from a growing insight that shame is inseparable from the development of self and each person's subsequent experience of himself *as* a self. Thus experiences which take the form of violations of or attacks on the self disturb at the most primitive (early) levels each person's sense of his or her own being, and as such are likely to be deeply traumatising. Certainly shame seems to predate all other human emotional experience, an occurrence paralleled in Jewish tradition. In Genesis, the first book of the Torah, shame is the first human emotion that is unambiguously mentioned, echoing the idea that it is embedded in the deepest part of our psyche. Genesis Chapter Two describes the newly formed Adam and Eve, in their innocent state, as "both naked, the man and his wife, [yet …] not ashamed". However, as soon as they have eaten of the forbidden fruit of the tree of knowledge, "the eyes of both of them were opened, and they knew that they *were* naked" (Genesis 2, verse 5). Thus Genesis refers to the rise of human consciousness of self—a consciousness which in itself cannot be separated from the human capacity to feel shame. The story of the garden of Eden and Adam and Eve's expulsion from it is a striking metaphor for human awakening to itself. The paradisaical state in which everything is provided for man clearly denotes the idyllic state of merger that is the infant's earliest experience with his or her mother. The "expulsion" from this state expresses the infant's gradual awareness, as yet preverbal, that there is a self and there is an Other, and that the encounter between the two is not always pleasurable: a very early stage in life which Margaret Mahler called "the psychological birth of the human infant" (Mahler, Pine, & Bergman, 1975).

Many psychoanalysts begin their explorations of shame with Genesis and with good reason, for the story encapsulates aspects of the most primitive part of human psychology. Genesis tells us of our anxiety as to how we are seen; it deals with our instinctive need to hide (protect) that which is most intimate and private about ourselves; and it refers to the relational context in which awareness of self, self in relation to other, self as seen by other, and its inherent potential for shame, takes place. For Adam and Eve, to be seen as who they are by the disapproving eye of God is terrifying. Expulsion from Eden represents the painful alienation from a contented, unconscious enjoyment of oneself. It also opens the way to human growth.

Because shame is so embedded in our psychological lives, it holds an almost polar position in our emotional landscape. Any event anywhere that touches, however distantly, on our sense of identity is likely to refer almost magnetically to this early emergence of self. Shame thus cannot fail to be a reference point in our conscious or unconscious relating to the Holocaust and to images associated with the Holocaust, even though, as ordinary Jews, we will never have been directly exposed to the extremes of degradation that victims and survivors underwent. There is something inherently shaming for Jews about the Holocaust because it touches with particular acuteness sensitivities that are bound up with our sense of identity *as* Jews. To be Jewish is to inhabit a self that is partially determined by "Jewishness". However understood, those who are born and have grown up as Jews can no more disavow their Jewishness than someone born and bred English or French can deny their Englishness or Frenchness. It is part of the family and community matrix in which we have grown: an identity that the toxic images of ourselves beamed back to us in "the Holocaust" profoundly attack.

In psychoanalysis, shame is understood as being intrinsically related to the development of self. Every individual is a unique self living in a world of Others through whom and with whom he or she must discover, validate, and express his own true identity. Mollon, for example, says:

> Since our sense of self is formed in the context of relationship with others, involving the capacity to envisage oneself in the eyes of the other […], it follows that shame is inherent in the formation of the self. (Mollon, 2002, p. 11)

while Wright talks of the way in which:

> shame forces into awareness some aspect of oneself that one had not realized, and can therefore enlarge self-awareness and give a clearer sense of one's own identity. (Wright, 1991, p. 30)

In this way of thinking, shame is an inevitable consequence of the encounter with "the Other". At the earliest stages of infant development this is a *necessary* encounter with the Other in the form of the mother, in whose eyes and facial responses the infant first experiences himself as someone "seen": seen either with a love and responsiveness which affirms the infant as a valued and cherished self; or with blankness, even hostility, an experience which communicates to the infant the very opposite about himself. Many writers speak of the concrete physicality of face and eyes in these early encounters, indicating how, right from the start of our lives, shame is intimately tied to being in someone else's gaze and the internal experience of *being seen*:

> When the mother looks into the baby's eyes, what the mother "looks like is related to what she sees there", and because the mother from the beginning holds her baby in mind as a whole person, the baby who looks into the mother's face "sees himself or herself". When this necessary mirroring communication does not take place, however, such babies "look and they do not see themselves". [...] [O]ne crucial component [of the structure and experience of self] concerns the sense of who one is for the other. (Mollon, op cit., p. 10, citing Winnicott)

> The mother's face is still here, but no longer as the sun that shines and warms. Her look is cold, and she stands at a distance; she looks *at* me, and the stark outlines of a visual form, the spectre of myself as she sees me, haunts the space between us and holds us apart. (Wright, op. cit., p. 24)

Mollon and others consider that a crucial consequence of the experience of being "looked at" in a distant or unempathic way is a "splitting" of the self, between the self as "subject" and the self as "object". When the self is experienced as a subject, one is an "I" at the centre of one's own experience, relationally engaged with another "I" in a process of mutual enjoyment and discovery. When the self is experienced as an object, however, one is no longer an "I" but has become an "it". "I" is outside the "it" looking at it, with contempt, judgement, disgust or derision. These separations (or, as Mollon calls them, alienations from self) are common to all conscious experiences of embarrassment: one is simultaneously conscious of oneself and self-judging, as though looking on oneself from outside. A common example in relatively benign conditions is its manifestation as nervousness, even panic, when called upon to answer a question in class or to give a talk in public. It is a state of acute dysphoria.

This "shame-ridden state of being an object for the other" (Mollon, op. cit., p. 44) was central to experience in the camps quite simply because Jews *were* objects for others. In Nazi eyes all camp prisoners were more-or-less contemptible "objects" to be used, but in Nazi typology Jews were at the bottom of the heap. Depending on the nature of the camp, most Jews were condemned to death straight away; some were selected for their temporary usefulness; none had any intrinsic value. It is arguable that one of the qualities that enabled some people to survive (and all survivors emphasise that luck was the over-riding factor in their survival) was some retained capacity to exist as an "I", the subject in one's own life. The "*Musulmänner*" whom Levi describes could not survive because they had already disappeared as subjects: they had become "its", "the drowned, [...] an anonymous mass [...] of non-men [...], the divine spark [already] dead within them" (Levi, 1987, p. 96).

But a crucial factor in shame is *self*-consciousness. Whilst in the camps, the moment-by-moment imperative to survive—to stay upright during hours-long roll-calls, to find ingenious ways of securing more bread, to find shelter from the elements—suppressed virtually all other considerations. It was only once the experience was over that survivors had the possibility and space to look back, and this almost certainly explains why, as Levi and others attest, feelings of shame and self-disgust arose *after* liberation rather than during the camp experience itself, once there was space and time to recover a sense of the selves they were, rather than the ones that the camp experience had forced them to become. It is this seeing oneself *as though* through another person's eyes that is the hallmark of shame. Nor was this only an experience for camp survivors in the Holocaust. A study of Jewish children separated from their parents and hidden (for their own survival) in wartime Belgium also reveals that, when the now-adult children began decades later to recover the early trauma of these experiences of parental separation, some also experienced overwhelming feelings of shame and guilt (Fohn & Hehnen-Wolff, 2010).

This sense of oneself as an "object", a state which we all share to some degree or other, is highly pertinent to the final part of this chapter, that of the way, of necessity, we have to relate to the Holocaust through images. I shall turn to this theme shortly. Before I do so I consider another core aspect of shame which Mollon discusses: namely, the association between shame and passivity.

"The submissiveness of the weak"

In reflecting on the relationship between guilt and shame, Mollon highlights a key difference between them.[18] Guilt, he thinks,

> seems to be felt in response to harmful or prohibited actions or phantasies of such actions. These are often of an aggressive nature.

> Shame, by contrast, is often to do with failures to do what is expected, and is associated with feelings of weakness. Aggression and guilt may be preferentially highlighted as a defence against feelings of weakness and shame—on the basis that it is better to feel strong and bad rather than weak. [...] [A] major component of the developing organization of the self is the transformation of passive experience into a more active mode—to do actively what was once suffered passively and thereby move from helplessness and shame to guilt. (Mollon, 2002, pp. 28–29)

A connection between passivity and shame forms the central thesis of Ronit Lentin's study, *Israel and the Daughters of the Shoah*. Lentin is an Israeli-born member of a family of Holocaust survivors whose concern is the way (as she sees it) the state of Israel structured a particular social discourse around the Holocaust ("Shoah") which was silencing of, and stigmatising towards, Holocaust survivors and their children. Lentin's book draws from the testimony of a number of women who were daughters of survivors, and it forms a study of the way in which Israeli social consciousness and political strategies have flowed out of the deeply felt shame which the Holocaust has triggered in this self-identified Jewish country:

> The young Israeli state constructed itself in opposition to the passivity implied in the discourse of Jewish victims allegedly 'going to their death like lambs to the slaughter.' It met Shoah survivors upon their return from the Nazi hell with silence [...]. (Lentin, 2000, p. 10)[19]

Crucial to Lentin's argument is her interest in women's experiences in the Holocaust, for she sees Israel as having constructed for itself a stereotypical "male" and "heroic" identity as a reaction against the supposedly "weak" and passive diaspora. In this latter association it was her interviewees who were left to experience the devastating effect of shame:

> Nava Semel speaks of [...] the shame involved in having been less than the Israeli male heroic stereotype. (Ibid., p. 108)

In Israel this shame was associated above all else with Holocaust survivors, to the extent that their children were disparaged—even humiliated—if their parents had retained their original Yiddish or German names:

> "A woman whose name was Yael Horovitz enlisted on the same day as I did. She was given exactly three minutes to change her name. [...] I felt as if they stripped her naked. [...] [It's like] this terrible process of stripping, when they tear off your clothes and dress you with something else. [...]" (Ibid., p. 50)
>
> "[some teachers] would mock my name [Friedlander] to a point that I really hated [it] and it took me years to understand that it's a ... respectable name like any other, that one didn't have to feel ashamed of it. They said, 'What is it, this diaspora name? What is it, a German name? Are you from Germany?' And the association was immediately the Nazis." (Ibid., p. 92)

Lentin postulates that the newly formed Israeli state saw in the Holocaust such a shaming image of European Jews passively going to their deaths that, in its need to create an image of an altogether different kind of Jew to embody the spirit of the new state, it systematically disparaged Holocaust survivors and their pre-Israeli lives while simultaneously constructing an alternative image of Jews as heroic and strong. "Israel", says Lentin, "was constructed on the repression of memory" of the Holocaust, so as to substitute for the annihilated diaspora "a new [Israeli] identity" (ibid., pp. 50, 51). This new identity was intentionally based on the notion of "*gvurah*", a word that best translates as "heroism".

Lentin's argument reaffirms the way in which Simon (Chapter One) saw Holocaust trauma enacted subsequently in Israel. The implication is that Israel (or its then leaders) identified particularly with the way in which Jewish men were rendered impotent and helpless during the Holocaust, and therefore acted to conceal and compensate for the shame and pain this triggered. Lentin particularly emphasises how perceptions of the humiliation of fathers in their role as protectors of their families fed through into a reworking of "maleness". As a result Israel promoted a culture that emphasised strength and a certain kind of militaristic "heroism" whilst scorning qualities they derided as "passive":

> "The only heroism Israelis valued was armed resistance, but survivors often felt that merely surviving was heroic." (Ibid., p. 120)

Echoing Lentin's thesis in fictional form is S. Yizhar's novella, *Khirbet Khizeh*. Published in 1949 by a former intelligence officer in the Israeli army during the War of Independence, this novella focuses on the forcing out of Arab residents from their village in 1948. The author contrasts the culturally dominant "strong" form of heroism with another, one perhaps less palatable but to him at least as powerful, and one which to the post-Holocaust reader is painfully evocative of the circumstances of the murdered millions:

> Those sights, screams that were screamed and that were not screamed, the confused innocence of dazed sheep, the submissiveness of the weak, and their heroism, that unique heroism of the weak who didn't know what to do and were unable to do anything, the silenced weak [...]. (Yizhar, 2011, pp. 109–110)

Lentin argues that in its formation Israeli culture was driven by shame-ridden associations with diaspora, particularly European, Jewish identity. In its efforts to hide from such feelings, the culture fostered an alternative image of Jews, but it could only do this by marginalising actual lived Holocaust experience with its real-life forms of survival, and other forms of experience which did not "fit". Lentin sees Israel as having constructed an antithetical split between Israeli Jewish identity and diaspora identity: a split which required passivity to be located with the diaspora while Israel appropriated for itself more potent definitions of heroism and courage.

Lentin's book provides a cogent description of how collective trauma can work in a discrete population such as Israel, a newly founded state faced with particular pressures such as the need to form a culture sufficiently compelling for its new collective identity. In this explanation, events which are felt as deeply shaming and therefore traumatising, even though not experienced personally by a majority of the population, contain enough felt relevance to people's own past experience and sense of identity to percolate through the population and, in the case of shame, provoke the impulse to hide those very feelings. A state has power to emphasise particular cultural values through its organisation and messages; thus collective behaviours set in, such as the deliberate (if unconscious) marginalisation (hiding) of survivor personal experience through cultivating a culture of silence. The traumatic shame becomes the domain of the silenced, and even while the population at large may talk in vague terms about "the trauma of the Holocaust", they repress the specificity of its shamefulness in their collective psyche.

"The Holocaust evokes shame, because shame was already there"

It is not easy to discuss shame without some reference to sexuality. Even Genesis makes the connection explicit. Adam and Eve's shame is felt by them specifically in relation to their sexual being, the exposure to view of their genitalia: that which, amongst other things, makes them not only different from each other but capable of an autonomous and exclusive engagement with each other. The Genesis story reflects the fact that before all other influences on the formation of self, whether family, religion, or culture, from the moment of birth we are defined by our gender and our sexuality. For most of us, it is an immutable part of who we are. The experience and expression of self that shame reflects back on us is therefore inseparable from our sexual sense of self.

In relation to what is evoked in ordinary Jews by the Holocaust, this is difficult territory to chart; in the absence of much interview material, I can only hazard guesses. I probably would not have ventured into this area at all had it not been for Richard, who was vehement in his view that shame of a sexually related kind was the pre-existing basis for Jewish trauma and therefore not separable from underlying feelings of shame stirred up by the Holocaust. For her part Lentin is also insistent that, over and above the way Israeli men (in her view) reacted to "the shame of the Holocaust", the sexual shame and humiliation of women in the Holocaust is a grievously marginalised subject in most Holocaust explorations, a marginalisation that adds to the intense feelings of shame that many women survivors already felt and which compounds that dimension of trauma in the shared unconscious. What cannot be spoken about or given voice in some creative form cannot be worked through. Thus there are indicators that this linked sexual dimension of shame and trauma is relevant to this study, even if the direction of travel is not entirely clear.

To Richard, there is an underlying culture of traumatic shame amongst Jews which he relates to the practice of circumcision of male infants. In his view the act of circumcision, at an age when there can be no question of the infant's consent, places Jewish males virtually from birth in the place of victim, an archetypal state which he sees as deeply embedded in the Jewish psyche:

> "The whole thing on circumcision [...] isn't directly related, but if you relate it through shame I can connect it to Auschwitz. [...] [Circumcision is] utterly traumatic, the child does not understand this. [...] If you circumcise a Jewish boy, what you're doing is telling him ... [...] I reckon the way the Jewish identity is so strong is through circumcision. It's like a brand [...]: you can't put the piece back. That's you forever a Jew, through something which has been taken away from you with a knife. That actually is traumatic. [Shame is] evoked by circumcision, which actually means that it's there, which is why you're available for Holocaust. [...] Of course [the Holocaust] evokes shame, because shame was already there."

For Jews this is a highly controversial position, and one which Howard completely refuted:

> "I don't know much about it so my responses are entirely ill-informed, but they're also entirely contemptuous. [...] I distrust that anybody can actually know what their feelings or response or reaction was; there is so much back-editing of 'what I think I probably would have felt' [...]. I don't trust it. I don't believe that small babies are yet sufficiently coherently formed, mentally, emotionally, interactionally, that their responses have any direct consequence long term."

Nevertheless, there was, quite independently, an echo of Richard's feelings in Caroline's. Like Richard, Caroline only has sons; like him, she chose at the time not to have her sons circumcised, although her reasons were different and her ideas have changed:

> "I've married someone who's not Jewish [and] I'm not religious. [...] My first son was born in France and if I had wanted him to be circumcised my husband would have agreed to it; but I didn't. I wasn't religious and the image that immediately came to mind was Nazis lowering boys' trousers to see if they were circumcised and if they were Jews. I thought, 'It's unfair, why should I brand my son when it didn't matter?' I thought it didn't matter to me. I'm not going to

> transmit the religion to him, I'm not going to bring him up Jewish, why should I brand him and possibly put his life in danger? It was only when I moved to the States where they have a completely different attitude and circumcision is done routinely for health reasons and not for religious reasons that I realised you can have a different approach to it. Had I known at the time, I think I would have circumcised my sons. [...]
>
> So would you say I've been traumatised? Yes, maybe—because that was my reaction."

Caroline does not mention the word "shame", and she is also considering the question of trauma from her own perspective, not that of her sons. Richard is considering both, and he will certainly be able to identify more particularly with his sons because he is male. However, Richard also observes that a critical dimension of this "primitive" trauma is the response of the infant boy's parents at the time of the procedure:

> "I gave a talk against circumcision to eighty Jews [...] and they kept attacking me. [...] After about five attacks [they stopped]. Then the women [started to speak] and said, 'I wouldn't let a knife go to any other part of my child, why should I let that happen?' 'I prayed for a girl so I wouldn't have to make the decision.'
>
> I went to one of these *mila*, or *brit*, and I watched, and all the men closed their eyes."[20]

Whether or not the physical act of circumcision is a trauma for an eight-days-old male infant, it seems not unlikely that it evokes deeply ambivalent feelings in the parents, as both Caroline and Richard have commented. In psychoanalytic thinking, one of the key issues associated with shame is the way it arises in the earliest interactions between mother and infant. A mother burdened by a sense of guilt (albeit subsequent relief) at the physical act of a knife being taken to her newborn infant is at this level of her being already compromised in the joy and pleasure she takes in her son and will subtly communicate this to him. Both parents are caught in a double-bind. The ritual condition for a Jewish male to belong within Judaism and the Jewish community is that of being circumcised, a procedure in which the parents' pride is also fraught with anguish. Being Jewish comes at a cost.

There is no equivalent ritual for girls in Judaism, which leaves certain gaps in Richard's argument that these circumstances create an underlying condition of shame for all Jews. However, the fact that circumcision is inflicted on the Jewish male's penis, his sexual organ, raises important questions as to the symbolic meanings a boy or man may subsequently give to this form of ritualised exposure and its association with an inherent helplessness to change a given condition of one's identity. This relates to the way in which menstruation is regarded in traditional Judaism: it is seen as unclean, requiring monthly purification before any sexual contact or even any physical contact with a man can take place. Thus from the moment an orthodox girl reaches the age of puberty and begins to menstruate, she is exposed to the message that her attainment of conscious sexuality is tainted. She must keep her menstruation, her sexuality, hidden from the gaze of men. By no means unique to Judaism, such traditions ensure that certain aspects of oneself connected with sexuality are associated from the outset with shame.

All these associations turn on questions to do with exposure; with being seen as flawed in some way that one is helpless to change (the given nature of one's body); with being seen not as a whole "subject" to be loved in entirety but as a series of part-objects (one's penis, one's menstrual blood) which are unacceptable in the eyes of the community and therefore of one's parents. They are all shame-ridden, and as Richard suggests, potentially provide fertile ground not only for shaming *experiences* but for shaming *associations*. For Lentin points out that there was a duality of sexual shame connected to the Holocaust: a duality which was both physical and symbolic. Men and women equally were routinely stripped and paraded naked. However, while men were commonly beaten, women were physically subjected to rape, sexual abuse, enforced prostitution, and medical experimentation inflicted deliberately on their reproductive organs: assaults which were also catastrophically emotional in impact. Men's sexuality was attacked symbolically, through their being rendered impotent in their emotionally vital capacity to stand up for themselves and to protect their women and families. These are powerful emotional triggers for ordinary Jews, whether men or women. In our, ordinary Jewish, ambivalent relationship with the Holocaust, we are both exposed to descriptions and images of these experiences and simultaneously keen to avoid them, because our inner identifications with them are so painful.

Hannah Holtschneider considers that there is something extremely problematic about the way we "receive" material about the Holocaust and the way it then conditions our responses. As she points out, the vast majority of the actual images we see of the Holocaust, received through books, documentaries, and in museums, are photographs or film taken by and from the vantage point of the perpetrators.[21] Inevitably, the Jews we see in those photographs are reduced to *nothing more than* the status of victims: victims, moreover, filmed in the very state of their own humiliation. They are images of Jews naked and about to be shot, like the one Janina Struk discussed in a *Guardian* article in 2004: rounded up in ghettos; in camps dressed in striped pyjamas, their gaunt faces staring out at us from behind barbed wire fences (Struk, 2004). In her preliminary study of Holocaust Memorial Museums, Holtschneider suggests that:

> How the Nazis conceptualised Jews is a powerful structuring device for Holocaust exhibitions whose master narrative follows perpetrator history and the impact of the actions of the victimizers on the victims. [...] [V]ictims' reactions to persecution are slotted into this master narrative as illustrative devices, not having any structuring authority of their own (Holtschneider, 2007, p. 91)

and:

> the victims become victims because they are identified as Jews by the Nuremberg Laws, and Nazi racist categories thereby become the vehicle for portraying Jews [...]. By allowing Nazi categories to control the narrative unchallenged, the possibilities of understanding the victims' lives and deaths from their own perspectives are severely curtailed. (Ibid., p. 93)

What this implies is that when we look at such images (or contemplate them in our imaginations) we are looking at those Jews as Others, as "objects" whose lives have not only been divested of all dignity but of all meaning other than their status as victims and the manner of their dying; objects with whom we have an ambiguous relationship and towards whom our feelings are ambivalent. If, as ordinary Jews, we identify with them, we have to feel shame; if we disidentify, we must feel guilt, as Doris did:

> "Another thing I feel guilty about with the Holocaust, [is that] so many of the six million were Jewish people whom I wouldn't feel I totally identified with anyway. [...] ... they're totally different people. You see, it's the difficulty of identifying because they're different sorts of Jews from me."

But it is not only we who contemplate these images in the privacy of our own minds. These "objects" are on full display to the whole world. Alongside the grotesque and lethal caricatures contained in *The Protocols of the Elders of Zion*;[22] alongside Shylock, and Dickens's "the Jew" Fagin; alongside the current image of Jews as aggressive colonisers and occupiers; and alongside Nazi depictions of Jews as "vermin",[23] we also have to live with this image of ourselves as an ongoing inheritance. It is not one that can be entirely shame-free.

CHAPTER SIX

"So conflicted"

In the preceding chapters, I have been considering how trauma can be understood both as a personal and as a metanarrative amongst ordinary Jews contemplating the Holocaust. I have deconstructed trauma and looked at it through its clinically understood dimensions: for trauma is not "one thing" but is constituted by a multitude of experiences, feelings, and fantasies which interact with each other, giving rise in individuals to a complex, frequently indescribable, internal world for which the word "trauma" provides both a shorthand description and a starting point for exploring its living presence in someone's mind and soul. Although it cannot be assumed that the dimensions I have discussed fully represent trauma—as though it were ever possible fully to describe something which of its very nature is complex and subject to change—these dimensions have clinical validity. Trauma is, at least partly, composed from deeply painful loss; from anger that has no expectation of a constructive outcome; from fear, tied (often realistically) to an experience of helplessness, which together lock people into victim positions; from guilt as an unconscious attempted antidote to helplessness; and from shame, the earliest and most primitive form of self-abnegation. In various ways these aspects all emerged in the narratives of those whom I interviewed.

In these earlier chapters, I have been tracing how this very specific "Jewish" trauma, prompted by thoughts of the Holocaust, is experienced as traumatising at different levels. At one level, it activates experiences, sometimes only partly conscious or even unconscious, that are personal to each individual and that have nothing as such to do with the Holocaust. At another level it is traumatic in a collective sense: while the Holocaust symbolises and embodies experiences which are innate in all human beings, it also symbolises and embodies experiences that, transgenerationally transmitted and ready to be triggered by current circumstance, are more specifically tied to the condition of being Jewish. I distinguish between "symbolise" and "embody" intentionally: the Holocaust was undoubtedly an embodied, material event, and because it actually happened in all the horrific detail we know so much about, it has an exceptional power to represent in a symbolic sense all that is most chaotic, depraved, and terrifying in the human soul.

In this chapter, however, my focus shifts away from the detailed deconstruction of trauma per se and towards the subject that dominates Jewish post-Holocaust narrative like none other: that is, Israel. Israel, the state founded in the immediate aftermath of World War Two as a kind of compensation by the world to Jews for what they had suffered during the Nazi years, is far from being "just" a state. No country formed under conditions of such trauma can escape its impact, but Israel has laid a particular claim to it. Israel is the repository to varying degrees in its own mind, in the minds of Jews worldwide, and in the mind of the world at large, of vast amounts of hope, expectation, despair, and opprobrium, much of which sits in the context of the Holocaust past. It is impossible to think about the psychological impact that the Holocaust has had on ordinary Jews without also considering how—and why—the impact is transferred on to and into Israel. Such transference takes place partly in response to Israel's own deliberate agenda-setting, but partly also because post-Holocaust diaspora Jews have been presented with an unprecedented situation in which to reconsider who and what they are: a situation in which there is, for the first time in two millennia, a "Jewish state" or "a state for Jewish people" in the land historically associated with the founding of Judaism, and that, in consequence, fundamentally shifts the parameters by which diaspora Jews define who and what they are.

At various points in earlier chapters, I referred to ways in which particular dimensions of trauma might lead to a Jewish hope directed towards Israel. In Chapter Four, for example, I observed that Israel is explicitly viewed by many ordinary Jews as the one safe place they could go to if all else failed, a perception that clearly derives strength from what happened in Europe under the Nazis as virtually all countries were occupied, all escape routes closed, and Jews were trapped with no prospects other than a one-way ticket to Auschwitz. Edward clearly thinks this view of Israel as a safe refuge is decidedly optimistic in present circumstances. He describes Israel as "the most dangerous place in the world for Jews", and like many contemporary Jewish writers who share this view, is deeply critical of Israel's increasing intransigence towards Palestinians:

> "Shut up shop, we arm ourselves to the teeth against a hostile world, we encourage all Jews of the world to come here, but we don't allow Palestinians whose families lived in the area to come back. It's a profoundly pessimistic world view. I don't think it's done Jews any good either."

At the same time in Chapter Four, I suggested that Israel does not just act as the idea of an *actual* home but symbolises refuge in a much wider sense. Israel, I suggested, also sits in the psyche as a fantasy home, the home that all of us yearn for, where we can be safe, protected, wanted, and free from both external and internal persecutions. In this juxtaposition of outer and inner views of "home", Israel becomes doubly potent, and, in its inevitable failure to meet expectation, doubly disappointing.

In this chapter, I contemplate ordinary Jews' (post-Holocaust) position in relation to Israel with one main premise in mind. This concerns the psychological experience of conflict: more especially, conflict that is unresolved. Unresolved conflict, I will argue, is a hallmark of trauma. The continuing conflict, which is such a feature of Israel's present existence, is, I suggest, both a manifestation of Israel's unresolved state concerning its own Holocaust inheritance, and a condition which distracts diaspora Jews from freely exploring their own relationship with the Holocaust and their own future in a diaspora world in which the Holocaust happened. Both circumstances act to perpetuate a traumatic legacy.

Israel is indelibly associated in everyone's mind with a conflict that never finds resolution and over which the rights and wrongs are ceaselessly fought. In the eyes of certain commentators this external conflict is predicated on another, one innate to Israel's self-conception. Jacqueline Rose, for example, speaks of "the inner conflict that Israel has always had with itself" (Rose, 2005, p. 54). In this, Rose is referring to an internal tension arising from two radically different concepts of "Israel": Israel as the fount of Jewish spirituality and inspiration for Jewish life everywhere; and Israel as, simply and prosaically, a nation-state "like any other". Rose follows the thinking of key figures—Martin Buber, Hans Kohn, Ahad Ha'am, Hannah Arendt—all of whom wrote passionately about the development of Zionist thinking. She describes, for example, how Buber wrote in May 1948, shortly after the establishment of the state of Israel that:

> At the heart of Zionism [...] there is an "internal contradiction that reaches to the depths of human existence." Two notions of national rebirth. Both require a return to Palestine. But whereas one desires to become a "normal" nation with "a land, a language and independence", the other, outside political time, aims to restore the spirit. (Rose, op. cit., p. 70)[1]

"Today", Rose goes on to say, "David Grossman makes the same link as did Buber between inward and outer havoc" (ibid., p. 72).

The idea of there being a tension, a conflict, a contradiction, at the heart of Israel's formation, which plays out in the realm of the externally familiar conflict, is thus not new. What may be new is to see this as a crucial element in the way that Israel relates to the Holocaust, and by extension how the Jewish world outside Israel relates to both. Into the internal split between two notions of what Israel *is* or *is meant to be*, falls the Holocaust, along with its traumatic burden. As with the land itself, Israel's reaction to the Holocaust has become increasingly one of appropriation: to all intents and purposes, Israel has converted the Holocaust from being a tragedy shared by all Jews and with many layers of potentially unfolding significance, to something akin to national property. This radically affects the way in which others—Jews and non-Jews alike—might relate to the Holocaust.

Ordinary Jews express many conflicted feelings over Israel, and this has partly to do with the way in which our Holocaust past has become conflated with Israel's present. Israel's deterministic view of European history confuses ordinary Jews' capacity to seek their own "meanings" to the Holocaust; at the same time, it contaminates diaspora memory of the Jewish past in Europe. In line with Herzl's view that only a Jewish state could "solve" the problem of anti-Semitism, Israel has made a powerful effort to appropriate "the meaning" of the Holocaust as one which *only* leads to the founding and upholding of the state; but this places diaspora Jews in a very ambiguous position. The Holocaust implicitly posed questions as to what remained *of* the diaspora in Europe, but Israel now questions what remains *for* the diaspora: what it *may be* as well what it might do. Israel's self-positioning blurs distinctions between the Holocaust—a specific historic catastrophe particular to European (and Christian) history—and the State of Israel as one consequence of that tragedy, but by no means the only one. This shrouds the very real possibility that the Holocaust has a significance in its own right for those of us who continue to live in the diaspora and are part of the continuing unfolding of European and western history. When the Holocaust and Israel are collapsed into each other, two questions, two issues and two needs are treated as though they were one and the same. More fundamentally, this blurring distracts diaspora Jews from our own task of relating to the Holocaust as a diaspora event that belongs with us. Diaspora Jews have the right, indeed an obligation, to absorb the events of the Holocaust in their own way, as they continue to construct a diaspora future with its own life. Thus diaspora Jews, too, live in an unresolved conflict: not just about Israel and *its* future, but about the Holocaust, its implications for diaspora life, and who, or what, Israel is for us in determining that.

Conflict unresolved is inherently part of a traumatised state. We can see this even in the simple sense that military and civil conflicts perpetuate traumatic events: traumas continue in Israel (and amongst Palestinians) because there is a continuing, unresolved, and violent conflict. Woven into my thinking in this chapter, and to return to the theme of Chapter Two, is the connection between trauma and loss, and how trauma is perpetuated by the *failure to mourn*. Levy and Lemma think of trauma as a "perversion of loss": that at the heart of trauma lies a loss so painful that it has never been properly mourned, and it therefore sits in the unconscious enmeshed in unresolved and conflicted feelings; always ready to be provoked; never fully laid to rest. Trauma, loss, conflict, and mourning are all involved in ordinary Jews' complex emotional relationship with Israel.

A state of conflict

"Conflict" is seldom far from people's thinking in relation to Israel. Over the decades it has become the norm to refer to the state of affairs in which Israel resides in terms of a—or "the"—conflict: the "Arab–Israeli conflict", the "Israeli–Palestinian conflict", the "Middle East conflict". One has to consider whether this state of affairs is purely an external matter relating to an historically common-enough conflict over right to land, or whether it runs more deeply into a state of mind that is at war with itself. In 2008, former speaker of the Knesset Avraham Burg wrote of his "uneasy feeling" in relation to Israel's own psyche "that Israel will not know how to live without conflict" (Burg, 2008, p. 14). Burg prefaced this statement by speaking of how the conflict has come to permeate even the substance of his own language, creating in him two distinct psychic worlds: a potent illustration of the way in which language is never merely a neutral vehicle for expression but acts to shape and reinforce perceptions of reality:

> In Israel I live in one language, that of tensions and traumas, conflict and confrontation. Outside of Israel I use a different language, of building bridges, understanding, forgiveness and of concession. [...] As the years pass, the schism between the two languages I use deepens and tears me apart. [...] Israel accentuates and perpetuates the confrontational philosophy that is summed up in the phrase, "The entire world is against us." (Ibid.)

In this linguistic conflict, Burg cannot reconcile a split world in which trauma and conflict are disconnected from understanding and mutuality. Inside the country of his birth he experiences a deepening crisis: a *weltanschauung* in which there is little or no space for "Other", whether people or perspective. He could well have gone on to describe how such an orientation feeds both a continued state of defensiveness and a continued state of alert against potential intrusions by "an Other". The separation wall between Israel along with its settler areas in the West Bank, and Palestinian territories, is as much psychological as it is physical.

Burg is not the only Israeli Jew who feels a profound dismay at the corrosive psychic split which the relentlessly maintained external conflict engenders inside Israel. Speaking partly of the death of his son in the 2007 war in Lebanon, David Grossman, one of Israel's leading writers, declared that apart from the "horrible, outrageous waste" of the death of young people,

> no less horrible is the feeling that the state of Israel has, for many years now, criminally wasted not only the lives of its sons and daughters, but also the miracle that occurred here—the great and rare opportunity that history granted it, the opportunity to create an enlightened, properly functioning democratic state that could act in accordance with Jewish and universal values. A country that would be a national home and refuge, but not *only* a refuge. It would also be a place that would give new meaning to Jewish existence. A country in which an important, essential part of its Jewish identity, of its Jewish ethos, would be full equality and respect for its non-Jewish citizens. Look what happened. [...] When did we lose even the hope that we might someday be able to live different, better lives? (Grossman, 2007, quoted in Cooper, 2008, p. 190)

Grossman's passionate words reveal an anguished sense of betrayal and loss, an anguish which implicitly refers back to that "other" ideal of Zionism which Buber and others espoused. The "criminal" waste of "the miracle"; the betrayed hope that Israel would have become "a place that would give new meaning to Jewish existence", a meaning that Grossman identifies with an "essential [...] Jewish ethos" of "equality and respect"—these arouse in Grossman a profound conflict with the country of his birth: a country to which, notwithstanding, he still feels fully committed.

Much continues to be written, inside and outside Israel, on the impact of the Holocaust *within* Israel: on the way "the tragedy in Europe" (to quote Rose again) not only creates its own shadow in Israel's actions but seeps into Israel's inner self-beliefs and psychic positioning. Grossman, Oz, Lentin, Yarom, Folman are but some of the Israeli creative artists who engage in painful self-examination. Questioning naïve hopes that Israel per se can be the answer to anti-Semitism, they see Israel's continued disturbance and wonder whether blindly continuing down the same path can ever result in the peace and freedom from persecution that Israel ostensibly craves. Outside Israel, many Jewish writers focus their attention, too, on the disturbing paradox that Israel, created as a place where Jews could safely be Jews, seems not only to flout Jewish ethics but negates what they see should be intrinsic Jewish learning from two thousand years' experience of how to live successfully alongside "the Other". Reflecting on Grossman's words (above) and, no doubt, also on the venerated Babylonian Rabbi Hillel's "Golden Rule", "That which is hateful to you, do not do to your fellow",[2] Howard Cooper, a British Reform rabbi and psychotherapist, thinks of the

> Jewish religious perspective attuned to prophetic and, later, rabbinic Judaism's demand that justice be the guiding principle in the life of Israel. [...] Those who composed the canonical texts of the Torah made it the *sine qua non* of Jewish purpose: 'Justice, justice you shall pursue ...' (Deuteronomy 16:20a). Those of a genuinely religious disposition, those attuned to the spirit of historic Israel's prophetic consciousness, might say that, without adherence to the principles of justice, the Jewish people have no *raison d'être* and 'Israel' has no moral right to existence. (Cooper, 2008, pp. 185–186)

In *The Question of Zion*, Rose, like Lentin, ponders on the post-Holocaust shame-inheritance built into Israel's core structure that caused Israel so powerfully to reject its European past in favour of an heroic future, thus embedding, if not actually causing, a violent split in Israel's founding psyche (Rose, 2005, ch. 3). One might wonder whether it is really possible to jettison one part of the past (the traumatic pain) without equally throwing out that which, ideally, you would want to keep (the accumulated wisdom and its associated sustaining ethos). The psychic conflict in Israel thus acquires two layers: one between who and what Israel is to be in the world; and one over Israel's relationship with its own diaspora past. In Israel, both stay unresolved, and Israel's own trauma continues.

Here, I am less concerned with Israel's relationship with the shared Holocaust past than with how ordinary diaspora Jews feel about it. Yet the conflicts, the disturbance, the contradictions inside Israel cannot be confined to Israel itself. Worldwide, this small, identifiable community to which I and some fourteen million others belong is too interconnected for that. Many interviewees felt a gut kinship with Israel; it is "family":

CLIVE: "Countless Jews at the time of the '67 war suddenly realised viscerally that they had to support Israel. 'It's ours.' They felt strongly, 'It's family, you've got to connect'."

CAROLINE: "If we thought of Israel not as a country but as family ..."

DORIS: "I have what is obviously ... I can only say a tribal connection ... Everything that happens that I disapprove of, it's like your child misbehaving, you know what I mean, it's the family."

VICTOR: "Somehow or other, I'm associated."

Whether we feel the "tribal connection" strongly or weakly, most ordinary Jews have friends, family, or both living in Israel; like it or not, their fate is our concern. So, predictably, diaspora Jewish sentiments partly mirror those within Israel, reflecting a community torn between its own high ideals and aspirations, and the awfulness of grim realities past and present.

If the official organs of British Jewry are to be believed, the majority of ordinary British Jews embrace, or are assumed to embrace, a conformity to Israel's "orthodox" line about itself.[3] Such positions were, of course, represented amongst my interviewees; here seen first in Sonia's angry defensiveness, then in Leah's heroic fantasy.

For Sonia, the lesson of the Holocaust simply means that Israel is "absolutely necessary":

> "I'm ... absolutely in no doubt [...], staunchly supportive [...]. It was absolutely necessary to establish a place where the survivors of the Holocaust could go. Any thought of anyone refuting that evokes feelings of anger in me.
>
> It was absolutely necessary. From my understanding ... the host population wasn't prepared to work with us, they weren't prepared to work with Jews [...], they were given the opportunity to work with Jews and live and cohabit peaceably and unfortunately it wasn't to be, and the only alternative was for Jews to protect themselves and the rest is history, as they say, with the conflict and the segregation and the life as it is now. But ... absolutely Jews have a right to be in Israel, absolutely. They have a right really to be anywhere but they chose there, their homeland and [...] ... you only have to look at a map and see the tiny geographic area inhabited by Israel, surrounded by twenty-two hostile states, all rooting for its destruction, and then any normal balanced person, Jewish or not, should be able to see what's just and what's not."

Leah, too, is thinking about "the right to live as a Jew", but she identifies this with a right *to die*, heroically, as a Jew. Israel for her is associated with a Masada-like last-ditch stand, a fight to the end: the antithesis of what Jews caught up in the Holocaust were seriously able to do:

> "[I]t's Israel and anti-Israel that dominate my thinking at the moment and they're very linked up with the Holocaust and the question of survival. […] I keep saying to my husband, I want to go to Israel. I would rather die with my back against the wall fighting, than go down in some ridiculous pogrom, anti-Semitic attack."

Others take a diametrically opposite view, expressed through a kind of dis-identification, a desire to keep away physically and emotionally. Olivia and Richard, both first-generation British of Arab-Jewish descent, speak of distancing themselves from Israel:

OLIVIA: "Personally speaking, I don't buy the connection between the Holocaust and, 'We've got to have our own country'. It's spurious to me. I do think there's something to the argument that Jews will be persecuted wherever they go because of their Otherness and because … they will remain 'other'. […] That doesn't justify the founding of the country, necessarily. I would rather argue, let's embrace 'otherness' […].

The nationalist, Messianic, recovery of 'ancient nation' feeling that you get in Israel which I've always felt alienated from … at an emotional level I've never been able to go there. I sometimes wonder why I don't feel anything for Israel except mild annoyance. Visiting Israel is fine but I can't fall in love with the place. The last time I went was really unpleasant and I couldn't run away fast enough. I just don't have a sense of attachment to it. I've a much greater sense of attachment to Baghdad. But that's partly political, it must be, it's the only way I can rationalise it."

RICHARD: "There's a bit of me that says, 'Don't monopolise the suffering'. [I]t was gruesome in its … coldness, but there have been other instances which proportionately are … . I don't know what it's done to Israel, because they're treating the Palestinians like they were treated. I both feel sympathetic and, well, 'Haven't you learnt?' But I'm out of that.

> I won't go to Israel and I'm a bit ashamed when I read about what Israel does."

Even Bernice's ostensibly straightforward identification with Israel can be read, if her word "heat" is given broader meaning, as an unconscious recognition that the only way she can manage her unease is to place a physical distance between herself and the conflict:

> "I'm Zionist. I most likely would be living in Israel if I wasn't *allergic to the heat*." (my emphasis)

Each of these "ordinary Jews" seeks, in her or his own way, a defensible ground to stand on in relation to Israel: whether a political critique, an emotional withdrawal, or a moral justification. To live consciously with conflict means having to live with feelings that pull in different directions and that may continually change under the impact of conditions and events. Speaking in 2007, Simon, for example, described the way his emotional ground has been vulnerable to shifts:

> "At the moment I'm very keen on supporting Israel. I've still been very critical of Israel, especially when Israel or supporters of Israel seem to be using the Holocaust to claim some special kind of moral exemption from normal rules about how to treat people; or, indeed, comparing Arafat to Hitler, as some people used to do, just as Arafat used to compare Israelis to the Nazis, so [there is] this [...] evil exploitation of the Holocaust wrongly, on both sides of the Israeli–Arab conflict, where both sides get accused of acting like Nazis or being Nazis. That's really horrible, maybe inevitable, but it's wrong.
>
> I've become perhaps [...] less optimistic than I used to be about all sorts of things in society generally, but with the huge growth as I see it in the last couple of years particularly, of a kind of anti-Israel feeling in large sections of British society and certainly the British media, which instead of just questioning the rightness of things Israel does [shifts] to questioning the very existence of Israel. It seems to me that this has become increasingly acceptable. That's made me really alarmed [...] and has changed my personal stance on a lot of things and a lot of ways in which I react. Whereas once I would have come

> out 'all guns blazing' denouncing Israel, I tend not to now because I think that … I don't think the existence of Israel is directly under threat geopolitically, but I do think that if the assumption that Israel's existence is illegitimate is allowed to go unchecked for too long, it could present a very dangerous situation in the future for Israel and hence for the Jewish people."

Simon is describing being in an emotional trap. He is caught between two powerful but conflicting desires: to challenge Israel for its flouting of certain moral codes that he holds dear; and to defend the *principle* of Israel against attacks by those who also flout a moral code—one which requires respect for the (Holocaust-driven) reason for Israel's very creation, however problematic this "solution" became. Simon experiences "the question of Israel" as an invidious choice between survival and morality; but it is also possible to discern in him a continued anguish over the seeming unresolvable-ness of the Israeli–Arab conflict, which leaves him in no peace. His anger at "this […] evil exploitation of the Holocaust […] on both sides" reflects an unhappy awareness that, although it would be tempting to try and resolve his dilemma by embracing one or other side of what to others is a simple black-and-white situation, this particular conflict, external or internal, is not going to go away. It is an example of the way Israel has manifestly failed to fulfil its imagined, and much-desired, role for Jews as a haven from conflict and oppression. Emotional affinity with an ongoing external conflict precludes inner peace.

Like Simon, Doris also feels torn between two contradictory stances on Israel. She feels perfectly entitled to be critical of Israel, but set against this is her distress that Israel acts in ways that are so at odds with what she understands Jews to be "for":

> "According to my own standards of rationality and political analysis, I am very emotional […] about Israel. I have two parallel views on Israel. One is, I am perfectly capable of being critical about the government of Israel. I am British by nationality, I didn't vote for … they are … a foreign country which I was not responsible for electing the government of, and I am perfectly entitled to be critical as I am of any other country. However, parallel to that, I have what is … I can only say a tribal connection that … Everything that happens

> that I disapprove of, it's like your child misbehaving, you know what I mean, it's the family.
>
> It hurts me so much when I hear [of Israelis doing certain things]. I know armies behave like this. All armies of all states. [...] I don't want Jews to be associated with being bullying or killing innocent people. That's not what we're for. [...]. It's guilt by association as well, of course."

Victor experiences a similar dilemma, and his struggle to put this into coherent words is painfully evident. Growing from childhood to adulthood during the twelve years of Nazi rule, Victor remembers his post-war feelings of rage over the Holocaust, which initially sparked his decision to be an active player in the new state of Israel. His early enthusiasm soon gave way to doubts and anxieties, which even fifty years later he has not resolved:

> "Israel seemed to be one thing through which we could channel our anger ... [Now] I feel tremendously conflicted, such a sorrow that things haven't worked out. I certainly start off with the feeling that somehow or other, I'm associated. A feeling of responsibility, not a responsibility in actual deeds, which would be very tiny, but a feeling of responsibility, of emotional association [...] ... Because with a feeling of association one tends to make excuses or see the arguments for things, but there's another side to the argument which you discount. On the other hand ... early on ... [I had this] feeling that Palestinians are ... I realised this early on [...] I was upset when I saw people badly treated. Though again [then] I would make excuses for that. So, confused and conflicted feelings about it. This feeling of association, feeling of regret that it isn't the sort of country I imagined it would be when I was going out to build it in 1952. That lots of things started which I wouldn't like to be ... Though when I've been there, [...] one still gets a feeling of elation and enjoyment and association with it. Anger about all sorts of wrong decisions ... I don't know, *so conflicted*."

For Claud, who also lived through the war, the impact of all of this seems more depressing than anything else. Israel has not been the answer to Nazism "that one might have hoped for". He cannot resolve the conflict, he can only abandon the field to others: "let the future generations worry about it."

Ordinary Jews therefore live with a telling range of feelings in relation to Israel: a weight of difficult feelings—anger, defensiveness, guilt, shame, loyalty, annoyance, distress, confusion, depression; but enjoyment and pleasure are there, too. These feelings are also ones that people normally experience in relation to their own families, for it is in the family that conflict first arises, and Israel undoubtedly represents part of the larger family from which every Jew has come and where they hope always to be, in an untroubled way, "at home". But if Israel is at one level simply family, it is something else when it comes to the Holocaust and its aftermath. Ordinary Jews use Israel to symbolise certain things for themselves that the Holocaust attacked. But there is a conflict involved. Is it right for Israel—is it even possible for Israel—to carry this legacy on behalf of all Jewish people? Or have we missed something crucial?

Conflict and trauma, loss and mourning

The notion of conflict is central to the founding tenets of psychoanalysis. Freud conceptualised the oedipal conflict as a way to reflect the intrapsychic process through which each of us gains sexual autonomy. This drama describes the infant's shift in perception into realising that s/he is part of a triad involving two sexually different parents, as opposed to one of a duo with one parent exclusively devoted to him or herself. The infant attempts to cope with the loss of his unique status in the eyes of a single Other through seeking a new exclusive relationship with the opposite-sex parent. This necessarily involves a competition with the other parent, resulting in a conflictual (if unconscious) wish to fight off ("kill" in the original Oedipus myth) the same-sex parent in order to claim the other parent as his own. The resolution of this conflict comes at the child's acceptance of his/her loss: it is the parents who are the exclusive couple, and the child must follow her separate sexual path to intimacy.[4]

If Freud is the founding father of psychoanalysis, Melanie Klein can well claim to be the founding mother. Klein focused on the very early relationship of infant with mother and saw this as the earliest source of conflict in humans, one which operates through the psychological process known as "splitting". Human birth entails our first (and deepest) exposure to loss, as the human infant is thrust from the warm, all-encompassing safety and nurturing environment of the womb into a wholly unpredictable world. Klein thought that in their earliest weeks, infants experience the world as intrinsically split between two beings, one who acts to satisfy and one who does not (Klein famously described this as a split between the "good" and "bad" breast), while the infant simultaneously experiences himself as a helpless being who is merely "acted upon" by a random world. Klein went on to develop the idea that the infant thus feels helplessly at the mercy of his/her own torrent of feelings (distress, rage, fear, love, and hatred being paramount) without any means of containing these. It is only as infants gradually acquire capacity to act for themselves in some way that their world becomes less frightening and more amenable to influence, and they themselves can learn psychically to "hold" the world as one which contains both "good" and "bad"; but the primitive tendency to split, that is, to live in a psychological conflict between two polarised states, is something that we retain through our lives.

In its more extreme and unresolved forms, splitting is very dangerous, and Klein also saw it as the basis of paranoia. Dicks (1972), with extraordinary insight, traced its manifestation in the psyche of Nazi killers, showing how, in adverse cultural-political conditions, the damage done to individuals in childhood can be hijacked later by a political process and converted into mass destructivity.[5] It is also a form of splitting that underpins Lentin's study of Israel and its shame legacy. In her analysis, Israel split the Jewish world into "heroic" and "shameful" and repressed its deeply felt sense of shame at its Holocaust past by projecting all shame on to the survivors ("miskanim"), then pursuing an alternative ego identity in the form of a militaristic—and salvationist—heroism (a split uncannily like the one that took hold in Nazi Germany). It is a splitting that derives from the consequences of extremely painful loss. But splitting is a universal tendency in human beings: love and hate, good and evil, black and white, are human constructs which may appear to satisfy a primitive need for simple explanations but which in practice offer little guidance in the messy business of human affairs. It is therefore in principle to be expected that in the wake of what was essentially a violent acting out by Nazis of their split psyche, similar effects might continue to percolate through the post-Nazi world.

Like Freud, Klein saw the infant's engagement with conflict as a purely intra-psychic one. Later writers, notably Fairbairn, recognised that in reality the baby lives in a relational world, and that its developmental progress is as much interpersonal (one in which the baby's overwhelming feelings can, in the right conditions, be mediated effectively by a responsive mother) as it is intra-psychic. The nature of early care thus plays a critical role in developing our internal capacity to contain the psychic conflict of loss and trauma throughout our lives. In the case of "Mr. X", Lemma and Levy cite an example of how an internalised experience of nurturing care can sustain people in the most adverse circumstances. Mr. X was a young intellectual from the Sudan, who had been imprisoned and tortured to the point of death by being forced to stand for five days without food or water:

> He had given up hope and had known, with little care, that he was going to die. [...] At the very moment when hope was extinguished, his mother had appeared to him and saved his life. He described in considerable detail how she had walked up to him in the prison and sat down on a chair. She took him onto her lap [...], then, gently and tenderly, she had fed grapes into his mouth.

Lemma and Levy comment that:

> This patient's capacity to maintain a dialogue with this internal maternal imago tells us something about his early object relations and the levels of psychic integration he achieved. [...] His history reflected this. (Lemma & Levy, 2004, pp. 9–10)

Common to all these writers is their understanding that psychic conflict is a central outcome of trauma. Trauma itself always derives from loss (whether loss of the womb, loss of a loving mother, loss of the desired relationship with the opposite-sex parent), and in early development these losses are vital stages on every human being's progress towards autonomy and eventual maturity. However, these goals can only be achieved when the reality of the world is accepted and the emotional and psychic conflicts that stem from loss are ameliorated. We may speculate that "ongoing trauma" is a consequence of traumatic experiences which could not be worked through at the time and which have become "fixed" as unreconciled splits in the psyche. It is not therefore conflict per se which denotes ongoing trauma so much as the failure or inability to resolve the conflict which trauma gives rise to. In the aftermath of the Nazis' systematic association of Jews with "vermin", "infections", and "toxins", Israel might well counter-identify in a view of itself as pure, righteous, and beyond reproach. It is as though Israel cannot digest the painful history of Nazi degradation (and thereby reconcile the split) but can only seek refuge in, and hold fast on to, a diametrically opposed view of itself, as utterly "other".

Darien Leader argues that central to this process of resolution is what he, following Freud, calls "the work of mourning". Leader distinguishes between loss, grief, and mourning. Loss is the event or experience of losing, and grief the immediate emotional reaction; but mourning is an active process through which we gradually integrate a loss and eventually reinvest our emotional energies in new "love objects" (Leader, 2009, pp. 26–28). Levy and Lemma, too, are of the view that there is:

> a link between traumatic responses and a breakdown in the capacity to mourn. Instead, the course of mourning is somehow 'perverted' as a way of managing the unbearable and unthinkable nature of the traumatic loss. (Levy & Lemma, 2004, p. xvi)

These writers all thus link the pain of unmourned traumatic loss with the continued manifestation of trauma in someone's life. Conflict will be integral to this as we struggle to reconcile two opposing impulses, desires, needs: at its simplest, the desire not to feel pain—in a sense "to die" emotionally—set against the need to work through the pain and be fully alive. It is no accident that the title of Ruth Kluger's Holocaust memoir, both in its original German and in the English version, is *Still Alive*. In this Kluger was expressing her personal desire to stay psychically alive despite her Holocaust experiences, and in her particular case this involved facing her conflicted feelings towards her mother.

In the context of today's predilection for Holocaust memorialisations, it may seem strange that I am here discussing mourning as one that is key for ordinary Jews in their relationship with the Holocaust and with Israel. To repeat a reference in the Introduction, Peter Novick critiqued "excessive or overly prolonged mourning" in the minds of American Jews in their responses to the Holocaust. But there is a profound difference between *remembering* and *mourning*. Much of what might pass for "mourning" by Jews in respect of the Holocaust looks perilously like an endless repetition rather than an emotional confrontation: a repetition of names, of sites, of dates, of events, whose objective may be little other than to continually reinforce in us a sense of horror and to remind us of our moral responsibility "to remember". Gideon describes being exposed from a very young age in Israel to a statutory requirement "to remember":

> "You have Yom Hashoah in Israel, and […] it's not something you can ignore. The air raid siren goes off and … There's this tradition in Israel, Days of Remembrance […]. Everybody [at school] would stand up and try not to giggle for a minute and that would be Holocaust Day, and also Yom Hazikaron. You couldn't possibly not know about it, even at the age of six. It's a different question what you know about it […].
>
> When I was a child, I was resentful of all this Holocaust business. Having the Holocaust poured down your throat. We hated it, we would tell Holocaust jokes, we would try not to giggle during the ceremony. We hated the fact that it was rammed down our throats endlessly, all the time. 'Remember, you're here because of the Holocaust' […]. As if it was in some way our fault, our business. […] Depending on the teacher or person […] it was the most terrible thing that ever happened ever, anywhere. […] You were supposed to treat it with the greatest reverence, you had to be very serious, glum. You had to appreciate just how horrible it was, and if you didn't want to appreciate it, 'Let me tell you, show you a picture'."

Leader suggests that there is a specific difficulty involved in mourning the Holocaust:

> Every attempt to give the Holocaust a narrative frame risks turning it into a story of heroism and valour or of death and defeat. This is because human narratives follow certain set patterns. […] [T]hat is precisely what makes a single story inappropriate for representing anything to do with the Holocaust. (Leader, 2009, p. 32)

Simply re-presenting icons from the past risks reducing the Holocaust to a litany, imbued with suitable horror but devoid of any real life, which eventually people may walk past without noticing, or even start resenting as Gideon did. Leader observes this deadening effect in relation to a piece of artwork called the "J-Street Project" by Susan Hiller, intended to "remind" us of the historic presence of Jews in Germany:

> The serial, list-like quality of 'J-Street' […] frustrates our desire to create stories. […] The signs catalogued […] have been restituted exactly as before. […] Rather than the in-depth exploration of a single street, the characters that once inhabited it, their lives, hopes and dreams, there is simply a visual list. […] It's as if nothing had happened inbetween […]: as if 'Jew Street' before and 'Jew Street' after the Holocaust were one and the same. […] [T]he people we see in the film […] stroll by without once noticing the signs. (Ibid., pp. 32–33)

Leader links such reducing with a "failure to mourn":

> It isn't just listing or reshuffling or recombining elements that constitutes mourning. Something more has to take place. (Ibid., pp. 33–34)

Mourning is a dynamic process which permits into the mourning space the collision of opposite feelings: above all the conflicting feelings of love and hate for the lost "object". "It isn't love, but the mixture of love and hate that matters," says Leader, pointing out that Melanie Klein and Karl Abraham, who followed Freud, both thought that conflicting love and hate "was central to all forms of mourning"[6] (ibid., p. 61). We do not think much about what we, the post-Holocaust Jews, might hate about the murdered millions, since to do so would seem a violation of their memory. Yet we cannot uncomplicatedly "love" so many people whose violent deaths robbed us of something important. Israel's own marginalisation of Holocaust survivors, too, surely has some hatred in it.

Psychically, Israel was founded too quickly in the aftermath of the Holocaust. The impulse to compensate for the lost millions and the lost Jewish world unconsciously colluded with an equal impulse to avoid the devastating loss and its implications. It used to be the case that, if a child died young, the parents were encouraged to "have another one as quickly as possible" in the simple belief that this would make up for the void left by the earlier death. A same-sex child would often even be given the same name as the lost one. It was invariably disastrous for the subsequently born child, who would almost always carry the feeling that s/he was there *in place of* another rather than *for* him or herself. I wonder if behind Israel's insistence that Palestinians "recognise Israel's right to exist" as an *a priori* condition of peace, this despite the fact that Israel does exist and its status as a state is not legally in question, lurks a hidden anxiety as to its own legitimacy: not in respect of the Palestinians, but in respect of the murdered millions. There is a powerful conflict ingrained in Israel from the start: how *could* it "replace" so many communities, such a rich and long-established world? Even more, how legitimate are its efforts now, given its disposition to marginalise diaspora history and view the present diaspora as little more than a support system for itself? Israel is not only in conflict with the Palestinians. It is in conflict with its own diaspora history which it partially hates even while Israel would not exist without it. Embedded in this conflict over history is the conflict of ideals which troubled Buber, concerning Israel's spiritual role in the world; a role which, if pursued, would inherently call for Israel's dialogic engagement with, and respect for, the diaspora.

By implication, ordinary Jews in the diaspora must be in conflict with Israel because implicitly we do not accept Israel's judgement that the diaspora has no further meaning. But we still hesitate to address ourselves to a critical question. If Israel is not the simple answer to the Holocaust that we might once have imagined, how do diaspora Jews now define their own post-Holocaust future? How do we place the Holocaust in its proper context, recover what is valuable from the past, and reinvest in a Jewish diaspora future in a way that allows us to relate freely, and as equals, to the state of Israel?

To mourn is to honour

> "To mourn is to honour. Not to surrender to this keening, to this absence—a dishonouring."
>
> —Anne Michaels, *The Winter Vault*

Israel was always meant to be a restitution for Jews. In physical terms it was, of course, an attempt to restore to the tens of thousands of European Jews who had been so violently dispossessed of everything—families, homes, relationships, property, old securities, a known place in the world—a place to live, and live openly as Jews. But in the wider context of Jewry, Israel was much more. It was to be a place in which *symbolic* losses could be recovered. I am not thinking here of the oft-invoked "restoration to ancient homeland" that has religiously become woven into the Zionist cause, so much as the more immediate losses of self and history which the Holocaust involved, and which above all are the inheritance of the more than half the world's Jews who live in the diaspora today. For so many of us, the Holocaust obliterated a sense of living connection with where we had come from, and the immediate physical disaster was compounded by the political split that fell over Europe in the aftermath of the war, in which the sites and scenes of so much destruction fell under Soviet control, and the loss of Jewish life from the old heartlands became further consigned to oblivion. For ordinary diaspora Jews, especially for those in my grandparents' generation for whom there were living memories involved, a personal iron curtain fell, between there and here, then and now; and there was a powerful emotional inducement to displace this unmourned pain into the vibrant and energetic new state.

Jacqueline Rose uses the psychoanalytic concept of "resistance" as a way of examining the underlying dynamics embedded in the poisoned chalice of Jewish-Israeli-Zionist post-Holocaust existence. "Trauma", says Rose, "enters the [Israeli] national psyche in the form of resistance to its own pain" (Rose, 2007, p. 6). In both the Freudian and commonplace use of the word "resistance", there is more than an element of conflict involved; moreover, such resistance is not confined to Israel. What are we in the diaspora to do with our own inheritance of painful loss? In the absence of discourse in my own family as to our history, it only seemed to start between the years of 1903 and 1905, less than fifty years before I was born, when my paternal grandparents arrived in London. I grew up with a strange sense of absent origins; a disconnect from that part of Europe where my ancestral line had probably lain for six or seven hundred years. To this day, I envy those of my British friends who could, if they wished, summon up evidence of their roots by a simple trip to the registrar of births, marriages, and deaths.

All loss functions symbolically as well as materially. Freud observed that when we lose someone, we lose not only the actual person—the "whom"—but what that person embodied for us—what we have lost in them. The death of someone important to us leaves a gap: something that Leader describes as "a hole in our psychical world" (Leader, 2009, p. 132). People we hold dear are such because they hold and give back to us something of ourselves, and their loss exposes us to a painful reminder of an empty space in ourselves, a space that is inherently difficult to visualise or find representational form for. "Lacan", says Leader, "called this the *object a*—a point of emptiness and loss that eludes ready visualisation or representation" (ibid., p. 133). This space can feel unbearable, and humans seem often to have an ingrained impulse to fill it quickly if they can. Alternatively, people can find themselves "lost" in it, a lostness which has a bearing on the ceaseless lamenting associated with depressive or melancholic states. Something has been deeply lost in a person's psyche, and to that person, nothing equivalent can be found.

In Chapter Two, I talked of the losses associated with Eastern Europe that, almost without exception, those I interviewed referred to when thinking about the Holocaust. I connected these losses in part to the actual family experiences in the background of most ordinary Jews: our descent from what was in effect a massive, albeit voluntary, displacement from home, family, country, which our migrant grandparents and great-grandparents went through in moving west. This, I suggested, was an experience of loss that was passed down to the next generation who would probably have met its impact through some kind of emotional absence in their parents, particularly in their mothers at a critical stage of infant-rearing; and indirect evidence for this could be gleaned from the widespread silence in the immigrant generation about their previous life, their own families, their experiences as young people growing up and so on. Its psychic impact, I suspect, will have been to have fostered an internalised experience in their children of something hauntingly lost *in* the parents, which in turn may have contributed to the hectic focus on material achievement amongst the first-born British or American generation: for in material goods we unconsciously seek consolation for our intangible losses.

What this psychic "lost space" signifies for post-Holocaust Jews is an ongoing sense of absence in respect of our own past and our own roots. What it further implies is an immense problem when it comes to "meeting" the existential reality of post-Holocaust Eastern Europe. There we meet an *outer* reminder of an *inner* loss, an immense gap that we do not, even in this present time, know how to fill. The juxtaposed meeting of outer reality with inner longing is painfully met in these words of survivor Roman Halter:

> "[M]y town was part of a dream, that I will come [back] there and certain members of my family will survive and some other Jewish people will come back, and there was a nucleus of a Jewish community and I will fit in. When I came there [...] the realisation was

> [...] I found there was just me and three sisters who by some fluke managed to survive. [...]
>
> I went for a walk to the lake and suddenly I thought, 'What is going to happen to me?' I suddenly felt this emptiness of everybody. Some members of the family died when I knew that they died, my father and grandfather, died of starvation in Lodz Ghetto, and I had to bury them [...] The cemetery was ploughed out, the synagogue was burnt down. There were hardly traces. [...] The Jews had disappeared, just like that." (Halter, 2005)

Like many survivors, Halter opted not to live in Israel but to settle in Britain after the war.

As much as it is a physical country, Israel therefore was and is desired by Jews *symbolically* to fill an empty space: the desolate gap in our continuity, the violent break with our own past. It would recreate for us a sense of belonging in both space and time; a country that would restore Jews to a sense of valued self-image in contrast to the degradations of Nazism; a place where to be Jewish was *normal*. For Jonathan, at least,

> "it's nice to have a state where they have a Sabbath that is Shabbos rather than Sunday, and to have everything closed down on Passover and Yom Kippur. I think that way of life in the state is great";

while Victor speaks of the "emotional strength" he gets from being in Israel, which comes through

> "the general pride [of] being associated with something which in the past has been very oppressed. Also this idea of its being our own ..."

But Israel comes at a cost. In the way Israel positions itself in Jewish life and history, the diaspora appears as little more than a prelude to the "return to Zion": a failed experiment to which the Holocaust was the ultimate witness, rather than a history with value and meaning in its own right. Victor goes on to comment:

> "I remember attending meetings before the state was set up where somebody was saying that it would be great if we had this state [of Israel] [in the way] that Italy can speak up for the Italians or whatever.

> [Now] on the contrary, [Israel's] often quite self-satisfied when there are atrocities against Jews in Argentina or in France or wherever. They use that to say, 'Why don't you come here?'"

The political and psychological pressures in Israel concerning survival and legitimacy lead it to look to the distant past for its own identity and rationale. Israeli historian Shlomo Sand observes that in Israel, the academic structuring of the study of history at Israeli universities disconnects Jewish history from "other" history. Israeli universities appear to split the study of history between two departments: one of "Jewish" history, and the other of "history", as though Jewish history had nothing to do with the history of the nations in which Jews have lived for so long.[7] A specific focus on a nationalist view of a distant past formed part of Israel's need to develop its sense of nationhood: the effect was, in the words of Moshe Dayan, one of the most prominent leaders in Israel's early decades,

> [to help] our imagination to vault over the past and return to antiquity, to our forefathers and the heroes of our nation. (Cited in Sand, 2009, p. 112)

"Vaulting over the past": it is a powerful phrase and sums up an attitude towards the diaspora. The effect continues into present times. In 2006, broadcaster Dennis Marks produced a series of radio programmes for the BBC on Sephardi history. After the Germans invaded Greece in 1943, the Nazis obliterated the Sephardi community in Greece almost as comprehensively as they did Polish Jews. Some ninety-five per cent of the 50,000 or so Jews in Salonika, a major Jewish settlement that had re-established itself under the Ottomans after the 1492 expulsion from Spain, were deported to Auschwitz, where Primo Levi admired their communal solidarity (Mazower, 2005, ch. 22). A museum of Sephardi history was later set up in Tel Aviv. Its apparent tribute to "a wide and fruitful scattering" is, as Marks points out, misleading. The emphasis is on a "scattered family" of Jews, "a nation doomed to destruction", and in reality the museum is dedicated to "the ingathering" of the scattered nation back to Israel, to the place where Jewish life now happens. Thus in Israel's eyes, Jewish history over two thousand years in the diaspora leads inexorably and only to the founding of the State, and the diaspora's history as of value in itself is negated.

This is highly problematic for Jews outside Israel. Diaspora Jews legitimately exercise the autonomous choice of continuing to live within the continuity of a long-established diaspora tradition, yet are effectively regarded with a degree of contempt by the very country which is of such immense emotional significance to them. Israel has only partially assuaged the longings and gaps left with Jews after the Holocaust. We are still confronted with unanswered questions of mourning concerning our own diaspora loss, but we cannot look to Israel to help us in mourning whatever we need to mourn in the Holocaust. On the contrary, Israel may even compound our difficulty in fully absorbing the impact of our painful past.

"One would have hoped for something better"

For all that issues concerning Israel are so frequently positioned as ones of physical or existential survival, the question is also one of image; or, more precisely, of self-image. One of the most grievous psychological impacts that the Holocaust has had for Jewry comes from the Nazis' attack on how Jews were seen. The legacy of shame which I discussed in Chapter Five creates an underlying vulnerability for Jews around their self-image, a question which has acquired a particular potency in the context of how the Holocaust is—and therefore Jews are—called to mind. As an antidote to the depravities of Nazism, Jews particularly needed a "good image" of themselves to turn to, and in 1948 Israel offered a powerful counter to the abject images of Jews that were so visible in the world's eye. Victor recalls his own feelings at the time:

> "It was the aftermath of the war, and the Holocaust, and our own personal situation, which comes back to … anti-Semitism: we didn't feel totally at home. And we were presented with this heroic enterprise which we could participate in."

But Israel, as we know only too well, is both subject and object of another conflict: one in which the very ideal of Israel is at stake. Rose points out that as a political philosophy Zionism always had a strong element of "redemption" in it, a pull that drew from Jewish religious longing (Rose, 2005, ch. 1). In the aftermath of the war, the new nationalist project could not fail implicitly to encompass a different Jewish longing for redemption: a hoped-for image of a pure Israel, a land unsullied by war, hatred, and repression, in which to recover an image of Jews wholly different from the degraded and despised one the Nazis left us. This desired image has been painfully eroded by the decades of conflict and oppression which Israel itself seems so set on maintaining, and the impact of this diminishment of pride and good self-feeling is painfully apparent. For Victor, "sixty years on" Israel's "heroic image" is looking "very tarnished", and he reflects on his lost ideals of Israel and Israelis:

> "For a long time I've resented the superior [...] arrogant attitude about Israel, by Israelis ... [...] It's funny thinking about visitors from Israel and their attitudes. When people say, 'We've got visitors from Israel', [it's] such a contrast to if you have visitors from Iceland, say. [...] Pride in all the things Israel ... [which is] often not justified. Now I think things weren't so good all the way through. Israel's feats of arms, cultivating the land, blah blah blah, weren't quite what we took them to be, [given] ... what we now know. I've done a lot of reading. This is the nature of human society and politics."

Claud, too, has revisited his younger enthusiasm for Israel and found the results depressing:

> "The only thing one can learn from what went on in Europe is that this is a very real possibility in our time, in our days, in our children's days, and I find that very depressing [...] when I think about it. You know, a fellow over there, with a nice German or Polish father, with a family, he could have easily have done the same things, [gone] home at night and chatted to his children and read them fairy stories [...]. [That] probably results in the strongest support for Israel than I would have had without that, because Israel's been quite a disappointment in some ways.
>
> I was very excited as a child, I sat up half the night listening to the United Nations vote coming in to partition Palestine and it hasn't been quite the success that ... [...] one might have hoped for. [...] It's a society as vicious and as corrupt as any other, unfortunately. One would have hoped for something better. I would have hoped that the divide or the hatred between religious and secular would not have been there. It is there. The last State of Israel lasted for about eighty years, but I don't see any historical necessity where this state should

> last. Of course, I hope it does; [but] I've got to the age now when it doesn't matter to me what happens anymore, let the future generations worry about it."

Perhaps most powerfully present for ordinary Jews in contemplating Israel, therefore, is an anguish at the loss of the redemptive, hoped-for, renewed image. This may go some way to explaining the pained fury that many Jews feel at the (admittedly, often vicious) attacks and criticism launched against Israel which stretches to the very justification for the state. In aspiring to become "a nation like any other", Israel has, most paradoxically, fulfilled itself in ways never consciously envisaged in 1948: "it's a society as vicious and as corrupt as any other". Israel presents us with conflicts about who we are and how we see ourselves, a conflict impossibly heightened by the humiliations of the Holocaust. This loss of how we wanted to see ourselves in the longed-for redemption is another we need to mourn.

CHAPTER SEVEN

Held captive?

> "The past does not change, nor our need for it. What must change is the way of telling."
>
> —Anne Michaels, *The Winter Vault*

Seventy years after the event, what do we *do* with the Holocaust?

Throughout this book I have posed the question not only of what constitutes "collective trauma", but what it is that constitutes *this particular* Holocaust-derived "collective trauma" in the minds and experience of ordinary Jews. The term appears increasingly often in relation to all manner of catastrophes and atrocities past and recent but, especially when separated from a direct relationship to the original experience, the parameters of "collective" trauma remain elusive.

The question is not helped by intrinsic difficulties in definition. Like "community", the very term "collective" is nebulous. For example, in respect of memory Novick (1999), drawing on Maurice Halbwachs (1992), writes about "collective memory", but Avishai Margalit resists the term "collective", preferring to talk instead of "shared" and "common" as distinct categories of memory. A "common" memory,

Margalit says, is "an aggregate notion": it aggregates the memories of all those who remember a certain episode experienced by each individually. A "shared" memory is not an aggregate of individual memories but is the process of distilling from a number of disparate individual memories into an overarching memory that can be narrated. In this process, everybody has a different perception of (therefore memory of) an event:

> A shared memory integrates and calibrates the different perspectives of those who remember the episode [...] into one version. Other people in the community who were not there at the time may be plugged into the experience [...] through channels of description rather than by direct experience. (Margalit, 2002, pp. 51–52)

Margalit's discussion reminds us that terms cannot be taken for granted; variations in meaning and precise definitions matter. Definitions are no less confused when it comes to the question of "collective trauma". Different writers have their own preferred terms, and the field is wide-ranging and unsettled. Alexander, for example, talks of "cultural" trauma:

> Cultural trauma occurs when members of a collectivity feel they have been subjected to a horrendous event that leaves indelible marks on their group consciousness, marking their memories forever and changing their future identity in fundamental and irrevocable ways. (Alexander, 2004, p. 1)

Volkan thinks in terms of "large-group trauma". He thinks of this as trauma which is in a particular sense "chosen" as an "ethnic marker" to represent and uphold the identity of the large group:

> Massive societal catastrophes [...] involve severe large-group identity issues. When the 'other' who possesses a different large-group identity than the victims humiliates and oppress[es] a group, the victim's large-group's identity is threatened. (Volkan, 2012, p. 14)

For Volkan, the trauma "chosen" is associated with an earlier generation's failure to complete crucial psychological tasks including mourning:

> Attempts to complete unfinished psychological tasks associated with the previous generation's or ancestor's trauma are handed down from generation to generation (shared transgenerational transmissions). All these tasks are associated with the shared mental representation of the same event and eventually this mental double evolves as a most significant large-group identity marker (*a chosen trauma*). (Ibid., p. 16)

Hopper focuses on the "social unconscious" as an element of collectivity inseparable from an individual's psychological functioning and belonging, since

> within the infinite context of time and space, the self belongs mostly to others, who may have lived far away and long ago. [...] The development and maintenance of personal autonomy can only be understood within the context of social, cultural and political constraints (Hopper, 2003, p. 19)

and he goes on to describe experiences of working in groups with people affected by what he calls "massive social trauma" (ibid., p. 72).

Thus it becomes clear that the term I have adopted in this book, "collective trauma", is fraught with definitional challenges. It has something to do with catastrophe; something to do with common experiences and with social connectedness; with memory personal and shared; with cultural markers; with identity and with belonging. We are in complex terrain.

While in previous chapters I considered how commonly recognised characteristics of trauma—loss, guilt, anger, and so on—surfaced in my interviewee narratives, these are best understood as feeling reactions *to* trauma, rather than the trauma itself. Core trauma at the heart of anyone's experience itself is never easily defined or grasped. It can be inferred but it remains on the whole a dimension of existence that, somewhat like black holes in space, is dense and absorbs energy; it refuses easy categorisations. Any exploration of "collective trauma" must, therefore, have in mind a dynamic which is similarly elusive and mysterious: possible to *feel* but inherently difficult to name other than in tentative and shifting terms. Furthermore, as Margalit and Hopper both point out, no collective/common/shared experience exists independently of the individuals who comprise a given "collectivity": memory and experience are intrinsically individual in nature. Hopper also observes that the self does not exist independently of others, before or contemporaneously. Thus "collective trauma", whatever it is, is *simultaneously* individual and social in nature. No group can be traumatised independently of the individuals in it; and it is through the experience of individuals that a broader experience can be recognised.

In Chapter One, I referred to Levi and Rothberg's discussion of "traumatic memory" as "a [key] phenomenon [linking] collective, historical experiences [...] with the psychic suffering of individuals." Alexander, Volkan, and Hopper all similarly indicate that memory and trauma are intricately related. A narrative process is involved whereby traumatic experience (individual or shared) is translated into how the experience is "remembered"—recalled—and then passed on. The process is by definition selective and meaning-laden. It is not necessarily the *actual* memory which matters so much as what the memory *signifies* to the one who remembers. De Vito, Cubelli, and Della Sala demonstrated this through examining individual memories of a highly memorable incident in Italy's recent past. In 1980 a massive bomb exploded in the main station at Bologna; eighty-five people were killed and more than 200 injured. The subsequent "shared" memory amongst local people is that the station clock stopped permanently at the exact moment of the explosion, and to this day the clock is perceived as "remembering" the event. Archive research of the station's records, however, revealed that the clock had continued working for sixteen years after the bomb; only then was a decision taken to keep it stopped in an act of symbolic memorialising. Yet thirty years later, the researchers found that eighty per cent of those interviewed believed that it had stopped permanently at the time of the bomb (De Vito, Cubelli, & Della Sala, 2009). Cubelli himself, who passed through the station daily during the sixteen-year period that it was still working, "remembered" the clock as stopped.[1] This illustrates, first, the adaptive nature of memory to later social and psychological need, and then the overriding importance of symbolisation. It appears that the need for symbolic representation of powerful experience is so strong that it obscures—even changes—actual memory.

Memories are never complete. Every individual's memory of his or her own life is made up of fragments which he or she has to hold together as disparate parts of a meaningful "whole". Symbolisation of "memories" gains its strength from a *present* need to have a coherent narrative of self, and a key function of symbolisation is to act in support of identity and meaning. The relationship between "collective" memory and "trauma" is, therefore, via the symbolic value attributed to an event: the feelings associated with an event profoundly influence how it must be kept alive.

Trauma's connection to memory manifests in the way in which time is collapsed in the continued experiencing of trauma. An original experience of a trauma occurred in past (finished) time, but memory of it happens in the present; this is true even when the memory is not a conscious one.[2] Memory revives without necessarily resolving past trauma, so that an original traumatic experience may become a source of ongoing trauma through being in the present traumatically re-membered, re-called, or re-experienced. This probably explains why the Bologna clock is falsely remembered as stopped. The memory had its own symbolic truth, in that in representing "stopped time" it accurately symbolised the timeless moment of shock: a psychological "stopping", for those affected by the event.

The attribution of symbolic value brings us to the question of meaning. Meaning becomes central to the whole experience of trauma and its memory, primarily because trauma *disrupts* previously held (if unconsciously so) meanings. A "collective" memory of trauma—which, as Margalit makes clear, increasingly becomes a *narration* rather than a memory per se—is "chosen" (in Volkan's term) because it encapsulates a core element of the past around which people can orient in the present. Through this, members of a community (however defined) unconsciously hope or seek to reconstruct meaning in the wake of the painful chaos of the disrupted past.

Survivor Jews, who can be considered a distinct population in their own right, unquestionably emerged from a massive *common* trauma—one that each of them had endured and had their own specific memories of—with enough cumulative potency to carry across from one generation to the next. Their "common" trauma, formed by their separate, then aggregated experiences, over time would converge into a shared narrative. Ordinary Jews, however, can be part of neither the "common" nor "shared" experience of actual Holocaust trauma. They can neither remember it for themselves, nor speak of it with direct knowledge to others. They are, if you like, "lookers-on", similar to Ruth's recollection of herself watching "old newsreel, documentary … archival material" on the television and longing to be able to rescue those who have long since died. It is, I suggest, inherent in the very experience of being on the edge of this disturbing history, bound to it through the ties of communal identity yet literally unable to speak of it, that a different kind of trauma resides: a trauma in which one's own narrative as an ordinary Jew can be so overshadowed by the traumas engendered by the Holocaust itself that it becomes correspondingly delegitimised as a valid narrative in its own right. As a result, ordinary Jews may lose sight not only of the meaning, but of the very existence of their own, distinct, Holocaust-related, experience.

"It stops you in your tracks"

In the psychic worlds of ordinary Jews, there is a two-layered, internally conflicted experience in relation to the Holocaust: of being *party to* a cataclysmic event without having been *part of* it; coupled with the absolute challenge of finding words for an experience intrinsically removed from the explicit suffering. This conundrum was a repeated, if indirectly expressed, feature of my interviews. It surfaced most often in the form of people's bewildered incomprehension expressive of how impossible they found it to locate words which could describe their reactions to this "thing", and such felt impossibility was particularly striking given how normally articulate most of my interviewees were:

HARRY: "I have been trying to unravel my jumbled thoughts concerning the Holocaust. There are so many feelings crowding in on each other, it is not easy to express them in words."

Some people focused on a particular aspect of the Holocaust's horrors that for them might stand for, or symbolise, "the whole"; even then, words failed them. Others fell back into a generalised statement of incomprehension. Throughout, there was a pattern of stopping and starting; of sentences half-finished, thoughts begun and abandoned. Few people have a neatly thought-through "take" on the Holocaust: how could they?

PEARL: "How do ordinary people get sucked into this? How do human beings get … into doing these … doing the bidding of that lunatic? […] [W]ho were these horrible non-menshen[3] that were doing this? Never mind Hitler and his gang, what about the ordinary men and women who became camp … And then would go home to their families and kiss their … That's when it gets me, that these are supposed to be human beings. How do you get human beings to behave like that? That I can't understand. I don't want to understand."

JONATHAN: "The first word that comes to mind is atrocity. The most shocking thing … how can you? … there's no scale. … [O] ne of the most disturbing things is the medical experiments. I'd say for people who were doctors to do the things that they did […] it's absolutely beyond belief in terms of its insanity."

LIMMUD WORKSHOP PARTICIPANT: "As I get older, I find a greater need to understand it, understand what happened. I just don't understand how it … how the whole Holocaust could … come about. I know the individual components, I know the story very well, I've visited Auschwitz … but none of it leads to any understanding of how it could have happened."

SECOND SPEAKER: "Can it be understood? Can anybody understand it? I think maybe it's something that's not understandable."

SONIA: "It's not normal; it's of a magnitude that is beyond comprehension."

CLAUD: "I don't understand, I don't understand. […] Incredulity […]: how people can behave like that?".

Observable both within and between these various narratives is an oscillation between chaos—where there is no understanding—and a search for focus, in which effort is made to give shape, and therefore symbolic value, to something graspable. Thus Pearl speaks at one moment, haltingly, of "ordinary men and women […] who […] would go home […] and kiss […]," and in the next, forcefully, of her utter bewilderment. Jonathan, similarly, stumbles as he talks of "the medical experiments" and "people who were doctors", and then refers with a compelling strength of feeling to his disbelief at the "insanity" of it. These internally conflicted monologues testify to the extraordinary difficulty of trying to grasp this multilayered, many-faceted *thing* we call the Holocaust: of trying to give it a shape which might, in an underlying hope, give rise to some degree of comprehension. Yet despite all attempts to bring it into the realm of concrete form, comprehension of the Holocaust eludes grasp. The most unambiguously expressed relationship is to its madness, to the "jumble of thoughts" and "crowded feelings" that Harry refers to. In this context, it is unsurprising that both the Hebrew words that have been applied to the events of 1933–1945 indicate in different ways ruin, desolation, and utter catastrophe.[4] These linguistic experiments express the extraordinary difficulty of referring to the Holocaust in a way that can convey the associated experiences of immensity, chaos, bewilderment, and bleakness.

Alice describes another way in which language stops. On a youth trip to Auschwitz, she was disturbed to find herself feeling *silenced* in the presence of others who were part of a privileged inner circle of survivor descendants and who thus seemed to have more "right" than she did to a relationship with the Holocaust:

> "On the trip that we went on there were only ... there were about twenty of us and only about three of us hadn't ... families hadn't been involved directly. Almost all of the other people's families were actually from Poland, and that surprised me. Because I didn't realise how many people have actually been involved in that way.
>
> In one of the first sessions we had to go round and say why we wanted to come on the trip and for the three of us who hadn't any direct relationship with the event, it felt almost like we had to justify it more because it wasn't directly associated with us. That was strange because I hadn't really thought I'd needed to do that before. [... .] Saying, I'm here because I'm Jewish not because my great-grandfather lived here or ... You've got a different type of relationship to it."

There is a psychic no-man's land involved in such peripheralising experiences. I discovered it most explicitly for myself when, during the last stages of writing this book, I attended a psychotherapeutic Holocaust "event" in Israel. This was a gathering between second-generation Israelis (children of Holocaust survivors) and second-generation Germans. Both during and after those few days, I felt myself absorbed into the heaviness of the history. It was clearly difficult enough for those Jews and Germans present, who were far closer in terms of *experience* to the event than I was, to speak together about what they felt. I simply did not know what to say. Like Alice, I struggled to know how to be there, and wondered what legitimacy I had, faced with the continued impact of terrible stories of separation, disappearance, loss, guilt, mental breakdown, and knowing that none of it was, in that extreme form, part of my personal history. Different degrees of connection to a traumatising event add to people's sense of apartness not only from the event itself but from each other, and this makes the task of connecting through speaking even more challenging.

Afterwards, various participants wrote of the "weight" of their inheritance:

> "What weight has a child who can hear but is forbidden to listen, who sees but must not understand, who talks but doesn't tell?"
>
> "The Nazi wish of extermination, not only the expulsion, of Jews from Europe is still felt by many of the children as if the right to live [itself] died."
>
> "The transgenerational heritage of feelings [is] very loaded."

One spoke of how the struggle to sort out "intensely ambivalent emotions" normally generates angry and aggressive reactions that themselves are frightening if they cannot be contained:

> "We all were [...] cautious. Anger and aggression were behind the door. [...] Usually this struggle transforms quickly into anger and aggression, but this time it didn't, and I personally appreciated this cautiousness and self-control. It helps for gaining confidence for further exploration and for feelings to unfold."

It is well documented that survivors went through terrible—sometimes lifelong—periods of silence about their experiences during the years of the Holocaust. For many, silence was simply a way of coping in the face of a world that had limited capacity to understand or confront survivors' awful experiences. Ernest Levy, the most famous survivor in Scotland, dedicated himself to speaking in a sustained effort to bring the Holocaust itself, and genocide more generally, into public and educational awareness in Scotland. It was not without personal cost, as Ruth saw:

> "A few years ago he wrote [in the *Jewish Telegraph*] that he had felt a compelling need to talk about his past and ... [...] do some exposure work [...] for the sake of history and future educational needs. But the more he did this, the more the nightmares affected him, disturbed him [...]".

Silence of a different kind took root in post-war Germany: the silence of a generation that wished to avoid their guilt. Gabriele Schwab, a German woman born into the post-war "perpetrator" generation, describes the "prohibition placed on language" that characterised post-war German culture, a repression which led to a confrontative, even violent, reaction in the generation who grew to adulthood in the 1960s and '70s. Schwab writes of how in her personal world she internalised the prohibition and found it impossible to speak "as the descendant of a perpetrator nation" without guilt and fear specifically associated with the act of daring to speak for herself. Even today, she writes, "If I [...] address the legacy of children of perpetrators in a public forum, I do so with some anxiety and unease" (Schwab, 2010, p. 77). These prohibitions are not merely cultural. When they invade the private and intimate space of the family, for the young and vulnerable members of the family there is no protection against internalising them. Schwab is thus describing how personal and public/cultural spaces merge: the politics of silence inside the family are matched by the politics of silence outside, and affected individuals are left with no separate space in which to define or express their own thoughts or experiences.

Silence is inherently part of the Holocaust legacy, and such silence becomes both individual and shared in its impact. Silence is also inherently part of trauma. Human beings are languaged animals; thought cannot take place without the medium of language. When trauma cannot be symbolised through being expressed—given shape—in language,[5] it can only be enacted: somatised, acted out through repetitive and compulsive behaviours, returned in the form of nightmares, and so on. Lacan (1949) observed that while coming into language itself reflects a traumatic interruption of primal connection to the mother(er), it is in practice the only way of giving shape and voice to trauma. It is through the relationality—intersubjective exchange—of language that all infants—all humans—gradually learn to express *in form* their inner experience, and to manage and master their inner worlds. The loss of language, of the simple ability to communicate, in words, what we are feeling, is a profound interruption of the experience of self. Bollas connects this to the experience of shock—inseparable from trauma—and to the corresponding experience of blankness, when one psychically enters into or is invaded by emptiness and feels lost:

> Certain facts of a person's life are almost always intrinsically traumatic: many things done create momentary caesurae (blanks) within

> the self. By naming such facts the analyst brings the caesurae to the consulting room—these blanks are evoked, their emptiness is felt, and trauma enters the analytic space. [...] It is not that it [the fact] means nothing; it bears nothingness in it [...].
>
> [W]hen the real is presented—as a thing done to us, or as a narrated thing done—*we do not as yet know how to think about it*. There is something *unthinkable* about such facts of life. [...] Shocked by the effect of a thing done, the subject may not know what to do with *it*. (Bollas, 1995, pp. 110, 112)[6]

Certainly, coming across the Holocaust "stopped" Sonia, and her ability to speak, dead:

> "It stops you in your tracks. It's not normal. It's of a magnitude that is beyond comprehension. [...] [Y]ou have to sit and think about it and give it space, and you realize, it's terrible. I can't even ... it can't even be put into words, the magnitude of the terribleness."

For ordinary Jews, silence and "unthinkability" derive from the position we occupy on the edge of this historically documented trauma. In effect, we have retrospectively become spectators of a macabre, ghoulish, and deadly drama, and like all spectators we are likely to feel powerless to do or say anything other than absorb what we are watching. When Weissman suggested that visitors to Holocaust museums and similar memorialisations are, in his view, inappropriately seeking to persuade themselves that they are "witnessing" what happened, he was trying to conceptualise a phenomenon that puzzled him. But he misses a crucial point. What if the Jewish consumers of Holocaust museums are there less because they *wish* to be witnesses than because they have no language for the fact that in a certain sense they already *are*? Gideon speaks of such an experience when he describes his sense of thinking about the Holocaust as akin to watching a drama relentlessly being played out:

> "The Jewish side of [...] seeing your destiny in the Greek tragedy sense—being hemmed in on all sides, losing any means of escape [...]. I'm going to die [...]. [...] Having no means to fight it ...".

Shocked by what was done, we may, indeed, not know what to do with it.

Loss of language, it has to be emphasised, is a real loss. We speak of being "lost for words", but such lostness is no mere technical aberration.

Language is so intrinsic to our humanness that its loss not only deprives us of a key way in which we know ourselves, but in losing it we also find ourselves "lost": disoriented and at sea. This loss returns us to a primitive, preverbal world of sensation, forcing us to re-experience our latent primitive fears and anxieties without the tools we need to negotiate and manage them. Encountering a repeated failure to *find words for* what we feel and experience when we contemplate the Holocaust is in itself a constantly painful loss. At the same time it is an experience in which we are also confronted with our loss of power to articulate, to give shape, to reacquire a sense of mastery: a further reminder of our original helplessness. Such losses are, I suggest, in themselves enough to trigger those other emotions associated with trauma: we are, for example, bound to feel both angry and bereft at being deprived of a skill so crucial to our ability to contain our primitive fears.

"It is completely gripping"

Loss of language is a serious disability, and one of the effects of such a loss seems to be that it traps people in a state of confusion in relation to something that they have an existential need to understand. Primitive humans developed mythical narratives to explain natural phenomena which they could not comprehend, a key function of which was to provide a framework within which meaningful actions could be devised. If the gods, or God, were angry (whether experienced through thunderbolts or floods, drought or pestilence), they had to be placated; some kind of sacrifice was necessary in order to atone. The absence of a containing narrative leaves us simultaneously exposed to both the chaos of the external events and that of our own inner reactions. The *incomprehensibility* of the Holocaust to most ordinary people leaves them extraordinarily ill-equipped to deal with it psychologically, and this, I think, is a key reason why so many writers speak of being in a state of mesmerised fascination with it. Jacobson calls it "the death-in-life grip those slaughtered five or more million had on our imaginations" (Jacobson, 2006, p. 8). Eva Figes talks of her "fascination with the methods of killing" (Figes, 2008, p. 140). In "The vicarious witness", Froma Zeitlin refers to the way in which writing about the Holocaust "has so gripped the modern imagination—of author, critic and reader alike" (Zeitlin, 1998, pp. 35–36). Certain interviewees were also aware of being caught in an internal reaction akin to a state of compulsive gazing:

GIDEON: "The more I think about it, the more interesting I find it. [...] I find it fascinating and horrifying. I suppose some people like approaching a horror film; I don't, it makes me cringe. But I do have this fascination with the absolute horror of the Holocaust. It is completely gripping."

LOUIS: "What is strongly in my mind [...] is how stupid it was. How completely counter-productive [...]. Then you realise, actually, you don't understand these people because it wasn't counter-productive from their point of view ... . you know, they were actually prepared to lose the war, if they ... if they won the Holocaust! [...] How can that make sense? [...] [T]here's something really strange about that, which I ... I find ... [...] to me is really odd and interesting in a repulsive way."

Schwab says that, "Looking at raw horror, terror or violence cannot but appall, but we also know of its inevitable attraction. And it is this same attraction that often becomes most appalling and haunting at the same time" (Schwab, 2010, p. 63). Repeated use of the term "gripped", "grip", "gripping" attests to a way in which Jews experience themselves as both *captivated by* and *captive to* something which has for them little clear narrative shape. It conveys a sense of not knowing what to do whilst simultaneously feeling compelled to gaze, and this suggests an unconscious hope that the repeated act of "watching" may eventually result in a "knowing". But "knowing" is not merely knowing "what it is"; it also leads in hope to our "knowing what to do". It is part of the complicated legacy of the Holocaust that the establishment of Israel, by far the most powerful *action* taken in the aftermath of the war, was driven not only by the external urgency to find a home for a quarter of a million displaced—and dispossessed—European Jews. It also took place in a psychological state of shock at what had happened. No coherent words, no comprehension, no genuine analysis was possible that might gradually assist integration of this dark catastrophe; only a turning to familiar interpretations ("we're the people that people hate") that would fuel the need to do *something* rather than be trapped in impotent horror. And since "Israel" as an idea had been over the centuries an intrinsic symbol of hope and wholeness for Jewish people, the foundation of the state seemed eminently fitted to fill the devastating void left by the catastrophe.

For individual survivors of the camps and the ghettoes, efforts were gradually made post-war to help them give progressive voice to their experiences. Henry Greenspan, one of the most notable scholars in this work, emphasised the need for a sustained dialogue aimed at helping survivors unfold and shape, over time, their own individual narratives. Greenspan comments that "survivors retell more than specific incidents they witnessed and endured. They also convey what it is to *be* a survivor—to be a person who has such memories to retell—which includes what it is to be the particular survivor they each, individually, are"; a sentiment again echoed in Ruth Kluger's assertion that "though the Shoah involved millions of people, it was a unique experience for each of them" (Greenspan, 1998, cited in Weissman, 2004, p. 117; Kluger, 2001, p. 66).

In more detail, Greenspan writes:

> it may be precisely the unfinished, contested, and *not* definitive character of survivors' recounting that offers us fullest access to its significance. That is, it is only as we learn to follow survivors' accounts *as* they become disfigured and finally fail—because the destruction is too vast, because the loss is too unbearable, because meaning becomes undone, because stories fall apart, because voice starts to strangle, because death again invades the recounter—that we begin to approach the Holocaust.' [...] [S]urvivors' reflections on the difficulties of recounting their Holocaust experiences, and their assessment of these experiences from a present perspective, are valued as part of their testimonies, rather than treated as obstructive expressions of 'common memory'. [...] The purpose of ... interpretation [...] is not to uncover what survivors 'really' mean or to substitute our words for theirs. Rather, it is to enter into the process by which survivors *find words and meanings at all* in the face of memories that undo their words and meanings. (Cited in Weissman, 2004, pp. 138–139, my italics)

And Rachel Baum, who reviewed the second edition of Greenspan's book, observes: "Whatever else may come out of listening to survivors [...], Greenspan reminds us that the beginning and end is the listening itself" (Baum, 2012).

Because the word "witnessing" is used very often in relation to the Holocaust, it is worth pointing out that it does not have a single meaning. In its most commonly understood sense, it is used to mean witnessing what happened *to others*, and this is certainly the position that visiting Holocaust memorial museums or simply looking at photographs or newsreels places people in. Those so "witnessed" are placed in the position of "objects" in the gaze of the putative "witness". This can be seen in the way interviewees sometimes referred to those who died as "other" Jews:

DORIS: "For years, I couldn't … I couldn't identify … it bothered me, it upset me greatly […] with the suffering of other Jews in the Holocaust."

ANTONIA: "It's definitely them, it's not us. […] every now and again, I think, it could have been us, but it wasn't. There is a definite distance and I mean we have no relatives who died, not a single one. […] That's why we … [we're] … not emotionally involved, so we can look at it fairly objectively."

OLIVIA: "[My parents talked about it as] a terrible thing that happened to other Jews."

However, in the domain of work with survivors, "witnessing" has acquired a different usage, one which refers to survivors witnessing *their own* experiences in their own words. Survivor writers such as Levi and Kluger essentially did the latter. It is a radically different position from the first use, since it places the survivor witness as the *subject* in and of their own experience, in a way that was a phenomenally important antidote to the objectifying experience of state-organised anti-Semitic murder and ultimate genocide. It is notable that child survivors Dori Laub and Henri Parens, who both became psychoanalysts and writers, eventually embraced subjective witnessing for themselves and found in it a way at least partly to free themselves from the devastating losses incurred in their lost childhoods (Laub, 2012; Parens, 2012).

In referring to such work with survivors my purpose is to emphasise the centrality of language—of creating a narrative—in the expression and gradual integration of trauma. "Narrative", as I use the term here, is not the narrated "shared" memory which Margalit and, further on, Yerushalmi discuss; it is the personal action of speaking (or writing) one's own story, and in so doing, discovering the significance of one's own experience. Ordinary Jews have no claim on the immediacy of Holocaust experience but this does not mean there is no experience to be "witnessed"; it is simply that the experience is a different one. Moreover, being *on* the edge, a spectator, particularly of something to which one is personally or communally connected, has its own specific character. When attention goes to the immediate sufferers, those at the edge are overlooked. They are not the actual victims of the disaster but have a different experience of suffering, of victimhood: one which is compounded by not being seen. This may partly explain the pull to identification with the actual victim; for if the observer's position is denied, identification perforce becomes the only "legitimate" way of connecting to one's own sense of suffering. When it is difficult to articulate *even to oneself* the distinctness of one's own separate experience of suffering, its legitimacy becomes compromised. Suffering does not have to be the same or equal in order to be, in its own way, real. Both Doris's and Antonia's apparent sense of "otherness" is qualified by genuine distress:

ANTONIA: "... we can look at it fairly objectively. [Yet] I think I find it very upsetting, yes. All right, you go to Yad Vashem and cry. [Pause] And you go to Washington, same thing, and you go to [...] London, not so bad, but you do, you go to Paris [...]: it's very upsetting."

DORIS: "The thing that really upset me for a very long time [...] wasn't even the ... [sighs heavily], it sounds awful, the gas chambers ... what used to really bother me emotionally when I first started thinking about it [...] because you can imagine ... we would all understand what it would be like ... I used to think, there they were in these trains for days, in these ... and there was no loo, what must have it been like? And this was so horrifying and so disturbing to me ..."

The dual meaning of "witnessing" also incorporates another important distinction. The first implies "looking at" or "seeing" what happens to others; the second involves speaking. The first is a passive position, the second active. Many of my interviewees spoke with great feeling about survivors they had known, and whose stories they heard, but overwhelmingly the way in which most of us spontaneously *think* of the Holocaust is through visual images. Without exception, we can immediately think of photographic images of Jews in various states of helplessness and degradation.[7] These images are powerful, but they are also frozen. They are not only (for the most part) images of dead people (people who subsequently died, often killed immediately or shortly after, the photographs were taken), but they are dead (frozen) images. Deadness, or frozenness, is core to trauma: feelings become deadened, in that they are unavailable to be felt.[8] Schwab talks of how, even though there was much "spoken" about the war in Germany during the decades afterwards, there was an absence of *emotional connection* with the facts of the genocide. The eerie fascination exercised by the Holocaust is in many respects a visual experience emptied of emotional response, one characterised by being in a state of frozen spectatorship. This sense of shocked, marginalised "witnessing" is also a state of captivity. Language, through its capacity to link thought to emotional experience, becomes an even more important, however imperfect, tool if people are to free themselves from an experience of frozen and uncomprehending horror.

"The Holocaust ruptures 'thought'"

A word which in recent times is often deployed to signify the enormity of the Holocaust is "rupture". A prominent voice in this was theologian Emil Fackenheim who had, according to Braiterman, "an ongoing preoccupation, not with God, but with revelation, rupture and the fragmentation of value" (Braiterman, 1998, p. 134). For Fackenheim, Braiterman observes, "the Holocaust ruptures 'thought'". Against this rupture, Fackenheim endeavoured to renew Jewish theological thinking linked to redefining "wholeness" in a way intended to take account of the "fragmentation" of previous Jewish thought and life. "This rhetoric of fragmentation", Braiterman says, "pioneers a unique theological stance. Fackenheim acknowledges that any post-Holocaust *tikkun*[9] remains incomplete at best. No redemption subsumes painful memories into a larger pattern of meaning and good. […] But", Braiterman continues, "Fackenheim tries too hard to mend a religious landscape constructed totally of unquiet fragments" (ibid., pp. 150–151).[10]

Braiterman sees that for Fackenheim and other contemporary theologians, the Holocaust forced a "radical rupture" between their theological reflections and classical Jewish traditions. Braiterman himself extends the notion of "rupture" further, into post-Holocaust aesthetics and particularly into the landscapes of art:

> I propose that post-Holocaust religious thought reflects the cavernous interiors and *ruptured landscapes* depicted in the paintings of Anselm Kiefer (Ibid., p. 170, my italics)

and he postulates that post-Holocaust theological thinking is trapped in a ruptured mental landscape between the recent past (represented in *Shulamite*, Kiefer's painting of a massive black and burnt-out crypt) and an uncertain future (reflected in *Flight into Egypt*, where two small figures trace an uncertain path through a desert to an unknown destination). "The fragility of good represents a theme that runs throughout the post-Holocaust literature. [...] [T]he survival of the Jewish people, [...] its rebirth in the State of Israel, [...] Jewish life and ritual [...] remain vulnerable, perpetually at risk, never taken for granted" (ibid., p. 178). In undermining confidence in these "goods", the Holocaust effectively ruptured all previous continuities of thought as to God, goodness, and meaning in Jewish life and teaching, and fundamentally challenged what was, after all, core to Jewish life down the centuries.

Fackenheim's idea that the Holocaust ruptures *thought* is intrinsically a rupturing of language. Language and thought are indivisible. Nor is language merely a question of words. Language concerns expressiveness; it gives a shape to what we feel that can be communicated to ourselves and to others. If the Holocaust ruptures thought, it therefore interrupts narrative; and narratives are central to the way in which we relate who and what we are, to and in the world. A catastrophic break in the continuity of narrative interrupts the experience of continuity of self, and this in turn threatens to open the "hole in our psychical world" of which Leader speaks. Jews historically *had* experienced ruptures before, but hitherto had found ways to re-establish a continuity of narrative and thus of (collective) self. The Holocaust disrupted this capacity to a depth never previously experienced, and this may partially explain the strength of feeling behind arguments as to the Holocaust's "uniqueness".

Historian Yerushalmi places the extreme psychological rupturing provoked by the Holocaust in the context of an earlier rupturing that had evolved in Jewish thought in the two previous centuries: a rupturing in tradition which in essence concerns the question of how we narrate *ourselves* through narrating our past. In Biblical and rabbinical tradition, "remembering" was central to the collective Jewish articulation of self; history as such was irrelevant. Jews were liturgically required to "remember" so as to maintain and continuously rework a belief in God as actively engaged with the Jewish people, and a conviction that Jews were on this earth to witness His presence. Narrated memory therefore served to uphold Jewish identity and purpose.[11] According to Yerushalmi, the expulsion of the Jews from Spain in 1492 provoked the first major rupture in this tradition. That expulsion was the greatest catastrophe of Jewish diaspora life to that date; it shook the Jewish world then, and even today stands as one of the great markers of Jewish diaspora experience. It provoked an unprecedented outpouring of work by contemporary Jewish writers, who for the first time started considering the event as something occurring within Jewish *history*. "Nothing that had happened in the Middle Ages", says Yerushalmi,

> not even the Crusader massacres, had engendered a comparable literature. [...] [A]bove all, we find a highly articulated consciousness among the generations following the expulsion from Spain that something unprecedented had taken place, not just that an abrupt end had come to a great and venerable Jewry but something beyond that. [...] It was felt to have altered the face of Jewry and of history itself. When Isaac Abravanel enumerated the sequence of European expulsions that began from England in 1290, he perceived the expulsion from Spain in 1492 as the climax [...]. (Yerushalmi, 1996, pp. 59–60)

Yet within a century, a new spiritual movement—Isaac Luria's Kabbalah—had reasserted the primacy of spiritual values. "Gnostic myth, and not history, provided the extra strength that Jewish memory needed for Jewry to survive its latest catastrophe" (ibid., p. xviii). Despite the rupture in Jewish life and the long-lasting legacy of loss in Sephardi communities, Judaism successfully found a renewed spiritual narrative that would reassert its sense of continuity.

Historiography is a much newer development in Jewish thought than in mainstream European culture, dating back no further than the nineteenth century, but its development reflected a significant change in the way Jews related to events, to themselves, and to the meaning of Jewishness. Emancipation, modernisation, emerging into the world beyond the ghetto: all established Jewish historiography within a modern concept of history and accelerated Jews' separation from their traditional tenets of spiritual life. The process pushed Jews into a search for new meanings to give to Jewish experience. Clive Lawton cites Jonathan Sacks, Chief Rabbi at the time, in saying that:

> "Until the Enlightenment Jews were confident that the strapline of the Jews was 'the people that God loves'; and therefore whatever

> happened was to be read through this experience. If people were unpleasant to us, they were jealous because God loved us; if people were nice to us, it was because God loves us; if things went well for us, it was because God loves us; if they went badly, God was chastising us because he really cares for us. Always that was the reassuring, optimistic, self-aggrandising conviction. At the time of the Enlightenment, people lost confidence in God altogether, the relationship was dead, He wasn't listening; so we constructed a different myth about the Jews: that the Jews were the people that people hated." (Personal communication, October 2006)

For Yerushalmi, the shift continues to pose an unresolved dichotomy between two modes of thought: the spiritual, embedded in the command "to remember", which could be understood as the bedrock of Jewish life; and the modern, given new form through a secular embracing of history. This dilemma, he suggests, "centres upon ruptures, breaks in continuity with many aspects of the Jewish past." To Yerushalmi, Jewish historiography stands

> in opposition to its own subject matter, since it cannot credit God's will as the active cause behind Jewish events, and it cannot regard Jewish history as being unique. [...] Judaism itself has become historicized [...]. With that process [...], Jewish memory and Jewish history begin to oppose each other. (Yerushalmi, op. cit., p. xix)

He sees its development as a response by Jews emerging from the ghettos and *shtetls* of the nineteenth century directed at framing a different kind of psychological continuity from that traditionally upheld:

> The modern effort to reconstruct the Jewish past begins at a time that witnesses a sharp break in the continuity of Jewish living and hence also an ever-growing decay of Jewish group memory. In this sense, if for no other, history becomes what it had never been before—the faith of fallen Jews. (Ibid., p. 86)

In this analysis, the Holocaust becomes a rupture within a rupture. Modern Jews let go of traditional modes of thought and life and embraced the modern world thus forcing a rupture with centuries-old, received meanings of Jewishness. But the Holocaust catastrophically exposed the fragility of the modern world with its apparent progressiveness, leaving Jews in many respects psychologically adrift. According to Lawton, ultra-orthodox Jews have responded by reasserting an unquestioning fidelity to God and spiritual tradition, thus ignoring any rupture:

> "What have the Charedim done as a consequence of the Holocaust? In a most remarkable way—because the Charedi communities were decimated—they said, let's rebuild […]. They didn't go why, or how […], they [just] quietly got on with rebuilding on two fronts. One, re-establishing the institutions wherever they could, in America or Israel; two, rebuilding their numbers. […] If you bear in mind that many leading Charedi Jews were destroyed in the Shoah, you would expect to find a Holocaust memorial or two somewhere in the Charedi world. Not one that I know of, not one. How do the Charedim commemorate the Holocaust? They have fifteen children.
>
> Being absolutely immersed in the traditional Jewish world [their position is], 'It's the same old same old. This happens from time to time. The world gets us.' Maybe we've not been as good as we could have been, maybe some are prepared to blame […] Reform Judaism or the Zionists, but one way or another we weren't getting it right. *Or* we can't know the mind of God. The Book of Job steps in at that point, *or* God punishes us for our misbehaviour, as we saw in the Destruction of the Temple. It's only as bad as the Destruction of the Temple. […] In classic, traditional Jewish form it's translated into behaviours, so the [underpinning] philosophy is hardly ever articulated. […] You won't find Charedim in Holocaust Museums and Memorial Parks: they don't do it." (Personal communication, October 2006)

Ultra-orthodoxy has been growing in appeal for younger Jews in recent years, a trend which is certain to be fuelled by a desire for familiar securities in a world full of uncertainty and rapid change. For the majority of Jews living in a modern and secular mindset, ultra-orthodoxy is not an option; rupture, however, still has to be confronted. Israel seemed to offer an immediate *practical* way to fill the gap and still *symbolically* offers the hope to which many Jews cling, of healing a ruptured past. But Israel alone is an insufficient answer to the rupture in Jewish diaspora experience. In its own internal tensions between democracy and religious identity, Israel has manifestly not resolved the contradictions between the spiritual/orthodox and the secular/modern. It would seem that diaspora Jews still need another way to confront rupture.

"I wouldn't know where to start"

Nobody actually confronts the Holocaust. We do confront the evidence and the physical consequences of it (absent populations, "killing fields" on which nothing will grow, memorial plaques); but mostly what we confront when we think of the Holocaust is a confusion of internal perceptions and reactions that we struggle to make sense of. Even Diana, who spent ten years working with survivors and helping them articulate their stories, did not quite know how to speak of her own reactions:

> "I have talked now and then about it, not deliberately, but it happens sometimes. […] I don't know [what would stop me talking deliberately about it] […] maybe I wouldn't know where to start."

Central to what I am exploring here is a thesis that language—the skill which helps us "make sense of" our world—is essential for "confronting" the Holocaust, but that ordinary Jews in their peripheralised position, related to the Holocaust but not part of it, find themselves robbed of speech: overwhelmed by feelings but incoherent; bereft of the words humans always need if they are to find meaning.

It has been said often that there *is* no meaning to the Holocaust and this is true enough in the sense that catastrophic events, whether natural phenomena or those fuelled by primitive and destructive hatreds, intrinsically lack meaning.[12] Nevertheless, this stops neither our impulse to find meaning nor our sense of desolation and disorientation in its lack. Human beings are not good at embracing emptiness or chaos. *Any* meaning, no matter how imperfect or counterproductive, is better than *no* meaning;[13] but the search for new meaning in the context of the ruptured narratives forced by the Holocaust is so difficult that there is a strong temptation to fill the space with familiar interpretations fuelled by primitive reactions: helplessness ("it was ever thus"), paranoia ("they'll always hate us"), or some equally self-limiting equivalent.

The word "meaning" necessarily occurs often in relation to such great rupturing events and experiences, for "meaning" is psychologically central to our lives. According to sociologist Peter Marris, nowhere does this become more apparent than in times of grievous loss. In *Loss and Change*, a study which mainly focuses on communities ruptured by change, Marris argues that major experiences of loss are experienced as painfully as they are by those bereaved because of the disruption of meaning in their own lives consequent on the loss. The meaning previously brought to the bereaved person's own life by the one(s) lost is central to the survivor's own sense of self, and it is the disruption of this meaning which brings such intense pain:

> The fundamental crisis of bereavement arises, not from the loss of others, but the loss of self. [...] When the dead person has been, as it were, the keystone of a life, the whole structure of meaning in that life collapses when the keystone falls. [...] To say that life has lost its meaning [...] describes a situation where someone is bereft of purpose, and so feels helpless. Familiar habits of thought and behaviour no longer make sense. *Nor can one escape from this distress by adopting new purposes since [...] purposes are learned and consolidated through a lifetime's experience, becoming embodied in the relationships which sustain them.* They inform the context of meaning by which life is interpreted, and so new purposes remain meaningless until they can be referred to those which have gone before. (Marris, 1986, p. 33, my italics)[14]

Marris calls meaning "a crucial organizing principle of human behaviour". As a consequence, meaning is central to all experiences of loss; and in all situations of loss, whether personal or communal, a similar psychological process of reintegration of whom and what has been lost is needed:

> When we lose [a crucial] relationship, the whole structure of meaning centred upon it disintegrates. [...] Meaning [...] makes sense of action by providing reasons for it; and the collapse of compelling reasons to act constitutes the trauma of loss. (Ibid., p. xvii)
>
> [...] Bereavement, [...] because it robs us of a crucial attachment, profoundly disrupts our ability to organize experience in a meaningful way. Correspondingly, social changes which disrupt our

> ability to interpret and respond to our world of experience are a form of bereavement. Both call for a process of recovery whereby the underlying structure of emotion and purpose can disengage itself from irretrievable assumptions and circumstances without losing its ability to generate meaning. [...] [T]he task of reintegration is essentially similar, whether the structures of meaning fall apart from the loss of a personal relationship, a predictable social context or of an interpretable world. (Ibid., p. x)[15]

Central to Marris's argument is his understanding of rupture as being *that which disrupts meaning*. Bereavement, he argues, represents a crisis of continuity in which the survivor has to work through a conflict between past and present. Grief:

> is the expression of a profound conflict between contradictory impulses—to consolidate all that is still valuable and important in the past, and preserve it from loss; and at the same time, to re-establish a meaningful pattern of relationships, in which the loss is accepted. (Ibid., p. 31)

The circumstances and nature of the loss also powerfully affect "the ability to construct or reconstruct meaning—to make sense of what has happened and assimilate it to present circumstances in a purposeful way" (ibid., p. xiii). Social upheaval can be:

> as disruptive of the meaning of life as the loss of a crucial relationship. Dispossession threatens the whole structure of attachments through which purposes are embodied, because these attachments cannot readily be re-established in an alien setting. [...] In all such situations, the ambivalence of grieving has to work itself out. (Ibid., p. 57)

I have particularly quoted Marris here so as to highlight further how enormous was the rupturing impact of the Holocaust, and to contextualise it as an experience that for Jews is one of profound loss. Marris connects loss to the interruption in continuity we experience in situations of major loss. I suggest that fundamentally the impact of such interruption is to disrupt the continuity of *narrative* that we develop throughout our lives. Narratives are key to the way we experience ourselves as individuals with meaning. It is in the construction and relating of our "stories", through relationship with others and with ourselves, that we learn that our lives are "meaning-full": in Winnicott's words, that we experience ourselves as "going on being". The tangible losses which the Holocaust involved—devastating enough for survivors—simultaneously invoked a more intangible shattering of continuities for Jews near and far: of family roots and connection to the past; the possibility of return and reconnection; confidence in one's unquestioned right to be in the world; the ongoing expectation of a Jewish life to which one may belong. In Group Analytic terms, this is a rupture in the communal matrix: the psychological holding space to which individuals entrust part of their personal narrative and which in the flow of "conversation" with its constituents evolves its own community narrative of identity.[16] When the matrix is shattered, it is a loss of home. Aspects of ourselves no longer have a place "to be", where our story is recognised and understood. This, as Marris points out, is one reason why the loss of a spouse or partner with whom one has developed a mutual life story can be so devastating. While ordinary Jews never experienced the immediacy of lost family and home in the Holocaust, it shook confidence in the continuity of a Jewish collective matrix and therefore implicitly poses for Jews an anxiety as to where to find a secure home for an important part of their own personal narrative. How, in the wake of the Holocaust, are Jews generally to "preserve [...] from loss [...] all that is still valuable and important [from] the past" and "at the same time, [...] re-establish a meaningful pattern of relationships, in which the loss is accepted" when what may have been valuable and important from the past was itself so lost? Are there still (and I would suggest there are) issues of incomplete mourning involved, for our ruptured past in Europe?

These losses of continuity and narrative are also framed by the legacy of ordinary Jews' own disrupted history. Most ordinary Jews inherit two particularly powerful recent histories: one, the intense physical and emotional upheaval involved in migration, which is the background family history shared by almost all ordinary Ashkenazi Jews and which, to all intents and purposes, disappeared as an emotionally lived experience from the discourse of Jews at the time and since; and second, the rupture in the psychological continuities of "Jewishness" which I have described in this chapter. These historic ruptures, incorporating losses of continuity of belonging and of self, constitute a shared emotional backdrop to ordinary Jews' psychological positioning vis-à-vis the Holocaust. They also offer a constantly available reference point from which all subsequent history may be interpreted consciously or unconsciously from a position of loss.

When Marris writes of the fundamental crisis of bereavement being less the loss of others than the loss of self, he makes a point particularly relevant for ordinary Jews. While the many losses involved in the Holocaust were not direct losses for us or our immediate forebears, they still represent something of ourselves. If meaning is central to human life and loss ruptures meaning, then the massive and complex losses involved in genocide can be understood as a terrible breach in a community's ongoing sense of itself; a self which will always need a continuously unfolding narrative of its own meaning.

Post-Holocaust reactions amongst Jewish communities can be thought of as deriving from strong impulses to fill such a breach rather than feel the full nature of its impact. Israel, I have argued, was the most immediate and tangible outcome of this impulse. Israel was, not least, a determined effort to reconstruct a sense of historic continuity via God's covenant to Jews in relation to "HaEretz" (the Land), and in so doing to "vault over" the recent, appalling rupture to the community's continuity. In *The Holocaust and Collective Memory*, Novick argued that in America the reaction was to appropriate the Holocaust so as to fill the growing gap in modern American Jews' sense of identity (Novick, 1999). French historian Esther Benbassa sees a more pervasive reaction in the way in which the concept of "suffering" seems to have become the central motif that defines being Jewish. "Suffering", she argues, is the new paradigm for Jewish identity. This reframing of "suffering", she suggests, attempts to provide Jews with a form of continuity from past to present: a continuity disturbed in the first place by the break with spiritual traditions, and more catastrophically by the rupture with a living past embodied in the Holocaust (Benbassa, 2007).

Each of these interpretations makes sense in the light of Marris's observations that communities as well as individuals afflicted by rupturing losses need sooner or later to re-establish a sense of continuity in their own sense of identity in order to direct future energy purposefully. What Novick and Benbassa describe, and what Israel embodies, are responses to rupture expressed in specific narratives which purport to, but actually fail to, provide Jews with a meaningful link to the past.

The difficulty is that none of these "solutions" deal with the emotional reality of the ordinary Jewish present: the confusion, shock, horror, loss of words at the all-too-recent past whose effects are still with us. Rather than helping ordinary Jews articulate their own sense of loss and rupture, the deficit is artificially supplied with quasi-mantras, or what Eric L. Santner calls "narrative fetishism". Language is taken on that is repetitive, predictable, and standardised: the Holocaust (or, more generically, genocide) "should never happen again"; "we (Israel) will take charge of our own destiny", "anti-Semitism is always ready to strike", and so on. Such phrases, I suggest, correspond to what Santner calls a "fetishistic" and Schwab an "empty" language: surface narratives that, Santner says, in practice serve "to expunge" rather than engage with the actual experience "of the trauma or loss that called [the] narrative into being in the first place." Santner contrasts such avoidant narratives with what Freud called "the work of mourning"—*trauerarbeit*: an active "working through" of the traumatic residue, however experienced. "Both narrative fetishism and mourning are responses to loss, to a past that refuses to go away due to its traumatic impact" (Santner, 1992, p. 144). As Schwab noted about post-war Germany where (in her experience) the form of language hid more than it revealed, empty language does little to heal the ruptures of self- or communal experience (Schwab, op. cit., ch. 2)

"It's all the disasters, isn't it?"

Jews have a very restricted perception of their own history. Asking most Jews to name the most significant events in Jewish history, as I sometimes did in interviews, elicits a telling list. Leaving aside the Holocaust and the foundation of the state of Israel—by far the two biggest events in Jewish life in the last seventy years—you will find that what most people automatically think of are most or all of the following: the destruction of the Temple(s); the siege of Mount Masada; the Crusades; the expulsion from Spain in 1492; and the Chmielnicki Massacres of 1648–49; or, as one person ruefully contemplating his own choices put it, "all the disasters". Few people think to include in their list the great migrations westwards of the 1880s–1900s, an omission especially remarkable given that that demographic shift became retrospectively the single biggest factor in modern Jewish history to ensure the survival of a Jewish population worldwide. More than half of today's Jews would not be here now were it not for those decisions taken by our grandparents and great-grandparents. Yet Jews seem wedded to a disastrous view of their own history and oddly resistant to thinking otherwise. Lawton, for example, recounts what happened when he offered a counter-cultural lecture to one Jewish group:

> "I [recently] gave a talk called 'Jewish History was a Ball.' I argued that we've actually had a marvellous time through the centuries, and we are so lucky to be Jews, because could you imagine what it would be like to be non-Jewish in terms of oppression and grimness? […] You've no idea how the audience hated this story.
>
> I asked them, 'What happened in the thousand years in Babylon from 400 BCE to 600 CE?' Blank. I said, 'Of course you don't know, because it was very nice.' We don't tell ourselves that story. We're great with the Spanish Inquisition, we're not so good with the Golden Age. We forget to notice. It might have been grim to be Jewish in the Middle Ages, but it wasn't such a ball to be non-Jewish in the Middle Ages, and we don't talk about that." (Lawton, personal communication, October 2006)

Like Benbassa, he notes how present Jewish identity was formed through the socio-psychological shifts of the eighteenth century, and that it continues to uphold itself no longer by reference to a spiritual tradition but instead to a perception of continually impending disaster:

> "We have a tradition of noting and recording our tragedies. We know about the Crusades and the Spanish Inquisition, but we never made them central to our awareness of ourselves until this last two hundred years. […] We've always had the narrative that Jews are in exile. […] That's in the liturgy. It's not the same as suffering dreadfully. […] [Once] Jews started to say, '[…] [Our suffering is] because they don't let us have our rights,' they reinterpreted the definition of suffering as meaning being exiled from contemporary civil life, like not being able to go to University. That wasn't what Jews meant when they were talking about the suffering of the Jews in the fourteenth century.
>
> […] At the time of the Enlightenment, […] we constructed a different myth about the Jews: that the Jews were the people that people hated […]. That's become the motivating story of the

> modern age. So if you try to get Jews to come inside a building to do something interestingly Jewish, they won't: 'It's not my thing.' If you say, 'Would you stand outside in the freezing cold with a walkie-talkie in order to deter the anti-Semites?'—'Absolutely.' It's become our narrative for who we are." (Ibid.)

Sonia exemplifies this. Until recently, her knowledge of Jewish history was so limited that:

> "I used to associate the Holocaust … as the 'only' Jewish history."

"Even today", Benbassa says,

> whenever Jewish history is mentioned, it is this memory of suffering that is cited first; […] it creates an identity for secularised Jews and, at the same time, cohesion in exile. [S]uch utilisation of the memory of suffering often stands in the way of a proper understanding of history, which makes it harder to maintain the appropriate distance between history and emotion, history and memory. Often, all that Jews […] retain of Jewish history is this discourse on suffering, because the real or imagined memory of suffering has long served in history's stead, and continues to do so today. […] Since the genocide, it has haunted us more than ever, tending to dictate an interpretation of the past as nothing but suffering, while closing off the present and future from the kind of hope that was once nourished by faith: a hope that is fragile yet was, only yesterday, omnipresent in Jewish life. (Benbassa, op. cit., pp. 30–31)

All nations have narratives of self, ways in which their people like to recognise themselves. Poles, like Jews, live with a narrative of suffering, one that in their case finds expression in their identification with the suffering figure of Christ.[17] A dominant Anglo-British self-narrative is that of a plucky island nation stoically resisting would-be invaders. Programmes about the Second World War are still part of our staple TV diet. Scots see themselves as a people oppressed by the English, a perception which always refers back to the story of the Highland Clearances. To Americans, the Statue of Liberty embodies their self-image as the champions of freedom. There is an existential truth in each of these national images but as dominant icons they occlude other stories which are more difficult or less desirable to tell. We know only too well how during the 1930s the narrative that came to dominate in Germany was the perception of Germans as humiliated victims of Versailles, a belief which helped fuel an overpowering drive to recast themselves as triumphant victors. The Holocaust was a devastating reality involving appalling suffering and shocking levels of commitment to destroy ordinary human beings. Yet even within the dominant picture of unremitting horror, there are glimpses of other realities: of courage, ingenuity, luck, humanity, and so on. With every "simple" picture of the Holocaust or of ourselves that we hold on to, we marginalise the complexity of all our stories. As Donald Bloxham puts it, "no one representation can adequately capture the essence of the past, for there is never only one essence" (Bloxham, 2009, p. 29). Trauma is enacted but never worked through in the repeated attachment to one view, one representation or one story.

"Who can you talk to about the Holocaust?"

In Chapter One I noted that the Holocaust is the kind of trauma that, consciously or unconsciously, demands meaning. By this I mean that, in the face of our incomprehension and bewilderment, we search for meaning as a way of giving ourselves a "purchase" on this seemingly unfathomable disaster. But the search for meaning, as Frankl wrote, is an active and continual process. Moreover, there is no single meaning that will be the same for all: "meaning" must always make personal sense, if it is to make sense at all. We still need, as human beings, to search for it.

Bollas writes of the analytic importance of "psychic elaboration" of the facts in an individual's life as a way of gradually detraumatising how traumatic "fragments" play out. "Facts" (i.e., actual events) create what he calls "hits" for people, and the therapeutic task is one of exploring such "hits" until their meaning becomes clearer for the individual "hit by" them:

> the presentation of the factual, the outcome of a deed done [...] is always somewhat traumatic. [...] Shocked by the effect of a thing done, the subject may not know what to do with *it*. Such a caesura becomes the potential matrix of psychic elaboration, if the individual can return to the scene of the fact done and imagine it,

> perhaps again and again. [...] [I]t may be that such facts nucleate into unconscious complexes, collecting other facts from life which increasingly gravitate into a particular mentality that derives from the *hit* of the fact. [...] [T]he analyst's interpretation of the patient's psychic reality, one derived from these associations, is intrinsically detraumatising, for it creates meaning where nothingness existed. (Bollas, 1995, pp. 112–113)

In the end, I suspect, it does not do justice to our separate experiences simply to speak of the Holocaust as "a collective trauma"; it is too complex to be reduced to a conceptual shorthand. The Holocaust was a massive event spanning many years, stages of development, countries, governments, episodes, and people. Trauma is an active pattern of human experience and reaction. Rather than "a" collective trauma, we would be better speaking of many different traumas, or many *aspects* of trauma, that our awareness of the Holocaust elicits in us. An equally important question is how we might recognise and face these. Ultimately, I would argue, meanings can only be found through language: through speaking and writing, and through the creation and renewal of narrative. And, to take further Margalit's observations on memory, as we cannot possess a shared meaning independently of the ones we have as separate individuals, finding meaning through our narratives is something we also have to do for ourselves.

Many interviewees commented on the benefit of speaking that the interviews themselves involved. The process seemed to be liberating; a chance to find out more clearly what they felt:

LIMMUD WORKSHOP

PARTICIPANT: "[Speaking together about it] was very worthwhile. I think it is one of the subjects that we all need to share our feelings with each other [about], and our knowledge and our lack of knowledge and our awareness, and it's only by these things ... [There were] things that are very deeply moving [...] that we actually hadn't thought about."

OLIVIA: "It's good always to clarify one's thoughts. I think we don't often pause enough to clarify our feelings about the Holocaust, and we have ready access to the kind of iconic publicly commemorated images that [means] it's very easy just to access that top level of engagement that [...] you already know about. So it's good to dig a little deeper."

SONIA: "It's been cathartic. And [...] I really think it's important. [...] [M]aybe [...] it can contribute to the healing process."

BERNICE: "I didn't know what I had to say until you asked me."

DORIS: "I realise from it that I'm on a journey ... I have been on a journey of understanding, reclaiming myself, which I haven't yet finished. That's the main thing."

Alice also described how going to Poland, and speaking to others about it both before and during, "settled" a latent anxiety in her:

> "Before the trip [to Poland], I was apprehensive and I talked to a couple of friends who had been on similar trips. [...] I thought I was going to find it a lot harder than I did. I thought I'd be a complete emotional wreck because I'm quite sensitive [...] ... But [...] it didn't hit us the way I thought it was going to. It was in a way reassuring that other people were experiencing it in the same way. [...] I think going there settled something in me. Because growing up, you hear all these stories and you hear survivors' experiences and you see pictures and it's building up this whole image in your mind about this event that happened, but actually going and seeing where it took place settles something. I don't really know how to explain ... [...] ... I think it was [something] like, you've seen it so it actually did happen."

But Gideon and Diana reflected on how difficult it can be to speak about it in normal life, outside a supporting framework:

GIDEON: "On the whole, who can you talk to about the Holocaust? [...] There's a limit to how much I can talk about it, as well."

DIANA: "I have talked now and then about it, not deliberately, but it happens sometimes. [...] I don't know [what would stop me talking deliberately about it] [...] maybe I wouldn't know where to start. [...] [T]he things I'm talking to you about today I have talked about before, but not linking them to this work that I did. [...] I wanted to sit down and talk about [other things]; but maybe there are links."

It is narrative, the forming and telling of our own stories, through which we constantly discover the meaning of ourselves and our lives. The search for authentic representational form, such as can be developed through narrative, is key to mourning and to the recovery of meaning and purpose in life. As an active process, narrative is also a vital antidote to helplessness. Ordinary Jews need to speak of their own experience of being on the periphery of the Holocaust story; to give life to this otherwise helpless sense of "spectating" and in so doing reclaim who they are as ordinary participants in an extraordinary communal history.

I called this chapter 'Held captive?' to suggest that without difficult explorations of loss and the painful process of developing our own narrative responses, we are effectively imprisoned in fixed views of the world and an unchanging experience of ourselves as helpless spectators of the worst imaginable horror. "How can you? … there's no scale" is one statement of shock that reflects a psychic experience of being trapped. Language is the most powerful tool available, and one we all share, that can bring air and light into this state: "to create meaning where nothingness existed." But it takes time and effort to find words and to shape more authentic narratives, through the painstaking processes of "psychic elaboration".

The formative story that all Jews share is that of the Exodus. Liberation from slavery in Egypt and accepting the Torah as a binding commitment to live ethically bound lives in a relationship with God is what made the Israelites Jews. The story of the Exodus, annually remembered at the beginning of Passover, is usually recounted either to remind Jews of their everlasting debt to God, or to prompt Jews to oppose all present forms of slavery. But there is another, inner, meaning to the story.

Between escaping from Egypt and arriving in the "Promised Land", the Children of Israel wandered for forty years in the wilderness, along the way receiving their revelation. The wilderness is a physical transition point between Egypt and the Promised Land, but it is also a psychological one between captivity—enslavement to old ways of living and thinking—and freedom—the freedom to choose how to live and whom to honour. The Promised Land cannot be reached without spending a long period bereft of familiar comforts and securities, uncertain as to where one is going. At one point the children of Israel reproach Moses for bringing them on this hazardous journey:

> All the congregation of the children of Israel came unto the wilderness of Sin […] on the fifteenth day of the second month after their departing out of the land of Egypt. And the whole congregation […] murmured against Moses and Aaron in the wilderness; And the children of Israel said unto them, Would to God we had died by

> the hand of the Lord in the land of Egypt, when we sat by the flesh pots and when we did eat bread to the full; for ye have brought us forth into this wilderness to kill this whole assembly with hunger. (Exodus 16, verses 1–3)

The Exodus symbolises all psychological journeys of recovery and growth. No Jew asked for the Holocaust to happen but it did; this fact leaves all Jews to deal individually and collectively with a powerful emotional legacy. "Collective trauma" is an imperfect description of the starting point. The journey into the sometimes desolate, sometimes turbulent emotional world of our post-Holocaust reactions has still to be mapped; but challenging as they may be to find, we do have words.

POSTSCRIPT

In over forty years of riding a bicycle, I have only twice had an accident. The first was about a month after beginning to work on this book; the second was three weeks after I had finished.

When in Chapter One I wrote confidently, about the first accident, that I had fully recovered, this was indeed the case. It was, I thought then, one of those unpredictable things which had just "happened". It had taught me something about the immediacy of a traumatising event, but otherwise I thought no more about it. The timing of the second accident, however, made me think again. For all my careful working through the various aspects of trauma Jews hit up against when they think of the Holocaust, I realised that these two unexpected accidents, occurring as they did in such a strangely synchronous relationship to this book, put me in touch with the Holocaust in a way I had not given closer attention to before; hence a postscript seemed to be called for.

Throughout the book, I had reflected on how our ordinary Jewish perceptions of the Holocaust impact on us: how it activates personal experiences and shapes our cultural inheritance; what use we make of it to interpret and relate to the world in which we live now. My orientation had largely been a direction of travel that flowed from *then* to *now*, for I had mostly written about how this particular past affects reactions, beliefs, and expectations in the present. The Holocaust is a history certain to arouse ambivalence amongst its principal inheritors. We want it enshrined in our history yet our relationship to it is hardly easy. It is in our cultural inheritance, but we don't know what to do with it. Partly out of duty and partly out of mesmerised fascination, we may read books, watch films and documentaries about it, go to museums and memorials, all of which involve taking in what other people have provided for us: selected information, interpretations, images. This is all part of an attempt to find a relationship with the Holocaust, but it is one which tends to keep us in the passive role of consumers and spectators. I had therefore concluded the book proposing that ordinary Jews need to become more *actively* engaged with the consequences of this legacy, through putting their own experience into words. In that way, I thought, the traumatic weight of the past could be digested and it need no longer hang so oppressively and unresolvedly over present and future.

We like to think of the past as something from which "we" (broadly defined) should learn certain lessons for our benefit in the present. In fact the past has a life of its own, and questions about our relating to it require us to address it in those terms. Traumatic pasts haunt because of the immense difficulty of engaging with what they contain. Often we oscillate between feeling helplessly overwhelmed and defending ourselves against that very feeling: by, for example, a utilitarian attitude towards the past as something to be used for our purposes and gratifications in the present. The combination of the two accidents, uncannily "topping and tailing" my entire project, brought something else into focus. I saw that what happens to us as we go through our ordinary, everyday lives in real time, provides another way of connecting to the Holocaust (or indeed any communal traumatic history): of understanding it *for itself* and not only as something there to serve us. The past is not a static entity; it had its own life, which if we want to, we can learn something about through the ongoing experiences of our own lives.

In the first accident, my world literally turned upside-down. I went head-over-heels over the handlebars of my bike and landed on my head. I have a permanent memory gap of the ten or fifteen minutes leading up to the accident and its immediate aftermath (for which I am extremely grateful), and will never know what caused it. Nor does this matter. What did matter is that my physical world and sense of physical security came apart. For two weeks my brain and body were terrifyingly disconnected. I could not move even around the confined space of a small house without an acute fear of falling and hitting my head again. My previous taken-for-granted seamless integration of thought and movement was frighteningly disrupted: nothing was normal; nothing could be relied on; every movement was fraught with danger.

Only in the aftermath of the second accident, did I grasp how much this experience captured something of Jewish people's experience under Nazi rule. The Nazis created a world in which all norms, all normal expectations, were violently turned upside-down. In that topsy-turviness where nothing can any longer be taken for granted, there is acute terror. How to move; what is safe to do; whom to reach out to; how to attend to one's basic survival needs—these and more were daily uncertainties of terrifying import for both victims and survivors of the Nazi regime. For a short time in my own life, I was given an intense experience of some of what being a victim entailed, without (thankfully) the deliberate and sustained cruelty that was the hallmark of the Nazi project. When I look back at this first accident, I have a more palpable sense of what it means to live in a world where there is no safety, no security, and where every step entails frightening risk.

The second accident was less potentially serious but had a more lasting effect. It occurred on another balmy day in late spring, shortly after I had returned from visiting Israel and the West Bank with members of my Jewish community in Edinburgh, a trip whose aim was to learn about the work of Israeli human rights organisations. The tour was very unsettling as it was bound to be, for much of what we encountered reflected how Israel, the too-quickly-founded, immediate inheritor of the Holocaust, continues to enact its own relics of trauma. Four days after returning home, quite distracted, I took a wrong turning, pulled into the kerb, lost my footing, keeled over sideways, and fractured my wrist. Complications seven weeks later required surgery, and for large parts of the summer and autumn I could not use my left hand.

Unlike the first accident, I was fully conscious throughout this one. I was also acutely aware of its long-drawn-out impact: weeks of considerable pain, shock, distress, and anger. I was especially angry at how little I could physically do; and one thing in particular that I could not do was write.

I had finished Chapter Seven arguing how important it is that ordinary Jews begin to structure a personally owned narrative about themselves and the Holocaust through the difficult task of putting their own words to their thoughts and feelings. Talking, I thought, was necessary if this history was to be engaged with in a more alive emotional way, and ultimately properly mourned for. Yet in the aftermath of the second accident, I suddenly couldn't write. As a ten-finger typist, typing is the way in which I translate my thoughts—my own words—into prose. What this meant, in effect, was that I couldn't "speak". For many weeks, therefore, this second accident gave me a direct experience of what it means not to be able to "speak" of one's pain and anguish. It echoed, I think, what victims endured and what survivors were left with; it also reflects that for ordinary Jews, too, speaking of what we want or need to say can be very hard.

I do not want to make too much of these experiences. I recovered, to a greater or lesser extent. Together, however, the two accidents and their aftermath obliged me to recognise that, whether we like it or not, sometimes we are faced with situations in which we have to think the unthinkable and speak the unspeakable. Not in order to add to our suffering, but in order to end it.

NOTES

Introduction

1. It is an interesting reflection of the cultural biases involved in studying the Holocaust that, according to Moyn himself, the controversy engendered in France was either little noticed or entirely forgotten about in America, where so much in the way of Holocaust studies takes place, until the late 1990s.
2. Weissman is particularly critical of writers such as Elie Wiesel, who explicitly asserts that no one who didn't go through the Holocaust can ever know it.
3. Elie Wiesel, a survivor of Auschwitz, along with Primo Levi, is one of the most prominent writer/survivors of the Holocaust. Through his writings he has achieved (and asserts) world status as "the authoritative" survivor. Alfred Kazin is a Jewish American writer and critic who, it would appear, initially sought to relate to the then recent events of the Holocaust through befriending Wiesel, but who later became estranged from him. Lawrence Langer is a literary scholar of the Holocaust whose work has been devoted to grasping the magnitude of its horrors. Steven Spielberg is one of the top Hollywood film directors whose 1993 film of the Holocaust, *Schindler's List*, has been both widely praised and criticised. Claude Lanzmann is a French film-maker whose lengthy (nine-and-a-half-hour) film about the Holocaust, *Shoah* (1985), used a

documentary technique comprising interviews both with survivors and with individuals who had been part of the organising machinery of the extermination camps.

4. While it is true that for some people no explicit confusion seems to arise, I think that efforts to label (or even deny) something as complex as the Holocaust as simply a "this" or a "that" arise from an internal world in which the confusion of feeling states and reactions is experienced as just too overwhelming.
5. Weissman critically cites, among others, Dominick LaCapra's (2001) term "secondary witness" and usages such as "vicarious witnesses" or "witnesses by adoption".
6. For example, Novick refers (1999, p. 5) to certain chapters in the Book of Esther, completely removed from modern Purim commemoration, which tell of the permission granted Esther to have slaughtered 75,000 wives and families of Haman and his genocidal cohorts. Novick comments that in the context of mediaeval Europe, these "memories" would have "provided gratifying revenge fantasies" to the Jews of the time.
7. The atmosphere in which this interview took place may bear comparison to May 1948 when the State of Israel was founded, and which for many Jews at the time involved a profound sense of relief, celebration, and—at last—acknowledgement.
8. I was particularly concerned to interview some Jews from a non-Ashkenazi tradition, as my assumption was that part of the post-Holocaust impact on Jews relates to the historic ties that most Ashkenazi Jews have to the old Jewish heartlands of Europe.

Chapter One

1. In *Moses and Monotheism* (1939), Freud made the first psychoanalytic attempt to theorise about a Jewish inheritance of shared psychic trauma, proposing that the origins of Judaism involved a deep-seated repression of guilt amongst Jews about an original communal act of murder. The book was, not surprisingly, highly controversial at the time, and Freud's speculations remained tangential to psychoanalytic thinking for some decades.
2. Based on a novel by Patricia Highsmith, this film tells of a charming psychopath who progressively engages in a psychotic world of pretence and murder.
3. The book in question, Lord Russell of Liverpool's *Scourge of the Swastika* (1954), was clearly a highly influential book in its day, since at least two

of my interviewees, both in their sixties at the time of interview, learnt about the Holocaust through reading it.

4. Throughout this book, I use the term "clinical" to indicate settings involving professional attention to wounds of the psyche. "Clinical" is often understood as specifically "medical", and "trauma" is a medical term applied by doctors to physical injuries. However, in Britain the psychological use of "clinical" extends to practice by non-medically trained psychologists, psychoanalysts, and psychotherapists.
5. Specifically, in Chapter Seven Bollas speaks of "emotional death" and of the "death of self" (p. 187); a "killed self" (p. 189); and a self frightened of coming into the excitement of being alive (p. 197).
6. Limmud is a Jewish educational event that takes place both in national and regional venues in the UK each year.
7. "*Shul*" is the popular term used by Ashkenazi (German and East European Jews) to refer to synagogue.
8. A "*kind*": one of thousands of children ("*kinder*"), rescued from Germany, Austria, and occupied Czechoslovakia, often through the efforts of British people, and brought over to safety in the UK. The last "*kindertransport*" left Prague on the eve of war in September 1939.
9. The Hebrew plural equivalent of "rabbis".
10. Account.
11. Archaeological evidence indicates that human settlements needed a minimum critical mass of human members before skill specialisation could develop, which in turn underpinned the capacity of human groups to organise for mutual advantage.
12. LaCapra is concerned to distinguish between what he calls a "dubious" identification with victims, and empathic unsettlement, which he describes as involving "a kind of virtual experience through which one puts oneself in the other's position while recognising the difference of that position and hence not taking the other's place." This is an accurate description of an empathic process crucial to the effective practice of psychotherapy.
13. See the ground-breaking work of John Bowlby, whose body of work on attachment, loss, and depression provided the clinical evidence underpinning the work of the object relations school of psychotherapy. See, too, James and Joyce Robertson's poignant series of films of children temporarily separated from their parents through hospital and other institutional forms of care (www.robertsonfilms.info).
14. Holocaust education in schools offers the younger generation some opportunity to process the impact, but from the point of view of learning rather than dealing with the depth of emotional reaction.

Chapter Two

1. Five million is the number cited in *The Scourge of the Swastika*, which was the book from which Jacobson's hero learnt about the Holocaust.
2. Specifically, Gubar cites Bauman's (1989) assertion in *Modernity and the Holocaust* that "[the Holocaust] stands alone and bears no meaningful comparison with other massacres"; Friedlander, who states in *Memory, History and the Extermination of the Jews of Europe* that "the 'Final Solution', as a result of its apparent historical exceptionality, could well be inaccessible to all attempts at a significant representation and interpretation"; and Lang for his declaration in *Act and Idea in the Nazi Genocide* (1990) that "all figurative representation [of genocide] will diminish the moral understanding of it".
3. *Kinder fun Maidanek* forms part of longer poem, *A kholem fun nokh Maydanek* (A dream after Maidanek), published by Zeitlin in volume one of his collected poems, *Gezamlte Lider* (1947). Zeitlin had left Poland for a short lecture tour in New York in 1939. While he was in America the Nazis invaded Poland, he couldn't return, and his whole family, including his only son, perished. He remarried in America but had no further children.
4. Jeremiah 31 verse 15. I first came across this quotation carved into stone at the entrance to an early Holocaust museum on Mount Zion in Jerusalem.
5. It should be noted that Hoffman was born in Poland and lived there till she was thirteen, at which point her parents moved the family to Canada. Her loss was therefore of an actual country which formed a central reference point for her childhood; her sense of loss and dislocation from the Poland of her youth is the subject of an earlier book, *Lost in Translation* (1989).
6. As an illustration of the close relationship between Romania and Nazi Germany, two Romanian battalions fought alongside German ones at the battle of Stalingrad.
7. According to Bloxham, the designation of Jews in Romania was complicated by the large numbers of Jews whom Romania had "acquired" as a consequence of territorial changes after World War One. Romania, evidently, did not deport its "old" Jews, but in nationalist terms saw the newly acquired Jews as "non-Romanian" and therefore expendable. The fact remains, however, that "in the region of 270,000 Jews under Romanian control died as a result of Romanian and German measures" (Bloxham, 2009, p. 114).
8. In Auschwitz main camp, different countries from which Jews were deported to Auschwitz have each been assigned a former barrack to

use as their own pavilion for exhibition purposes. The Dutch exhibition explicitly poses the troubled question, "How did we let this happen?".

9. Although estimates vary, it seems that about one in two German Jews and two in three Austrian Jews had made their way abroad by 1941. See, as one indicator, Helen Junz's study of pre-war wealth amongst the Jewish population in Nazi-occupied countries.
10. Gubar is particularly preoccupied with the psychological impact on those German Jews who left Germany of learning of the deaths of family members who were unable to leave, since both her mother's father and her own father committed suicide after the war.
11. For Sephardi Jews, the equivalent to Poland in terms of loss of a long-established and rich Jewish culture and way of life is Salonika (Thessaloniki) in northern Greece. Before 1939, some fifty thousand Jews lived in Salonika (one-fifth of the city's population). Over the course of a few weeks in early 1943, ninety-five per cent were deported to Auschwitz. See Mazower (2005).
12. One estimate is 2.4 million, but the real number is unknown. It is thought that as many as one-third of East European Jews left their homes in Eastern Europe to move westwards.
13. My father and his siblings certainly believed that their parents had fled the pogroms, although Pinsk, the Belarusian town where my grandparents came from, which lies just north of the Ukrainian border, records no pogroms there.
14. It makes little difference to my argument about the symbolic potency of Poland that not all Jews came to the west from Poland itself.
15. Coles refers to two specific episodes, both involving "unrecognised deaths", so as to trace the movement from loss via depression into the next generation's association with withdrawnness and silence. One occurred in Freud's early life, the other in that of the psychoanalyst A. Green. "The sibling deaths of Freud's uncle and Green's aunt must have augmented the depression of their respective mothers, but there has been a significant silence about these deaths in the writings of Freud and Green or any subsequent theorist. Nevertheless, these unrecognised deaths seem to cloud the emotional language of Freud's 'death instinct' (1920g), and the chilling language of Green's 'the deathly deserted universe' (Green, 1983). Their language is carrying the weight of their mothers' grief [...]" (Coles, op. cit., p. xx).
16. Studies indicate that the mental health disorder most characteristic of Jews is that of manic depression (now called bipolar disorder). Several of my interviewees themselves thought from their own observations that Jews seem particularly prone to serious depression. In an excellent paper, Naomi Dale (1988) discusses various causative influences

behind this epidemiological pattern, including anti-Semitism and Jews' historic position as outsider. However, as all the studies up to that point had been carried out on British and American Jews, almost all of whom would have been descended from Eastern European immigrants, the part played by migration in developing or reinforcing a tendency towards depressive disorders amongst Jews merits further attention.

17. "*Dayenu*"—"it would have sufficed"—refers to all the many good things God is described as having done for the Israelites during their journey from slavery to freedom.

Chapter Three

1. Not just Jews, of course. Incomprehension is a common reaction amongst people with no connection at all to the Holocaust.
2. Since the end of the war, considerable efforts have been devoted to investigating the question, how did the Holocaust happen? A vast amount of published research and study now exist, all of which shed light in different ways. What is important to recognise from my interviews is that many ordinary Jews are either unaware of these studies; or it is not delivered in a way as to reach them; or it simply does not address their fears. I suspect all three are implicated. The most widely delivered material about the Holocaust—TV documentaries—tend to focus on *what* happened rather than why. There may be an underlying assumption that the average viewer is unable to grasp complex analyses. I think this is a mistake; it abandons people to their inability to find adequate answers on their own, and leaves them vulnerable to ostensibly "simple" explanations.
3. "Frum" is a word used by British Jews to refer to those who are particularly orthodox.
4. To "make *aliyah*" is a Hebrew term used to signify Jews' "return" (effectively immigration) to live in Israel.
5. A Zionist Jewish youth group.
6. Victor had grown up in a largely non-Jewish area and throughout his childhood carried a sense of strangeness, for example in having a "funny name". He had also been evacuated, which "was complicated … because you weren't local anyway." Victor had never felt that he "belonged" in the "apparently homogeneous British society" of the 1930s and '40s.
7. A closely related example of how others have adopted the term "Holocaust" to refer to their own traumas is Tadeusz Piotrowski's *Poland's Holocaust* (1998). Piotrowski, an American of Polish descent, utilises the term "Holocaust" from the perspective that Poland as

a nation suffered uniquely in the Second World War, being at the frontline between the Nazis and the Soviets, both of whom, according to Piotrowski, carried out genocidal policies against the Poles. Piotrowski's book exemplifies what Krajewski describes as "a rivalry [between Poles and Jews] as to who suffered most": a competition which in effect closes down any appreciation of each other's experience (Krajewski, 2005, p. 89).

8. Finkelstein (2000) gets round this by using the term "the Jewish Holocaust" specifically to refer to the Nazi programme of destruction of the Jews.
9. A. Dirk Moses usefully discusses the complexities and controversies bound up in how different groups claim the right to terms such as "genocide" and "Holocaust" to refer to their own traumatic histories. Western societies largely ignore the genocides carried out under the force of colonialism, and centralise the Holocaust in memorials: hence the USA set up the first Holocaust Museum, focused on the European tragedy, whilst side-lining white American history in relation to indigenous Americans and to slavery. Moses argues that the colonial genocides of what he calls the "racial century" and the Holocaust form a continuum linked to the accelerating violence involved in nation-building, which began in the European colonial endeavour and culminated in the Holocaust (Moses, 2002).
10. Highers are the qualifying exams for university in the Scottish educational system.
11. The question of silence is, of course, absolutely relevant to discussions of the Holocaust, not least because of the serious self-questioning that post-war Germans had to undergo about their own silence in response to the evolution of Nazi policy. As an example of the literature, see Barbara Heimannsberg and Christoph J. Schmidt (Eds.) (1993): *The Collective Silence: German Identity and the Legacy of Shame*.
12. Art Spiegelman brilliantly illustrates one aspect of how cunning Nazi strategies were. Spiegelman's father fought with the Polish forces resisting the German invasion. He was taken prisoner as a Polish prisoner of war (POW), but then, along with all other Jewish Polish POWs, was offered release by the Nazis. This changed his status, from a POW with rights under international law to a civilian with no rights and who therefore was exposed to any kind of Nazi atrocity (Spiegelman, 2003, pp. 61–63).
13. "Primitive" is the term used by writers in psychoanalytic schools to refer to early states of infant experience, when an infant has to cope with the consequences of environmental (i.e., maternal/carer) failure to respond appropriately to his or her instinctive needs.

14. Murray Parkes, one of the key reference points in literature on bereavement, made similar observations of the presence of anger in situations of bereavement. See Parkes, 1970 and 1972.
15. *Licensed Mass Murder* is the title of a book by Henry V. Dicks, a psychoanalyst and psychiatrist. He was commissioned in 1971 to study a number of former Nazi personnel who were convicted and imprisoned for crimes against humanity, as part of the Columbus Centre's research into the relationship between individual psychopathology, social and political forces, and collective behaviour in the Nazi era.
16. Theologically, it is difficult to separate these two aspects, since in Jewish theology Jews' experience as a people *reflects* God. However, from a psychological perspective, social, cultural, and political experience in this world needs to be distinguished from spiritual beliefs.
17. Despite early success as a writer and a considerable output, it took Oz (2004) decades finally to write a memoir about his family and, in particular, his mother's suicide when he was just fourteen. The need to be silent can be very powerful, even for those skilled with words.
18. Bernice is here thinking of two separate events which took place in Poland. In 1941, Polish residents in the small town of Jedwabne killed several hundred Jews, also residents of the town and therefore neighbours. Though the Germans were in control of the area they did not participate, and the Jedwabne massacre is thus seen as a crime committed against Jews by Poles alone. In 1946, forty-two Polish Jews returning home from the camps to the village of Kielce were killed by a Polish mob, in what has come to be called a post-war pogrom.
19. Eliezer Berkovits, for example, used the term "holocaust betrayal". See Berkovits (1973), *Faith after the Holocaust*, p. 166; quoted in Braiterman (1998), p. 16.
20. See, for example, Marcus, J. R. (1938), *The Jew in the Mediaeval World*. Marc Saperstein provided a new introduction to the 1999 edition.
21. Of course, legal frameworks in the Middle Ages were different from how we now understand them. By and large, mediaeval laws were a combination of ecclesiastical—that is, Church—law, and laws laid down by the monarch or ruler. (In England these were amplified by the concept of "common" law: laws which grew up via custom and practice.) In other words, the laws which kept Jews in place derived principally from the two great mediaeval institutions of church and monarchy (or its equivalent), which is one reason why Jews depended to such a great extent on the favours and whims of rulers.
22. I have omitted here Busch's references in the quotation to the presence of fear and of guilt, as these are the subjects of later chapters.

23. Theodor Herzl's outrage at the Dreyfus affair, and his consequent establishment of Zionism as a political movement, is consistent with Bowlby's concept of "the anger of despair" as a reaction to the loss of relational engagement by and with the world. Zionism literally represented a position of "no hope" for Jews in Europe.

Chapter Four

1. "*Treife*" means non-kosher or unclean.
2. By far the most extreme modern example of such delusions is the forgery known as *The Protocols of the Elders of Zion*, a fabricated document purporting to reveal the existence of a small Jewish cabal conspiring to achieve world control. In *Warrant for Genocide* (1967), Norman Cohn traces the evolution of this from conspiracy theories originally focused on Freemasons in post-revolutionary France to its fully fledged anti-Semitic form in early twentieth-century Tsarist Russia. Eventually it was picked up by the Nazis and used by them as further "evidence" justifying their war against the Jews. Cohn explains how appealing such fantasies were in the nineteenth century, during a time of massive challenge to the old autocracies and hierarchies of Europe. Even today, the *Protocols* are in widespread circulation in some Arab countries, where they focus on beliefs about Zionist ambitions for world domination.
3. Traditional head covering normally worn by Jewish males for prayers.
4. In *From Pain to Violence: the Traumatic Roots of Destructiveness*, (2006, ch. 2), Felicity de Zulueta traces the way in which theological doctrines often set up psychological conflicts that can result in complicated emotional reactions and dysfunctional behaviour: for example, when sexual desire is conceptualised as sinful. In this she follows Fromm (1970), who observed that in Christian teaching, Augustine's doctrine of original sin set up an inherent conflict between sexual pleasure (=sinful) and sexual desire (=normal), leading to "moral prohibitions [which] always become a source of production for guilt feelings, which are often unconscious or transferred to different matters". In de Zulueta's analysis, the unresolved feelings of guilt are converted in certain conditions into violence.
5. Sand (2009) has questioned the commonly believed story that Jews were forcibly expelled by the Romans from the whole of Palestine and were thereafter doomed to live in exile. Jews were expelled from Jerusalem for political reasons but continued to live in various parts of Palestine, although the state of Judaea itself ceased to exist. There was in any case already widespread Jewish settlement throughout the Roman Empire,

suggesting that Jews at the time did not necessarily see their world in terms of "exile".

6. Lacan thought that such normal abandonment is an essential component to human growth and development, as it forces the substitution and development of language in the way infants negotiate their world.
7. Lacan used the term "motherer" to indicate that the principal person who cares for an infant stands in the position of the mother without necessarily being her.
8. The story of Adam and Eve and their expulsion from the garden of Eden symbolically represents human birth and the unavoidable discovery of one's own separateness. Masaccio's fresco of *The Expulsion from the Garden of Eden* in the Brancacci Chapel in Florence is one of the most acutely observed representations of the anguish involved in such loss.
9. It should again be borne in mind, as I discussed in Chapter Two, that most ordinary Jews today are descended from people who migrated within the last 120 years, and therefore that the emotional upheaval of *leaving* is very much a part of the present Jewish psychological structure.
10. In 2006, I ran a workshop on "Meanings of the Holocaust"' at Limmud, a major Jewish educational event that takes place annually in the UK. These comments were made during this group event.
11. The Community Security Trust is a UK body concerned with protecting British Jews from "bigotry, anti-Semitism and terrorism" (CST, 2010).
12. I am using the word "prejudice" here as a shorthand, to signify hostile and negative perceptions by one person or group in relation to another.
13. Wright is here quoting Winnicott (1971).

Chapter Five

1. The writers Leys cites here are Primo Levi, Bruno Bettelheim (himself a psychoanalyst), Elie Wiesel, and Ella Lingens.
2. There was a rich pedigree to draw on. Leys particularly cites the work of Freud, Sandor Ferenczi, and Anna Freud as significant influences on the thinking of American psychoanalysts working on the phenomenon of "survivor guilt" during the 1960s.
3. Leys' subject is the United States, but her general thesis, that is to say, the formulation of cultural identity, is applicable to any nation, including Nazi Germany at the time and Jewish collective identity today.
4. Tisha b'Av, the commemoration of the ninth of Av, when the Second Temple was destroyed. It falls somewhere between late July and early August, depending on the year.

5. The ship in question was the SS St Louis, bound for Cuba from Germany, with 937 Jewish people on board. They were refused entry to Cuba (they only had tourist visas), and the ship then sought refuge for them in the USA. The USA also refused entry, and the ship was forced to return to Hamburg. Most of the Jewish passengers did not survive the war. See Anthony Blechner's 1999 account, www.blechner.com.
6. Doris's experiences find an echo in Eva Figes' *Journey to Nowhere*. Figes' book partly concerns the experiences during and after the war of Edith, her family's former housemaid in Berlin. When Edith arrived in Palestine after the war, according to Figes, she "found herself ostracized because she came from Germany." "Yekke" was the common term of disparagement towards German Jews. "The word is supposed to originate from the German word for jacket, *Jäcke*. Myth has it that German Jews were so posh that they even dressed in town clothes when working in the fields. Underlying the epithet is resentment against a group of people who considered themselves socially superior." Figes, 2008, p. 125.
7. See my Introduction for Karpf's extended speculation on post-war Anglo-Jewish guilt. Karpf has usefully summarised some of the historic research on Anglo-Jewish attitudes to immigration in this period as a backdrop to examining her survivor parents' experiences when they arrived in Britain after the war.
8. Nor does this rule out the possibility that mixed feelings towards refugee and survivor Jews continued even after the war. I well remember my own mother's overt ambivalence in relation to my best friend's survivor mother, a Hungarian Jew who was undeniably—and worryingly—different from the Anglo-Jewish women my mother felt comfortable with.
9. The German Enlightenment, *die Aufklärung*, which freed German thought from the restrictions of mediaeval thinking, was powerfully echoed for German Jews by their parallel philosophy, *Haskalah*, championed by Moses Mendelssohn.
10. It emphasises the point to note that Marx, Einstein, and Freud—three of the most important intellectual influences in twentieth century life—were German or Austrian Jews.
11. So hard that every *shtetl* in "the old place" seems to have had to be replicated by its own synagogue in the East End of London. The eventual formation, respectively, of the "United" Synagogue and the "Federation" of Synagogues of Great Britain were responses to the continued factiousness between different *shuls* and communities. There is an old joke told about a Jewish castaway on a desert island. When found, he is discovered to have built two separate synagogue

buildings. His rescuers are puzzled about this, so he explains that the first is the one he goes to, and the second is the one he would never set foot in.

12. Reverend Ernest Levy, who died in 2010, was the best-known survivor in Scotland, mainly because of his own writing and his educational work in schools and the wider community.
13. It seems that, at Hitler's instructions, those parts of cities where it was known that Jews were particularly concentrated were deliberately targeted for bombing.
14. Laura Levitt makes a similar point, in the very different circumstances of American Jewry, in her book *American Jewish Loss after the Holocaust* (Levitt, 2007).
15. My mother's uncle was killed by the second-last V2 rocket that fell on London in March 1945. Writer Jonathan Freedland's grandmother was killed by the very last V2 attack: one in which 120 of the 130 fatalities were Jews. See Freedland, 2005, p. 220.
16. The most notable is the Shoah Victims' Names Recovery programme, run under the auspices of Yad Vashem Holocaust Museum in Jerusalem. It has documented the names of over half the six million Jewish victims known to have died under the Nazis.
17. Levi most notably recaptured the spirit of some of his campmates who died. In *The Drowned and the Saved*, he gives the briefest depictions of four men whom he saw as "the best, who died." This simple action, almost certainly a response to Levi's own feelings of guilt and obligation, is extraordinarily powerful in bringing these men back to life as individuals with meaningful lives (Levi, 1989, p. 63).
18. Mollon follows Edith Jacobsen in this line of thinking. See Jacobsen, 1965.
19. The reference "like lambs to the slaughter" comes from a question posed by one of the judges at Eichmann's trial to a survivor witness: a comment which Hannah Arendt described at the time as "silly and cruel".
20. *Brit* is the Hebrew signifying circumcision. It literally means "covenant", and derives from Abraham's original covenant with God through practising circumcision (Genesis 17).
21. The obvious exception to this is the footage taken by the Allies at Belsen when it was liberated. However, it is still footage of Others seen as victims, albeit this time from the perspective of "rescuers".
22. These images can be found in Norman Cohn (1967), pp. 183 and 185.
23. Nazi use of such terminology helped foster the psychological climate in which Zyklon B—the cyanide-based gas used in the gas chambers, and derived from rat poison—could be justified.

Chapter Six

1. Philosopher-theologian Buber is one of the most revered figures in twentieth-century Jewish history.
2. When a heathen who wished to become a Jew asked him for a summary of the Jewish religion in the most concise terms, Hillel said: "what is hateful to thee, do not do unto thy fellow man: this is the whole Law; the rest is mere commentary" (Talmud, Shabbat 31a). With these words, Hillel recognised as the fundamental principle of the Jewish moral law the Biblical precept of brotherly love (Leviticus xix, 18). Source: www.jewishencyclopaedia.com.
3. No single body represents the diversity of Jewish life in Britain today. The weekly newspaper *The Jewish Chronicle* is widely read for its coverage of Jewish interests; it allows for voices questioning of Israel but such views are swamped by lengthy coverage of Israeli affairs aligned with a mainstream Israeli perspective. The Chief Rabbi is the Chief Rabbi only of the United Synagogues of Great Britain, which does not represent all Jewish religious bodies. The remit of the Board of Deputies of British Jews is to represent Jewish concerns at government level, but its composition is overwhelmingly based on synagogue communities. All these bodies have generally displayed considerable reluctance to express any criticism of Israel.
4. In the light of changing family patterns there is a need for these core psychodynamic concepts to be re-evaluated. Growing numbers of infants are now born into and/or reared in same-sex parental units, and this has implications for the way we understand the unconscious dynamics of gender identity, gender attachment, and separation. At present there may be insufficient data available to study in adults the impact of new family structures, but this will change over time. One likely outcome eventually will be to develop distinctions between social parenting and biological parenting and their psychological impact on the child's unconscious. However, the fact remains that biologically we are all the product of male-female unions, and at the very least some of Freud's original conceptions are likely to continue to play out symbolically in the way in which individuals form their sense of self.
5. See also Michael Briant's (2009) paper building on Dicks's work. Briant describes Dicks as having traced the appeal of Nazi ideology "to conflicts created by an upbringing in a patriarchal, authoritarian society", which resulted in "the committed Nazi [tending to resolve] his oedipal conflicts by identifying with a harsh, authoritarian father figure, splitting off and projecting any thoughts, feelings, impulses or desires

that seemed inconsistent with that. Any hatred towards authority figures, for example, would be concealed beneath a mask of dutiful obedience." Briant connects Dicks's thinking with that of Winnicott, Money-Kyrle, and Gilligan, and goes on to argue that the role of fathers in transmitting models of male behaviour has been under-explored in the psychotherapeutic tradition.

6. Throughout Leader's discussion, he closely follows Freud's seminal work, *Mourning and Melancholia* (1917e).
7. It is perfectly normal for the teaching of history to be divided between the national history of one's own country, and the history of "other" countries. In my undergraduate history degree course teaching was, indeed, split between "British", "European", and "world" history. Sand's point, however, is that in Israel this teaching is split between two different *departments* of history, and is not merely a distinction made under the umbrella of one integrated department.

Chapter Seven

1. Cubelli presented this research at a seminar for the trauma, memory, and representation study group at the University of Edinburgh in January 2008.
2. Much early trauma is not available to conscious (mental) memory, but it is embodied. Prior to the brain's development, the infant's body is where physical and emotional experience happens. Early traumas can be "read" later through an individual's confusion of emotion and behaviours.
3. "Menshen": Yiddish word signifying humanity.
4. The earlier word *Churban*, derived from the root Hebrew word for "destruction" has now been superseded by the widespread use of *Shoah*, a word which, while it also means "destruction", has come since the Book of Job to signify a catastrophe of cosmic dimensions.
5. Trauma can, of course, be powerfully expressed symbolically through art. Even then, language is still needed in order to move beyond pure experience and into thought.
6. All the emphases in these two quotations are mine, apart from the last "*it*", which is Bollas's.
7. Simon's description (Chapter Two) of an internal image of bodies piled up in the gas chambers is a particularly potent example of the way in which we "hold" symbolic, visual representations of the Holocaust without necessarily having seen the actual physical image.
8. See references to Bollas in Chapter One.

9. Hebrew for "healing".
10. Braiterman is here commenting on Fackenheim's 1982 book, *To Mend the World*.
11. This emphasis on memory is normal in traditional communities. The practice of history can only develop when there is documentary and archaeological evidence, together with the knowledge of how to interpret it. Before history comes myth: "mythos" simply means "story", which in English we derive and distinguish from "history". "Myth", "story", and "history" are all variations on the ways in which we narrate and relate to a meaningful past.
12. The confrontation over meaning *vs*. meaninglessness is at the heart of the theodicy/anti-theodicy arguments which dominated Jewish theological thinking post-Holocaust and which Braiterman explores throughout *God After Auschwitz*.
13. Suicide is the most obviously extreme form of how individuals arrive at an ultimately self-destructive "solution" to their lives. This is seldom because there is *no* meaning, but rather because the meanings which the individual gives themselves, while distressingly hostile, are paradoxically "comforting" alternatives to their terror of emptiness.
14. This comment by Marris is particularly relevant to my argument that the founding of Israel psychologically happened too quickly. The magnitude of the losses sustained—personally, communally, culturally—was effectively bypassed, and the losses themselves then became displaced into Israel itself. For example, Israel's cultural devaluing of the European identities of its survivor population became another loss unconsciously embedded in the social psychology of the new state.
15. Marris illustrates how the existing robustness of social structures influences recovery from grief in instances of collective disaster through comparing two similar situations which had very different outcomes: the destruction of a mining village in Buffalo Creek, West Virginia, in 1972 when a dam burst; and the engulfing of the village of Aberfan in Wales in 1966, when a coal tip above the village collapsed. In the first, the responsible government department perpetuated the disruptive impact of the disaster by resettling the scattered surviving community in camps, an action which destroyed all possibility of the community recovering social cohesion and a sense of continuity. In the second, the villagers acted together, channelling their collective anger in pushing successfully for changes in government policy on the positioning of coal tips. In the process, the village recovered a sense of itself as purposeful.

16. "Matrix" is linguistically related to "the womb", and is intentionally used in Group Analysis to signify the potentially containing and nourishing space of a group; a place where we can metaphorically grow.
17. See Krajewski (2005) on "Catholic-Jewish Dialogue in post-war Poland", in *Poland and the Jews*, Chapter Eight. Krajewski makes the point that a competition over "suffering" has overshadowed post-war dialogue between Catholic Poles and Jews.

BIBLIOGRAPHY

Abley, M. (2004). *Spoken Here: Travels among Threatened Languages*. London: Arrow.

Abraham, N., & Torok, M. (1994). *The Shell and the Kernel*. Chicago: University of Chicago Press.

Arendt, H. (2005). *Eichmann and the Holocaust*. London: Penguin.

Bettelheim, B. (1960). *The Informed Heart*. New York: The Free Press.

Biale, D. (1986). *Power and Powerlessness in Jewish History*. New York: Schocken.

Bowlby, J. (1979). *The Making and Breaking of Affectional Bonds*. London: Tavistock.

Covington, C., Williams, P., Arundale, J., & Knox, J. (Eds.) (2002). *Terrorism and War*. London: Karnac.

Daniel, J. (2005). *The Jewish Prison*. Hoboken, NJ: Melville House Publishing.

Edmundson, M. (2007). *The Death of Sigmund Freud*. London: Bloomsbury.

Fairbairn, W. R. D. (1952). *Psychoanalytic Studies of the Personality*. London: Routledge & Kegan Paul.

Frosh, S. (2013). *Hauntings: Psychoanalysis and Ghostly Transmissions*. London: Palgrave Macmillan.

Goldberg, D. J. (2006). *The Divided Self: Israel & the Jewish Psyche Today*. London: I. B. Taurus.

Goodman, N. R., & Meyers, M. B. (Eds.) (2012). *The Power of Witnessing: Reflections, Reverberations and Traces of the Holocaust*. New York: Routledge.

Grossman, D. (2008). *Writing in the Dark*. London: Bloomsbury.

Hoffman, E. (2005). *After Such Knowledge*. London: Vintage.

Karpf, A., Klug, B., Rose, J., & Rosenbaum, B. (Eds.) (2008). *A Time to Speak Out*. London: Verso.

Kirkwood, C. (2012). *The Persons in Relation Perspective*. Rotterdam: Sense.

Kriwaczek, P. (2005). *Yiddish Civilisation*. London: Weidenfeld & Nicolson.

Mitchell, J. (1986). *The Selected Melanie Klein*. London: Penguin.

Robertson, J., & Robertson, J. (1989). *Separation and the Very Young*. London: Free Association Books.

Young, J. (1993). *The Texture of Memory: Holocaust Memorials and Meaning*. New Haven, CT: Yale University Press.

Zsolt, B. (2004). *Nine Suitcases*. London: Pimlico.

REFERENCES

Abarbanel, A. (2006). A few notes to clarify my trauma theory in relation to the Palestinian/Israeli conflict. Webpage http://avigail.customer.netspace.net.au/trauma.html, September 2004 modified June 2006. (Last accessed September 2006).

Alexander, J. C. (2004). Towards a theory of cultural trauma. In: J. C. Alexander, R. Eyerman, B. Giesen, N. J. Smelser & P. Sztompka (Eds.), *Cultural Trauma and Collective Identity* (pp. 1–30). London: University of California Press.

Ayers, M. (2003). *Mother–Infant Attachment and Psychoanalysis: The Eyes of Shame*. London: Routledge.

Baum, R. N. (2012). Rethinking Holocaust testimony: A new approach to survivor accounts. *H-Judaic*, H-net reviews, August 2012.

Bauman, Z. (1989). *Modernity and the Holocaust*. Ithaca, NY: Cornell University Press.

Benbassa, E. (2007). *Suffering as Identity: The Jewish Paradigm*. London: Verso, 2010.

Berkovits, E. (1973). *Faith after the Holocaust*. New York: Ktav.

Bhugra, D., & Becker, M. A. (2005). Migration, cultural bereavement and cultural identity. *World Psychiatry, 4*(1): 18–24. World Psychiatry Association. Online website, www.pubmedcentral.nih.gov. (Last accessed March 2014).

Blechner, A. (1999). *The Voyage of the St. Louis*. Online website www.blechner.com. (Last accessed March 2014).

Bloxham, D. (2009). *The Final Solution: A Genocide*. Oxford: Oxford University Press.

Bollas, C. (1995). *Cracking Up: The Work of Unconscious Experience*. London: Routledge.

Bowlby, J. (1973). *Attachment and Loss, 2: Separation, Anger and Anxiety*. London: Hogarth Press.

Braiterman, Z. (1998). *(God) After Auschwitz: Tradition and Change in Post-Holocaust Jewish Thought*. Princeton, NJ: Princeton University Press.

Briant, M. (2009). Psychotherapy and "the plague": some contributions to the understanding of a recurrent threat. *British Journal of Psychotherapy, 25*: 39–55.

Browning, C. R. (2004). *The Origins of the Final Solution*. London: Arrow.

Burg, A. (2008). *The Holocaust is Over*. New York: Palgrave Macmillan.

Busch, F. N. (2009). Anger and depression. *Advances in Psychiatric Treatment, 15*: 271–278.

Caruth, C. (1995). Trauma and experience: introduction. In: C. Caruth (Ed.), *Trauma: Explorations in Memory*. Baltimore, MD: John Hopkins University Press.

Cohn, N. (1967). *Warrant for Genocide*. London: Eyre & Spottiswoode.

Coles, P. (2011). *The Uninvited Guest from the Unremembered Past*. London: Karnac.

Cooper, H. (Ed.) (1988). *Soul Searching: Studies in Judaism and Psychotherapy*. London: SCM Press.

Cooper, H. (2008). Living in error. In: A. Karpf, B. Klug, J. Rose & B. Rosenbaum (Eds.), *A Time to Speak Out* (pp. 182–195). London: Verso.

CST (Community Security Trust) (2010). Website: www.thecst.org.uk.

Dale, N. (1988). Jews, ethnicity and mental health. In: H. Cooper, (Ed.), *Soul Searching: Studies in Judaism & Psychotherapy* (pp. 68–79). London: SCM Press.

De Vito, S., Cubelli, R., & Della Sala, S. (2009). Collective representations elicit widespread individual false memories. *Cortex, 45*: 686–687. Online website: Elsevier: www.elsevier.com/locate/cortex.

de Zulueta, F. (2006). *From Pain to Violence: the Traumatic Roots of Destructiveness*. Chichester: Whurr.

Dicks, H. V. (1972). *Licensed Mass Murder: A Socio-psychological Study of Some SS Killers*. London: Heinemann.

Evans, N. J. (2005). "Memory, reality and the Great Migration". Lecture delivered at Limmud seminar, Glasgow.

Fackenheim, E. (1982). *To Mend the World*. New York: Schocken.

Figes, E. (2008). *Journey to Nowhere*. London: Granta.

Figes, O. (2007). On *Start the Week*. London: BBC Radio Four: 8 October.

Figes, O. (2007). *The Whisperers*. London: Allen Lane.

Finkelstein, N. (2000). *The Holocaust Industry: Reflections on the Exploitation of Jewish Suffering*. New York: Verso.

Fischer, E. (1994). *Aimée and Jaguar*. London: Bloomsbury, 1995.

Fohn, A., & Heenen-Wolff, S. (2010). The destiny of an unacknowledged trauma: The deferred retroactive effect of *après-coup* in the hidden Jewish children of wartime Belgium. *International Journal of Psychoanalysis, 92*: 5–20.

Folman, A. (2008). On *Front Row*. London: BBC Radio Four: 10 November.

Fraiberg, S., Adelson, E., & Shapiro, V. (1980). Ghosts in the nursery: a psychoanalytic approach to the problems of impaired infant–mother relationships. In: S. Fraiberg, (Ed.), *Clinical Studies in Infant Mental Health* (pp. 164–196). London: Tavistock.

Frankl, V. (1946). *Man's Search for Meaning*. Boston, MA: Washington Square Press, 1959.

Freedland, J. (2005). *Jacob's Gift*. London: Hamish Hamilton.

Freud, S. (1917e). *Mourning and Melancholia. S. E., 14*: 237–257. London: Hogarth.

Freud, S. (1920g). Beyond the pleasure principle. *S. E., 18*: 1–64. London: Hogarth.

Freud, S. (1939). *Moses and Monotheism. S. E., 23*: 7–137. London: Hogarth.

Friedlander, S. (1993). Trauma and transference. In: *Memory, History and the Extermination of the Jews of Europe*. Bloomington, In: Indiana University Press.

Fromm, E. (1970). *The Crisis of Psychoanalysis*. London: Harmondsworth.

Garwood, Dr. A. (1996). The Holocaust and the power of powerlessness: Survivor guilt an unhealed wound. *British Journal of Psychotherapy, 13*: 243–258. (Reprinted in: C. Covington, P. Williams, J. Arundale & J. Knox, (Eds.), *Terrorism and War* (pp. 353–374). London: Karnac, 2002).

Garza-Guerrero, A. C. (1974). Culture shock: its mourning and the vicissitudes of identity. *Journal of the American Psychoanalytic Association, 22*: 408–428.

Green, A. (1983). The dead mother: In: *On Private Madness* (pp. 142–173). London: Karnac, 1996.

Greenspan, H. (1998). *On Listening to Holocaust Survivors: Recounting and Life History*. Westport, CT: Praeger.

Grossman, D. (1989). *See Under: Love*. London, Jonathan Cape, 1990.

Grossman, D. (2007). Looking at ourselves. *New York Review of Books, 54*: 11 January.

Gubar, S. (2003). *Poetry After Auschwitz: Remembering What One Never Knew*. Bloomington, In: Indiana University Press.

Halbwachs, M. (1992). *On Collective Memory*. (Ed. and trans. L. A. Coser). Chicago: Chicago University Press.

Halter, R. (2005). Missing. On: C. Wheeler, *Coming Home*. London: BBC Radio Four: 11 May.

Hartman, G. H. (1996). *The Longest Shadow: In the Aftermath of the Holocaust*. Indiana: Indiana University Press.

Heimannsberg, B., & Schmidt, C. J. (Eds.) (1993). *The Collective Silence: German Identity and the Legacy of Shame*. San Francisco: Jossey Bass.

Hilberg, R. (1985). *The Destruction of the European Jews* (revised edition). New York: Holmes and Meier.

Hoffman, E. (1989). *Lost in Translation*. London: Random House.

Hoffman, E. (1998). *Shtetl*. London: Secker & Warburg.

Holtschneider, K. H. (2007). Victims, perpetrators, bystanders? Witnessing, remembering and the ethics of representation in museums of the Holocaust. *Holocaust Studies: A Journal of Culture and History, 13*: 82–102.

Hopper, E. (2003). *The Social Unconscious*. London: Jessica Kingsley.

Huntingdon, J. (1981). "Migration as part of life experience". Paper given at the New South Wales Institute of Psychiatry seminar in cross-cultural therapy. University of New South Wales, School of Social Work.

Jacobsen, E. (1965). *The Self and the Object World*. London: Hogarth.

Jacobson, H. (2006). *Kalooki Nights*. London: Jonathan Cape.

Jacobson, H. (2011). *Desert Island Discs*. London: BBC Radio 4: 11 February.

Jewish Encyclopaedia (online website): www.jewishencyclopaedia.com. (Last accessed March 2014).

Julius, A. (2010). *Trials of the Diaspora: A History of Anti-Semitism in England*. Oxford: Oxford University Press.

Junz, H. B. (2001). Report on the Pre-War Wealth Position of the Jewish Population in Nazi-Occupied Countries, Germany, and Austria: How the Economics of the Holocaust Add. Report of the Independent Committee of Eminent Persons. Online website: www.clintonlibrary.gov. (Last accessed 2014).

Karpf, A. (1997). *The War After: Living with the Holocaust*. London: Minerva.

Kluger, R. (2001). *Still Alive—A Holocaust Girlhood Remembered*. New York: The Feminist Press.

Krajewski, S. (2005). *Poland and the Jews: Reflections of a Polish Polish Jew*. Kraków: Wydawnictwo Austeria.

Lacan, J. (1949). *Ecrits*. (Trans. B. Fink). New York: Norton, 2006.

LaCapra, D. (2001). *Writing History, Writing Trauma*. Baltimore, MD: John Hopkins University Press.

Lang, B. (1990). *Act and Idea in the Nazi Genocide*. Chicago, IL: University of Chicago Press.

Laub, D. (2012). Testimony as life experience. In: N. R. Goodman & M. B. Meyers (Eds.), *The Power of Witnessing* (pp. 59–79). New York: Routledge.

Leader, D. (2008). *The New Black*. London: Hamish Hamilton.

Lemma, A., & Levy, S. (2004). The impact of trauma on the psyche: internal and external processes. In: S. Levy & A. Lemma (Eds.), *The Perversion of Loss* (pp. 1–20). London: Whurr.

Lentin, R. (2000). *Israel and the Daughters of the Shoah*. New York: Berghahn.

Levi, N., & Rothberg, M. (Eds.) (2003). *The Holocaust—Theoretical Readings*. Edinburgh: Edinburgh University Press.

Levi, P. (1958). *If This is a Man*. London: Orion, 1960.

Levi, P. (1981). *Moments of Reprieve*. New York: Simon & Schuster, 1986.

Levi, P. (1989). *The Drowned and the Saved*. London: Abacus.

Levin, B. (1987). *To the End of the Rhine*. London: Jonathan Cape.

Levitt, L. (2007). *American Jewish Loss after the Holocaust*. New York: New York University.

Levy, S., & Lemma, A. (Eds.) (2004). *The Perversion of Loss*. London: Whurr.

Leys, R. (2000). *Trauma—A Genealogy*. Chicago: University of Chicago Press.

Leys, R. (2007). *From Guilt to Shame: Auschwitz and After*. New Jersey: Princeton University Press.

Mahler, M. S., Pine, F., & Bergman, A. (1975). *The Psychological Birth of the Human Infant: Symbiosis and Individuation*. New York: Basic Books.

Marcus, J. R. (1938). *The Jew in the Mediaeval World*. Cincinnati, OH: Hebrew Union College Press, 1999.

Margalit, A. (2002). *The Ethics of Memory*. Massachusetts: Harvard University Press.

Marks, D. (2006). *The Search for Sepharad* (1). London, BBC Radio Three: 30 April.

Marks, D. (2009). *Yiddish: A Struggle for Survival*. London: BBC Radio 3: 30 November.

Marris, P. (1986). *Loss and Change*. London: Routledge & Kegan Paul.

Mazower, M. (2005). *Salonika: City of Ghosts*. London: Harper Perennial.

Mendelsohn, D. (2006). *The Lost: In Search of Six of the Six Million*. London: Harper.

Michaels, A. (1996). *Fugitive Pieces*. Canada: McClelland & Stewart.

Michaels, A. (2009). *The Winter Vault*. London: Bloomsbury.

Minghella, A. (Dir.) (1999). *The Talented Mr. Ripley*. USA: Paramount Pictures.

Mollon, P. (2002). *Shame and Jealousy: The Hidden Turmoils*. London: Karnac.

Molodowsky, K. (1946). *Der melekh Dovid aleyn is geblibn* (King David Alone Has Remained). New York: Farlag papirene brik.

Moses, A. D. (2002). Conceptual blockages and definitional dilemmas in the "racial century": genocides of indigenous peoples and the Holocaust. *Patterns of Prejudice, 36*: 7–36.

Moyn, S. (2005). *A Holocaust Controversy: The Treblinka Affair in Modern France*. Lebanon, NH: Brandeis University Press.

Novick, P. (1999). *The Holocaust in American Life*. USA: Houghton Mifflin.

Okri, B. (2008). Under the surface is the nightmare of history. But some kind of beauty won the election. In: *Road to the White House. The Times*, 8 November, p. 16. Available at: www.thetimes.co.uk.

Orbinski, J. (2008). *Start the Week*. London: Radio Four, 11 June.

Oz, A. (2004). *A Tale of Love and Darkness*. London: Chatto & Windus.

Parens, H. (2012). A Holocaust survivor's bearing witness. In: N. R. Goodman & M. B. Meyers (Eds.), *The Power of Witnessing: Reflections, Reverberations and Traces of the Holocaust* (pp. 87–103). New York: Routledge.

Parkes, C. M. (1970). The first year of bereavement. *Psychiatry, 33*: 444–467.

Parkes, C. M. (1972). *Bereavement: Studies of Grief in Adult Life*. New York: International Universities Press.

Pearlman, L. A., & Saakvitne, K. W. (1995). *Trauma and the Therapist*. London: Norton.

Piotrowski, T. (1998). *Poland's Holocaust*. Jefferson, NC: McFarland.

Robertson, J. & J. (1967–1973). *Young Children in Brief Separation* Film Series. London: Concord Video and Film Council. See webpage www.robertsonfilms.info.

Rose, J. (2005). *The Question of Zion*. Princeton, NJ: Princeton University Press.

Rose, J. (2007). *The Last Resistance*. London: Verso.

Russell, E. F. L. (Lord Russell of Liverpool) (1954). *The Scourge of the Swastika*. London: Cassell.

Sand, S. (2009). *The Invention of the Jewish People*. London: Verso.

Santner, E. L. (1992). History beyond the pleasure principle. In: S. Friedlander (Ed.), *Probing the Limits of Representation: Nazism and the "Final Solution"* (pp. 143–154). Cambridge, MA: Harvard University Press.

Schwab, G. (2010). *Haunting Legacies: Violent Histories of Transgenerational Trauma*. New York: Columbia University Press.

Spiegelman, A. (1996). *Maus—A Survivor's Tale*. USA: Pantheon Books.

Steinberg, P. (2001). *Speak You Also*. London: Allan Lane.

Steiner, J. -F. (1966). *Treblinka: La Révolte d'un Camp d'Extermination*. Paris: Fayard.

Struk, J. (2004). The Death Pit. *Guardian*, 27 January. Available at www.guardian.co.uk.

Swire, J. (2010). *Taking a Stand*. Dr. Jim Swire in conversation with Fergal Keane. London: BBC Radio Four: 2 February.

Valencia, H. (2006). "Only King David remained …": Reactions to the Holocaust in the poetry of Kadya Molodosky. The Fourteenth Avrom-Nokhem Stencl Lecture in Yiddish Studies. Oxford: Oxford Centre for Hebrew and Jewish Studies. Occasional paper 6.

Volkan, V. D. (2012). Large-group trauma at the hand of the "Other": trans-generational transmission and chosen traumas. Conference paper: *Conflict and Reconciliation in Groups, Couples, Families and Society*, 24–27 May 2012 (pp. 14–18). Athens: European Federation for Psychoanalytic Psychotherapy in the Public Sector/Hellenic Society of Group Analysis and Family Therapy.

Weine, S., Muzurovic, N., Kulauzovic, Y., Besic S., Lezic, A., Jujagic, A., Muzurovic, J., Spahovic, D., Feetham, S., Ware, N., Knafl, K., & Pavkovic, I. (2004). Family consequences of refugee trauma. *Family Process, 43*: 147–159. www.FamilyProcess.org.

Weissman, G. (2004). *Fantasies of Witnessing*. Ithaca, NY: Cornell University Press.

Winnicott, D. W. (1971). Mirror role of mother and family in child development. In: *Playing and Reality*. London: Tavistock.

Winston, R. (2004). *Child of Our Time*, series four. London: BBC TV.

Wright, K. (1991). *Vision and Separation: Between Mother and Baby*. London: Free Association Books.

Yarom, T. (2008). Speaking at the Edinburgh International Film Festival. Edinburgh: 19 June.

Yerushalmi, Y. H. (1996). *Zakhor: Jewish History and Jewish Memory*. New York: Schocken.

Yizhar, S. (2011). *Khirbet Khizeh*. London: Granta.

Zeitlin, A. (1947). *Gezamlte Lider* (Collected Poems), volume 1. New York: Farlag Matones, 1957.

Zeitlin, F. (1998). The vicarious witness. *History and Memory, 10*: 5–42.

Zucker, S. (1995). *Yiddish: An Introduction to the Language, Literature & Culture*. New York: The Workmen's Circle/Arbeter Ring.

LIST OF RADIO PROGRAMMES, TELEVISION PROGRAMMES, AND FILMS CITED

Child of Our Time (2001–April 2007). Broadcast on BBC 4, UK (August 2007–2013). Broadcast on BBC 1, UK.
Coming Home (2005). Broadcast on BBC Radio Four, UK.
Desert Island Discs (1942–present). Broadcast on BBC Radio Four, UK.
Front Row (UK) Broadcast weekdays, BBC Radio Four, UK.
The Pianist (2002). Dir. Polanski, R. USA: Universal Studios.
Schindler's List (1993). Dir. Spielberg, S. USA. Universal Pictures.
The Search for Sepharad (August–September 2006). Broadcast on BBC Radio Three, UK.
Shoah (1985). Dir. Lanzmann, C. USA: New Yorker Films.
Start the Week (2007-present). Broadcast weekdays, BBC Radio Four, UK.
Taking a Stand (2007–2010). Broadcast on BBC Radio Four, UK.
The Talented Mr. Ripley (1999). Dir. Minghella, A. USA: Paramount Pictures.
The World at War (1973–74). Broadcast on ITV, UK.
Yiddish: A Struggle for Survival (2009). Broadcast on BBC Radio Three, UK.

INDEX